THE LANGUAGE AND GRAMMAR OF LOGIC

THE LANGUAGE AND GRAMMAR OF LOGIC

EDITED BY
JOHN H. PIET
AND
AYODHYA PRASAD

COSMO PUBLICATIONS
2000 INDIA

THE LANGUAGE AND GRAMMAR OF LOGIC

First COSMO Print 2000

ISBN 81-7755-009-8

This indipendent and complete volume has been derived from the set -
Encyclopaedia of ETHICS AND LOGIC

Published by
MRS. RANI KAPOOR
for COSMO PUBLICATIONS Div. of
GENESIS PUBLISHING PVT. LTD.
24-B, Ansari Road,
Darya Ganj,
New Delhi-110 002, INDIA

Composed at
Cosmo Publications

Printed at
Mehra Offset Press

CONTENTS

Chapter-1

Language and Logic

Chapter 1

THE COMPLEXITY OF VERNACULAR LANGUAGE SYSTEMS

What does it mean to *say* something in a vernacular language such as English, 'to sound right' and 'to make sense'? It is important to deal with language in general and with vernacular languages before proceeding to such metalogical questions as: What does it mean to say something in *logical* language? What is the specific character of this language, and what are the main problems associated, historically, with its construction?

One of the most remarkable things in the life of the one-year-old baby is the development of speech. 'The newborn baby and his mother often seem to have a feeling of complete wordless communication through the touch of their skin and the gaze of their eyes. The mother at moments may share the baby's "belief" that they are actually a part of each other. However, as the baby grows up he learns to see his mother as an individual separate from himself. Weaning forces him to accept the fact of the distance between them. The early unspoken physical communication is replaced by a developing means of communication—of sounds, gestrures, facial expressions. But sometimes to the baby it can seem very frustrating that he has to learn to tell his mother his needs and wishes in this way. The period after weaning can be one in which the baby is not only sad at the loss of close contact with his mother but also irritable or even angry with her for the distance she has put between them. However, as he learns to use words, this feeling of frustration goes. Through words he can communicate with his mother on a new more mature level, and he delights in this skill, which makes him more like his parents.' (Tavistock series on Child Development published by Corgi)

To a one-year-old language comes as a glorious *bridge* to mother after a growing awareness of separation. 'Bridge'—this is not a bad description: language has a referential force bending the attention of the hearer and a sense carrying the thought or feeling of the speaker. Once we know a language then any hearing of sentences in that language spans the distance between us and the speaker: an invisible network of social conventions and shared understandings bind us to him in the very act of hearing.

The science of linguistics contributes substantially to our understanding of language, its most basic sections being concerned with speech rather than writing. Speech is language in its primary form for the written word 'remains, for the most part, a substitute for speech, with logical and stylistic peculiarities best understood as efforts to overcome obstacles arising from the hearer's absence'. (Max Black, *The Labyrinth of Language,* p. 7) From linguistics we can construct the following schematic picture of the speech situation, this picture being of fundamental value for answering the question: What does it mean to say that a person's use of a particular language sounds right?

The existence of speech 'depends, in the last resort, on the trained capacity of human beings to produce distinctive sounds immediately recognizable by themselves and others'. (Ibid. p. 11) A normal four-year-old has the fundamentals of this skill and with increasing control of his articulatory muscles, he plays his vocal tract—a much more difficult skill than playing an artificial wind instrument. *Articulatory phonetics* describes our 'vocal repertoire—providing a verbal score, one might say, for the vocal tract's performances. Its distinctive vocabulary of labials and dentals, fricatives, liquids and the like, typically identifies vocal features in terms of the muscular adjustments ("articulations") needed to produce them.' But speech requires also that it be *heard* as such. How do we recognize and identify sounds as speech? To take a single detail, how is it that we hear the same word whether the speaker speaks quickly or slowly, calmly or excitedly, in this individual accent or that? Quite clearly, hearing is an active, skilful, abstracting process, drawing selectively on various physical and contextual clues. And natural language must facilitate this process, enabling the speaker to provide, with skill, a reasonable redundancy of clues.However, the proccess of hearing, so remarkable in what it achieves, remains mysterious in its own nature, although it is believed that to some extent the hearer relies on knowing where and how a speech-sound would be produced in his own speech tract.

It is evident that, physically, each language uses a definite set of sounds, i.e. it has a definite stock of phonemes or minimal units of sound-in speech, phoneme being a category word under each of which is grouped sounds which are physically and functionally similar. Thus each language is a distinct phonemic or phonological system and is studied as such in the section of linguistics called *phonemics or phonology.* In any given language only certain combinations of phonemes sound right and this fact is a constant source of clues which we use for anticipationg and identifying what a person is saying.

Speech as an acoustical event, uttered and heard, calls for an analysis which is physical, but much more than physical also, for speech is an intelligible utterance which 'makes sense'. We hear it as words and sentences in our language and such 'hearing' is a highly systematic, selective reaction to sound. Correspondingly, a special section of the science of linguistics studies the superordinate system of rules or syntax to which the basic phonological system of a language is subject for the purpose of achieving intelligible utterance. In this superordinate system or syntax, morphemes are the smallest units referred to, a morpheme being a minimal unit of meaning. Thus as well as simple words being morphemes, even a letter like 's' (which forms a plural or present tense) is a morpheme as is e.g. the adjectival ending 'al'. 'S' and 'al', however, are bound morphemes as they can only occur in combination with at least one other morpheme, whereas a simple word is a free morpheme, because it can occur alone. Morphemes are the building blocks of complex words, phrases, clauses and sentences; and grammar is the principal set of rules governing the structuring.

Of primary importance is the grammarian's grouping of words into categories on the basis of similar function, so that a word can always be substituted for any other word from the same category, without a sentence degenerating thereby into nonsense.

Thus, whether true or untrue, 'John is smoking a pipe' is as meaningful as 'Peter is smoking a pipe'—'John' and 'Peter' belonging to the same form-class, can be substituted, grammatically, for each other in any context. A special discipline, *Morphology,* is devoted to the construction and stydy of form-classes, organizing vocabulary (the material collection of individual words) on this basis. Grammar goes on next to the study of how words are systematically modified by prefixes and suffixes and how such modifications give rise to systematic variations of meaning. Finally it gives a precise formalization of acceptable structuring of phrases, clauses and sentences. Some of the requirements for acceptability may have become quite pointless as, e.g. rules for the gender of nouns and for the declension of adjectives according to gender, nevertheless grammar is a set of rules the penalty for not observing which is loss of speech—that we don't succeed in *saying* anything in the medium of the particular language. Essentially, these rules help to bring into existence a social medium both for expressing thought and for receiving directed thought.

Intelligible utterance cannot fail to bring into operaton, in however limited an extent, the whole language system—phonological and grammatical. Words function as elements of the system. Thus when we speak intelligibly it is not single words we use but the system; again what we hear and understand are systems of words rather than single words.

LOGICAL LANGUAGE

Logical language, like natural language, is an institution requiring social initiation. But it is designed for a far more restricted use, for what, in fact, is called a cognitive use: it is exclusively concerned with processing thought, whether formally as truth-claims (in standard logic) or otherwise (in many-valued logic). Since thought content (of any sentence or judgement) that is necessarily either true or false is called a proposition, and since well-formed expressions in any system of many-valued logic are also patient of evaluation in bivalent terms of truth and falsity, logical language is said to be designed precisely and exclusively for propositional use.

Further it is essentially a written language (the use of letters from known alphabets is incidental); thus it is not a phonemic or phonological system. Its symbols are ideographs standing directly for ideas and not in any way containing a code for pronunciation. In sum, it is a precision instrument for the writing of thought, designed to facilitate both the exact expression, and (to use the basic image in the technical term *implication*) the systematic unfolding, of thought content (the *lekton* of the Stoics). And its economy and power are both very striking: with a small number of primitive symbols and a minimal grammar governing formation and transformation (in proof) of expressions, it presents itself as an open system capable of generating an immense, systematic, range of rule-governed statements. And it has a great advantage over vernacular languages in that it need not be *redundant*: in everyday speech many clues converge to help the hearer interpret both sound and sense; in logical language one has not to compensate for the swift disappearance of sound-signals, and there is no indulgence to over-determination of meaning. As Wittgenstein reminds us, vernacular languages grow out of ordinary life and serve it, concretely, with a multiplicity of tools and of ways in which they are used:

> But how many kinds of sentence are there? Say assertion, question and command?—There are *countless*

> kinds: countless different kinds of use of what we call 'symbols', 'words', 'sentences'. And this multiplicity is not something fixed, given once for all; but new types of language, new language-games, as we may say come into existence, and others become obsolete and get forgotten... Here the term 'language-*game*' is meant to bring into prominence the fact that the *speaking* of language is part of an activity, or of a form of life.
>
> (*Philosophical Investigations,* § 23)

Vernacular language must take into account, express and serve the speaker's living situation and like the speaker, it is in abrasive reactive contact with concrete life; logical language, however, has not the function of ministering to intersubjective, psychic encounters between people, but simply and impersonally of presenting forms of thought.

THE LIMITATIONS AND CAPABILITIES OF LOGICAL LANGUAGE

The stipulated objectives that are built into the design of logical language increase its specific efficiency, but they also militate against the claim that the thought content of natural language can *always* be perfectly translated into logical language and that an *essential* function of logical language is to legislate and to judge clarity in other media, clarifying and remedying vernacular expresseion. The a *priori* uneasiness about such claims is justified when one comes to the difficulties which predicate Logic has in dealing with statements about the beliefs of a person and with statements that have dependent predicates.

In the medium of logical language since any wff is patient of being evaluated as either true or false and since the truth value of a complex expression is a function of the values of the constituent wff's, one can always substitute an equivalent wff for any of the constituent ones without altering the value of the expression as a whole. Taking *CKCpqpq* one can substitute *ANpq* for *Cpq* since they fulfil the same truth conditions; the result is *CKANpqpq* which is guaranteed to have the same truth value as the original from which it is derived. The rule of substituion is an inference license of the utmost importance in logical derivation and every application of it is intuitively valid in systems of logic where thought is processed *impersonally* as truth-claims, not *personally* as, e.g. a belief. In the latter case the rule of substitution cannot be applied: it is not valid to derive '*X* believes that the Tower of Pisa is not at an angle of 90° to the ground' from '*X* believes that the Tower of Pisa is leaning somewhat': *X* may not know anything about angles and degrees and therefore one cannot, with truth, describe his belief in those terms. The impersonal equivalence between 'The Tower of Pisa is not at an angle of 90° to the ground' and 'The Tower of Pisa is leaning somewhat' is not paralleled by an equivalence within the context of belief.

Logic is concerned with thought-content in the *formalized, impersonal,* context of truth-claim, assertion.It is not concerned with psychological conditions of belief, a conscious psychic event. It does not map thought content on to psychic, conscious attitudes; Thus its equivalences and discriminations are not at all mental. The result is that if one wants to formalize statements in natural language about beliefs one simply finds that the language and procedures of logic can deal impersonally with the content of a belief but that the psychic aspects and parameters of belief escape its net. *psychically* one cannot believe that a tower is or is not at an angle of 90° without knowing something of angles and degrees, but *implicitly*, in the content of sheer thought content, one is accepting the geometrical equivalent when one believes that the tower is leaning.

The difficulty involved in formalizing statements with dependent predicates arises from the fact that logic treats predicates as though they were independent of one another just as it treats propositions as being so. Thus while the argument, *Brutus murdered Caesar with a knife, therefore Brutus murdered Caesar,* is simple and seen, intuitively, to be valid it is not easy to formalize it in the medium of logical symbolism. Robert Ackermann points out:

> any attempt to abstract this argument... results either in an assessment of the argument as invalid, or in some PL forms which are clearly not appropriate. About the best attempt to obtain a most sophisticated PL argument consistency form which will show the argument to be valid depends on constructing some predicate expressions so as to produce this:
>
> (1) $Mbcd$
> (2) $(\forall x)(Mbcx)$
>
> To obtain this we have to take 'Brutus murdered Caesar' as equivalent to 'Brutus murdered Caesar with something', an intuition that is not easily extended beyond this argument. If Brutus is direct, strangling Caesar with his bare hands, or suitably inventive, sending Caesar off on a doomed mission, we would need to locate some other equivalence to effect an abstraction. It seems doubtful that an appropriate abstraction can be found to conclude that Caesar was murdered by Brutus from any statement of his having been murdered by some means or other, or in some place or other, or in some manner. (*Modern Deductive Logic: an Introduction to its Techniques and to its Significance,* pp. 159-60)

Although logical language is not a criterion of what all languages should be, viewed directly in itself it is a medium of formalization in the most exacting sense that is humanly possible. This is made evident by two facts:

(a) its use of variables to free it from reference (as distinct from application) to particular contexts. Since the time of Boole it has been explicityly and emphatically the aim of logic to write in a way that transcends contexts and is thereby *interpretable* for an indefinite range of contexts. Frege has been the great modern technician for this kind of concept-writing.

(b) by the problems that have arisen, historically, in the

designing of modern logical notation. Basic problems were encountered by Russell over the ten years devoted to writing the *Principia Mathematica* and gave rise to his important theories of (1) proper names, (2) definite descriptions and (3) levels or orders of language. Discussion, even controversy, about these theories makes it clear that it is the function of logical language to formalize in a way that is both exact and ultimate. We shall briefly review these theories.

RUSSELL'S THEORY OF PROPER NAMES AND HIS THEORY OF DIFINITE DESCRIPTIONS

For Russell the function of a proper name is simply to pick out an individual; there is no structure to its significance: it simply picks out. The function of naming cannot be exercised if the individual does not exist, so a symbol is not really a proper name if the individual it purports to name does not exist. Further, an existential expression of the type 'Patrick Jones exists' is not a genuine statement at all: the word 'exists' only appears to be a predicate, it does not perform any function that is not already performed by 'Patrick Jones' which picks out the existent individual. Russell indeed emphasizes that in having a category of symbols that are proper names, Predicate Logic is making a certain ontological presupposition, namely that the world it is dealing with is a world of individuals. Technically of course the proofs of predicate logic presuppose that there is at least one individual in the world.

Natural languages do not seem to conform, however, to Russell's theory of proper names. They seem to frequently discharge the function of naming through definite descriptions which (1) can have a rich structured significance, as, e.g. 'The present President of the United States of America'; and (2) may have no real individual corresponding to the description even though it is perfectly intelligible, as, e.g. occurs in 'The King of France'. In Russell's theory the presence of a definite description in a statement means that we are not naming any individual, we are not talking about a subject but about a linguistic expression. Thus properly formalized the vernacular sentence 'The King of France is bald' would read: For all values of x and y the following expressions (propositional functions) are true: 'If x is the King of France x is bald' and 'If y is the King of France, y is identical with x'. For Russell this formalization is the only acceptable way of reconciling the fact that the original statement is meaningful and yet that there is not any King of France. And when we use the word 'exists' with a difinite description we are really talking about an expression and saying that there is at least one value of the variable in it for which it will be true.

Taking the three sentences:

(1) The King of France is bald;
(2) The golden mountain does not exist;
(3) Scott is the author of *Waverly*;

their formalizations are:

(1) $(x)(Fx \rightarrow Bx).\ (y)\ Fy \rightarrow\ x = y;$
(2) $(x) — (Mx\ .\ GX);$
(3) $(x)(\ SX \equiv Wx)$, i.e. x is Scott $\equiv$ x wrote *Waverly*.

It is useful to note that in dealing with a vernaculare argument which contains a definite description, whether or not one needs to analyse it in Russellian fashion depends simply on what is necessary to display the force of the argument. The importance of Russell's theory lies in its insight into the design and presuppositions of logical language.

RUSSELL'S THEORY OF TYPES

In 1903 Russell wrote that a doctrine of types afforded a possible solution to his famous Paradox of Classes. After trying to solve the various paradoxes by other means he developed a theory which became known later as the Ramified Theory of Logical Types and he incorporated this in the *Principia Mathematica.* In the 1902s Ramsey's work on the paradoxes made possible a great simplification of the theory of types. At that time the simpler form became known as the Simple Theory of Types (and was often identified with Russell's 1903 version to which it is quite similar), and the complicated version in *Principia Mathematica* was called the 'Ramified' or 'Branch' theory.

According to Russell, if language is to be immune to paradox it must obey an inbuilt type-theory according to which its parts of speech form a hierarchy, falling into separate categories (e.g. names and predicates) with no element eve performing the function of an element from another category, and some elements not being predicable of others. This is fundamentally the Simple Theory of Types.

Further, in the Ramified Theory, propositions must be seen to form a hierarchy, the basic or first order propositions being those which are not themselves about propositions; the next (second) order of propositions are about the first order ones, and the *n*th + 1 tier is about propostions of the *n*th order. In *principia Mathematica* (p. 42) it is pointed out that 'the words "true" and "false" have many different meanings, according to the type of proposition to which they are applied'.

This hierarchy of propositions does render language immune to the liar paradox but not to others. As a solution to these the Ramified Theory provieds a complicated hierarchy of propositional functions. 'One dimension of this ramified hierarchy of functions divides propositional functions into functions of individuals (functions of type 1), functions of functions of individuals (functions of type 2) and so on. When functions of more than one argument are considered, this one dimension of the hierarchy becomes quite complicated itself... The other dimension... cuts right across the Simple Type Theory. For each type, the functions of that type are divided further into infinitely many *orders'*. (Irving Copi, *The Theory of Logical Types,* pp. 82-3)

Russell's theory was so restrictive that it jeopardized the derivation of a great deal of classical mathematics. To safeguard this derivation he introduced an axiom of reducibility which asserts that to any function of any type, any order and any number of arguments there corresponds a predicative function (i.e. a function of the first order) that is formally equivalent to it—the same in type and holding for exactly the same arguments. However neither the Ramified Theory nor the anxiom were ever generally accepted.

It is important indeed not to see the theory as either descriptive or prescriptive with regard to natural languages but as recommendations for the designing of a special artificial language which will render it immune to paradox and will further the specific objectives of mathematical logc. Bar-Hillel comments:

> The attempt to impose a type hierarchy upon natural languages seems misguided and linguistically pointless. The concerns of Russell and other authors about how to formulate the theory of types in English (or any other natural language) without violatign. the theory in its very formulation (e.g. by speaking of all types) are now no more than interesting curiosities. (*Encyclopedia of Philosophy,* vol. 8, article on Theory of Types, p.171)

Today an idea suggested by Russell in 1922 has been developed into a doctrine of levels of language—language, metalanguage, metametalanguage, etc.—which is very useful for handling paradoxes. In his introduction to the *Tractatus of Wittgenstein* he said:

> These difficulties suggest to my mind some such possibility as this; that every language has, as Mr Wittgenstein says, a structure concerning which, *in the language,* nothing can be said, but that there may be another language dealing with the structure of the first language, and having itself a new structure and that to this hierarchy of languages there may be no limit.

This levels of language doctrine which received an important technical presentation from Tarski, has a good deal of affinity with the Ramified Theory but possesses none of its negative effects on mathematical derivations.

CONCLUSION

Logical language is a medium for *formal presentation* of thought content (the Stoic *lekta*) rather than for *personal expression.* It is designed to facilitate rigorously exact and explicit proof; to exclude paradox; and to express laws that transcend particular contexts and are thus patient of unlimited interpretation.

Chapter-2

Two Basic Concepts: Meaning and Truth

Chapter 2

LANGUAGE AS MEANINGFUL

It is expected that when a language system is used properly it 'makes sense' and is not 'meaningless'. Linguistic utterance or writing is intelligible: it can be understood no matter what level of life or science it relates to. Bohr used the striking metaphor: we humans live suspended in language. At this point we are going to focus the medium of language as a constructed, coherent, understandable entity; we are not dealing at all with its truth or falsity and in so far as the concept of meaning or meaningful is used we must be quite sure that it is disengaged from the concept of truth.

In the case of logical language rules for constructing wff's constitute an adequate source and criterion of its intelligibility. A logical expression has *form or intelligibility* when it is grammatical. By the use of variables (i.e. blanks) logic transcends contexts instead of setting contexts by rich object words, and thus accord with grammatical rules achieves intelligibility (i.e. the intelligibility that is natural to logical statements) in a way that is fully defined and is patient of exact application. Within logic, therefore, problems of discriminating between meaningful and meaningless statements are solved by referring to the notation and formation rules of the language used. Further the transformation rules must be such that correct use of them guarantees that any theorem generated from wff's will itself be a wff.

Indeed in working out to the full any particular system, modern logicians apply both formation and transformation rules in a purely formalistic way, confident in a resultant coherent intelligibility.

The constitutors of logical meaning (i.e. of the form of

intelligibility that is natural to logical statements) are the operators. In propositional logic we have *N*-statements, *C*-statements, *A*-, *K*-, *E*-, *D*-statements, whose intelligibility is truth-functional in definition; in predicate logic the intelligibility is forms of attribution general and existential; in modal logic the intelligibility is forms of necessitation, possibility, impossibility and contingency. Later we shall discuss in detail the nature and functioning of logical operators; at the moment we are concerned in a general way, with the contrast between logical and natural language.

In his introduction to Wittgenstein's *Tractatus Logico-Philosophicus,* Russell said:

> ... logic has two problems to deal with in regard to Symbolism: (1) the conditions for sense rather than nonsense in combinations of symbols; (2) the conditions for uniqueness of meaning or reference in symbols or combinations of symbols. A logically perfect language has rules of syntax which prevent nonsense, and has single symbols which always have a definite and unique meaning. Mr Wittgenstein is concerned with the conditions for a logically perfect language—not that any language is logically perfect, or that we believe ourselves capable, here and now, of constructing a logically perfect language, but that the whole function of language is to have meaning, and it only fulfills this function in proportion as it approaches to the ideal language which we postulate.

This passage brings out the fact that modern logic begins by designing as perfect a language (for its purposes) as possible, where 'meaningfulness' and 'grammaticality' coincide, and it expresses the view that, ideally, the same coincidence should be true of natural languages.

Turning to natural languages does the 'meaningfulness', 'intelligibility', 'acceptability' of speech and writing coincide with their grammaticality? From the beginning of this century, with the work of Russell on paradoxes and the revival by

Husserl of belief in a universal grammar, attempts were made to devise a system of rules acceptable and powerful enough to decide, with respect to any expression of everyday speech, whether it were meaningful or meaningless. The works of Rudolf Carnap are a *locus classicus* for the view that such a system of rules can be discovered for each language. He did not believe in a single, universal grammer; indeed he opposed such a concept with a 'principle of tolerance' towards conventional variety of linguistic forms. But he believed that a syntactical method for detecting pseudo-statements could be worked out in each language:

> ...the whole theory of language structure and its possible applications in philosophy came to me like a vision during a sleepless night in January 1931, when I was ill. On the following day, still in bed with a fever, I wrote down my ideas on forty-four pages under the title 'Attempt at a metalogic'... At that time I defined the term 'metalogic' as the theory of the forms of the expressions of a language. Later I used the term 'syntax' instead of 'metalogic', or in distinction to syntax as part of linguistics, 'logical syntax'. [In other words his specific interest in syntax was in its capacity to generate and to decide intelligibility—that is the force of the word 'logical' rather than any suggestion that it was a syntax of an ideal logical language.] These shorthand notes were the first version of my book *Logical Syntax of Language* (1943-6). ('Intellectual Autobiography' by Rudolf Carnap, pp. 53 and 54 of *The Philosophy of Rudolf Carnap* edited by Paul Arthur Schilpp)

Later Carnap concluded that a purely syntactical theory of a language was not sufficient for his purpose; its metatheory must include semantics and pragmatics. Noam Chomsky was a pupil of Carnap and his work in linguistics has been very much influenced by Carnap.

The substance of a metatheory of language and meaningfulness may be presented, simply,against the background of specific problems and paradoxes posed by the following sentences:

> Socrates is redness.
> Socrates redness internationally.
> Colourless green ideas sleep furiously.
> Saturday is in bed.
> Today is Monday but I don't believe it.
> This statement is false.

Let us use the term theory of a given language to signify the formulation of its notation together with a set of rules that will generate all the possible meaningful statements in that language, and only meaningful statements. This set of rules will consist of:

(a) Syntactical rules which, independently of the meaning of words, govern their proper combination.A passage from Chomsky provides a good example: '...given an appropriate rule, it can be proved that the word-series "Pirots karulize elactically" is a sentence, provided only that "Pirots" is known to be a substantive (in the plural), "karulize" a verb (in the third person plural), and "elatically" an adverb...The meaning of the words is quite inessential to the purpose, and need not be known.' ('Systems of Syntactic Analysis', *Journal of Symbolic Logic, 1953)*

The two sentences 'Socrates is redness' and 'Socrates redness internationally' violate syntactical rules of the English language.

(b) lexical rules which are concerned with the word stock (vocabulary) of a language and determine for each item other words with which it may combine and words with which it may not combine. When words go together in definable combinations (e.g. 'night' and 'black'; 'coloured' and 'green') they are said to *collocate.* Collocations are part of the total meaning of a word and words cannot be used outside the range of their collocations without a loss of meaning.

The sentences 'Colourless green ideas sleep furiously' (Chomsky) and 'Saturday is in bed' (from Ryle) violate lexical rules.

(c) pragmatic rules which govern those aspects of linguistic form that derive from the user. Thus a statement is formally an assertion and a truth-claim. Pragmatic rules don't allow us to build into an assertion a denial that it is an assertion, or into a truth-claim a claim of falsity.

The sentences 'Today is Monday but I don't believe it' and 'This statement is false' violate pragmatic rules.

Wittgenstein showed that it was wrong to regard logical language as an underlying infra structure present, to some extent, in every natural language. Indeed in his later life he did not think of language in terms of an underlying system of forms. It was Chomsky's achievement to go outside formal logic in providing such a system, combining Carnap's formation and transformation rules with Wittgenstein's deep and surface structures.

Chomsky envisaged a limited Phrase Structure Grammar which would produce a number of terminal strings to be called the *kernels* of a language. All other sentences of the language would then be produced by the operation of transformations upon these kernels. A phonetic representation of each sentence would be produced by the operation of morphophonemic rules upon these transformationally derived sentence forms. A listing of the phrase structure and transformational rules used in the derivation of a sentence would constitute its *structural representation.* Chomsky often refers to the structure of a kernel as the 'deep structure' of *any sentence derived from it;* and the representation of the same sentence that a phrase-structure grammar would give, he calls, by contrast, its 'surface structure'. Both transformations and kernels are to be thought of as finite inventories, presumably stored in the memory of some computer or other device. (Yorick Alexander Wilks, *Grammar, meaning and the machine analysis of language,* published by Routledge and Kegan Paul, pp. 60-1) [Instead of 'kernels' Chomsky speaks now of the 'base component' of the whole grammar.]

There are three ways in which Chomsky views a transformational generative grammar: (i) as a model for sentence producton; (ii) as a model for a brain mechanism; and (iii) as a model for what people say about the grammatical structure of their language... It is the last of these that Chomsky has in mind when he speaks of competence...Chomsky thinks that perfomance models (models of what people actually say and write) are too difficult to construct, and also that grammaticality is *not appropriate* to performance. The appropriate notion there, he says, is 'acceptability'. (Ibid.,p. 69)

I claim that there can only be perfomance models, and that when Chomsky talks of competence models he is necessarily talking about models for certain selections from among possible performance. (Ibid., p. 70)

THE FORMATION, SPECIFICALLY, OF LOGICAL MEANING: LOGICAL OPERATIONS

Our metalogical discussion is concerned with the formation of meaning in the sign medium of logical notation. Every well-formed formula achieves meaning or intelligibility; it expresses and processes thought-content that is relevant to the science of logic. However, in itself, each formula is a *sign construct* and must be studied as such before, humanly, we can speak in general of the constitution of *logical meaning* or of *logical thought-content.* The present discussion will include some treatment of the terms *proposition* and *logical operations;* these and other elements will reappear at the philosophical level of reflection appropriate to the later section on the philosophy of logic.

The whole function of language is to have meaning, and the grammatical use of logical notation produces statements that have logical form or intelligibility, that make logical sense. Logical operations are varieties of ways in which we achieve meaning by the use of logical notation. The sign constructs indicate this variety of meaning: *pq; ECpqANpq; Fa; Fabc; (x)Fx; (Ex)Fx; (x)(y)Fxy; (x)(y)(z)Fxyz; (Ex)(y)Fx→ Fy; Lp; Mp* (or *NLNp*); *Up* (or *LNp*); *Zp* (or *NLp* or *KMpMNp*); $a = b \equiv (ab' = 0)$. $(a'b = 0)$; $a + b = -(-a \times -b)$. It is clear that in each case meaning is a function of the sign-construct as a whole and as a unit, even though in the process of sign-construction we may look on the variables as devices for transcending particular refrence and on the constants (or functors) as specific determinants of sense. Indeed constants are often called operators. One must remember, however, that the metaphor, *operation,* is best linked with the fact that meaning is a function of the sign-construct as a complete whole: indeed the sign-construct is a whole and not merely a sum of symbols: its constituents signify only in relation to one another as a totality. And instead of speaking of logical operations we could equally well speak of 'making logical sense', 'bringing into existence logical meanings, logical intelligibilities'. However, the metaphor operation does draw attention to the fact that the sign-construct has its meaning only in *use,* i.e. as *thought* by writer or reader.

The various sections of logic are charaterized by differing types of sense. In propositional logic meaning is presented in terms of the force it exercises when propositions are subjected to truth–falsity evaluation. The kind of intelligibility that is brought into existence by the use of *p,N,C,K,* etc. is truth-functional, i.e. such that the truth or falsity of every wff is determined, functionally, according to the truth or falsity of its constituent propositions. Thus *N, C, K,* etc. are called truth functors and are defined by truth-tables. Similarly the meanings of *N*-statements, *C*-statements, *K*-statements, etc. are discriminated by the matrix lines of their truth-tables.

It is important that when we speak of *N* as the negator, *C* as the implication sign, *K* as the conjunction sign, etc. our mode of speech does not obscure the fact that what has meaning is the sign-construct as a whole. This is particularly important in dealing with negation as a logical operation: being negative or positive is a feature of meaning; negative meaning is achieved by a particular type of use of logical notation. Thus the function of negation is performed by the total sign-construct, not by *N* which exists only in the totality. Further, as Wittgenstein pointed out, both *p* and *Np* lead us back to the same state of affairs which either verifies or falsifies our positive and negative meanings. In dealing with the concept of truth it will become quite clear that being negative or positive is a feature of *meaning,* where being true or false is a feature of *correspondence* between our meanings and the facts.

Predicate logic 'makes sense' in a way quite different to propositional logic: an identification is made of an individual, a dyad, triad, etc. and an attribution is made. Predication admits not only of a referential force that is individual but also of one that is systematic. The latter poses the problem of achieving generality of meaning. Modern logic does so by the use of individual variables and by quantifying their variability. Thus when one uses a universal quantifier one signifies that the range of predication is no less than the whole scope of the variable; when one uses an existential quantifier one signifies that the predication holds for some (indefinite) individual in the world we are talking about. It is a feature of predicate logic, of course, that it cannot speak of a world completely empty of individuals.

Eliminating the verb of existence modern logical notation has achieved a clear simplicity in the representation of predication (e.g. *Fa*) and of generality within predication (e.g. *(x)Fx, (Ex)Fx*). There is a welcome departure from grammatical symbolism (the *S* and *P* of traditional presentations) and generality is displayed as formation, the function *Fx* being incomplete potential material for the generalization *(x)Fx*. This quantifier-functor-argument structure also displays the logically heterogeneous nature of identification and attribution which are both necessary for predication but require, graphically, the use of symbols that belong to absolutely different categories (*x, F*). It is to Frege and Russell that we owe the insistence that the relation of a name to the thing named, and the relation of a predicate to what it is true of, are quite distinct and that the distinction must appear in the notation we use to achieve predicative meaning.

Finally, for a person who uses any of the well-known languages of the world, nothing could be more familiar than the subject-predicate mode of speech. It is important to note that linguistic scholars are by no means sure that all peoples do use natural language to make sense in this type of way.

In class calculus sign-constructs fall, simply, into two main categories: (a) *names* of complex classes generated by Boolean operations on simple classes (e.g. $a + b; a \times b$); (*b*) *statements* which chart the intelligibility of class space by expressing laws governing possible relationships between classes, e.g. $a \neq o \equiv (Ex)(x \in a)$. The meaning of these statements has always a truth-functional or predicative *form;* what is new in this extensional study of predicates is the objects referred to: classes, their equalities and inequalities, class inclusion, class membership.

Modal logic brings us to the spectrum of logical options in the certification of truth-claims. *LP* is a simple construct but very rich in its signification and implications: the meaning (or thought-content)as *truth claim* is certified as being necessitated. Other certifications may be simply compatible with truth (*Mp*) or be incompatible with truth (*Up*) or be that of falling neither under necessitation nor impossibility (*Zp*). In every case the notation is so used that what is processed through the meaning is a modal claim to truth.The modality of this claim is a function of the sign construct as a whole; it is *meant* and requires a special use of notation to achieve the formation of this meaning. The meaning or thought-content, modal in form, is either true or false, i.e. one can always say of a modal statement: if this is what is meant then it is true or false to say this.

Of course the introduction of the concept of modification and range as inherent possibilities for truth claims involves, *for calculation purposes* (if for no other reason), the setting up of many-valued tables in order to be able to operate a complete truth-calculus. Thus many-valued logic can begin, quite naturally, as a calculus for model logic.

'WHAT IS SAID' AS DISTINCT FROM THE 'SAYING'

When the *saying* of something is distinguished from *what is said* we describe it as grammatical, clear, polished, idiomatic, spoken with a good accent, loud, excited, nervous, blurted out...etc. We are dealing with the qualitative use that is made of the medium; we are evaluating (e.g.) English sentences not that which is said by them and could be said also in German, Irish, Chinese, etc. Proposition is the technical word used for something I say; the same proposition can be expressed in different sentences (German, English, Chinese, etc) and the same sentence can express different propositions (e.g. 'I was born in China') according as various people use this sentence. It is the proposition that is properly true or false not the sentence, and again it is what is said (the proposition) that is properly described as provable, derivable, exaggerated, implausible, etc. Frege put is as follows: 'The sentence has a value for us through the sense that we apprehend in it, and which we recognize as the same in the translation too. This sense I call "thought" (Gedanke). What we prove is not the sentence but the thought. And it makes no difference what language we use for that purpose.' (*Uber Logik und Mathematik,* 1914) It was to express this fact that Frege prefixed a $\vdash$ to every sentence in logical language when he was formulating propositions or deriving theorems.

It is interesting to note that the most fundamental section of formal logic is propositional logic where one begins with the simplest formulation of what is said—the propositional variables *P, q, r, s, t.* (Frege would prefix $\vdash$.) The tautologies of this section are needed for proofs in predicate logic where the formalization is more complex being in terms of individual variables, quantifiers and predicate letters.

A natural language pre-exists any particular use we make of it as a brain skill possessed by many people, as a mental competency, a vocabulary and a grammar. When these are brought into use in a normal way, meaningful speech is generated. But it is important to note that when we focus speech as meaningful, intelligible, understandable, we are not examining what is said but the quality of our use of the medium in saying what we do say. It is the constructed sentence as such that is meaningful and we speak of the meaning as being clear or ambiguous, controversial or indisputable, etc. On a last analysis while our saying must 'sound right' and must 'make sense' it is precisely what we say that is alone true or false.

THE FUNCTION OF A CONCEPT OF TRUTH WITHIN LOGIC

Logic is not concerned with all forms of meaning, e.g. with those that constitute prayers, commands, exclamations, but with those only that have the property of being appraisable as either true of false. Indeed the term proposition is very accurately described as meaning or thought-content which has the property of having to be either true or false. Thus logic is concerned basically with the fact that, in our speech and in our thought, we can achieve an intelligibility which, through having its being in a sign-context of speech and thought, is also, in some way, appraisable in relation to facts. The notation of logic is such that every logical operation is of its nature the processing of a potential truth claim, and in every section logic evaluates its propositions, seeking to sift, derive and organize those that are always true and so construct the body of logical truth.

Thus, a concept of truth is called for both in philosophy of logic (elucidating the nature of propositions as potential truth-claims) and in metalogic. Here in metalogic our concern is to make explicit such concepts as are operational in formal logic especially the concept of proposition as distinct from sentence and the kind of concept of truth that, technically, is necessary and sufficient for the problems and processes of formal logic.

A CONCEPT OF TRUTH SUFFICIENT FOR METALOGIC

Since the time of Frege logical notations have been chosen as simple and powerful media for propositional use in two senses of these words: (1) with regard to any wff, *what it says* is said in an eminently clear and economic way: thus the *propositions* which logic discovers and proves are presented in almost ideal sentences; (2) their symbols are predominantly concerned with formalizing entities that are either propositions or are constitutive of propositions. Even in class calculus one's long-term objective is to discover (indirectly) truths about predicative propositons; in many-valued logic we are evaluating propositions although we are not concerned to do so in a framework of truth and falsity; and, of course, in standard logic (outside class calculus) we are directly and explicitly concerned with propositions as entities which are essentially and properly truth-claims. Since it is what is said that is essentially and properly a truth-claim, logic may be described as the formal study of what is said. (In the psychic medium of thought what is *judged* is a truth-claim.)

Since the time of Frege there has been a thorough-going rejection of psychologism in modern logic, a rejection that is implicityly emphasized by the strictly formal character and formalistic method of mathematical logic.

However, with regard to the concept of truth whose philosophical elaboration has been attended, throughout history, with difficulty and controversy, a notable effort has been made to develop a philosophically neutral theory by disengaging truth from the context of proposition, treating 'true' as a predicate of sentences. This effort culminated in the classical paper of Alfred Tarski in the 1930s, *The Concept of Truth in Formalized Languages.* It crystallized two significant processes within Polish philosophy of the 1920s; (1) an acceptance of the classical concept of truth as conformity of thought with reality, the defence of this concept being sustained over many years by Twardowski, Lesniewski, Lukasiewicz, Ajdukiewicz and

Kotarbinski; and (2) concern for semantic analyses, a systematic study of philosophical semantics being due mainly to Lesniewski.

Church interprets Tarski's definition of truth very exactly:

> As appears from the work of Tarski, there is a sense in which semantics can be reduced to syntax. Tarski has emphasized especially the possibility of finding, for a given formalized language, a purely syntactical property of the well-formed formulas which coincides in extension with the semantical property of being a true sentence. And in Tarski's *Wahrheitsbegriff* [this German translation had an important appendix to the polish paper and is the basis of the standard English version] the problem of finding such a syntactical property is solved for various particular formalized language, [including the language of standard mathematical logic]. (*Introduction to Mathematical Logic,* Vol. 1, p. 65)

Professor Skolimowski comments:

> Church's is perhaps the most accurate and proper interpretation. Tarski's definition of truth, considered as finding a purely syntactical property of the sort specified by Church, is without question the task which he set for himself. (*Polish Analytical Philosophy,* p. 48)

Other evaluations emphasize either a philosophical neutrality in Tarski's work or the view that underlying its formal, syntactical character there is an acceptance of the classical concept of truth. Thus Max Black says:

> The neutrality of Tarski's definition with respect to the competing philosophical theories of truth is sufficient to demonstrate its lack of philosophical relevance [because] neither this, nor any formal definition of truth, goes to the heart of the difficulties which are at the root of the so-called philosophical problem of truth. ('The Semantic Concept of Truth', *Analysis,* March 1948, p. 61)

For Karl Popper, however, Tarski's work enabled exact scientists and philosophers of science to openly adhere, in their work, to a correspondence theory of truth:

> ...before I became acquainted with Tarski's theory of truth, it appeared to me safer to discuss the criterion of progress without getting too deeply involved in the highly controversial problem connected with the use of the word 'true'. My attitude at the time was this: although I accepted, as almost everybody does, the objective or absolute or correspondence theory of truth—truth as correspondence with the facts—I preferred to avoid the topic.For it appeared to me hopeless to try to understand clearly this strangely elusive idea of a correspondence between a statement and a fact......All this was changed by Tarski's theory of truth and of the correspondence of a statement with the facts. Tarski's greatest achievement, and the real significance of his theory for the philosophy of the empirical sciences, is that he rehabilitated the correspondence theory of absolute or objective truth which had become suspect. He vindicated the free use of the intuitive idea of truth as correspondence to the facts. (*Conjectures and Refutations,* p. 223)

In other words, Tarski's work was not a philosophical enquiry into the nature of truth but he accepted the classic concept of correspondence as a basis and although he did not examine, explain or justify the concept on philosophical grounds, neverthless it possessed form, precision and validity in his work.

In Tarski's paper one encounters both the power of a deceptively simple discovery and, to use the words of A. N. Prior an 'extraordinary precision, elegance and thoroughness' of elaboration which makes the paper one of the classics of modern logic.

The simple basic discovery is that to talk about the truth of sentence one must construct and use a metaloanguage which can speak about both the sentences of the language in question and about the facts to which they refer. Such a metalanguage is described as 'semantical' by Tarski; a metalanguage which can speak about sentences but not about the facts referred to is called 'syntactical'. The need and use of a semantical metalanguage may be exemplified as follows: *the sentence 'Snow is white' corresponds to the facts (i.e. is true) only if snow is white*. However, here the only metalinguistic sign drawing our attention to the fact that we are speaking in a metalanguage is the use of single quotation marks: these are used to signify that we are naming (mentioning) a sentence in the English language; the English language itself is retained as a proper part of the metalanguage to speak of the facts, i.e. of that which will verify the sentence. In a perfect metalanguage every category of level of reference would have a special symbolism and this happens, of course, in metalanguages for formal logic.

Tarski works out the definition of a true sentence in the language L. This sepecific, rigorous and difficult part of his paper brings out two essential points: firstly, for Tarski a definition of truth is relativized to a particular language and cannot be extended as a formulation for true sentences of other languages; secondly, a definition can be worked out only for sentences of a formalized language, i.e. of a language whose elements and structure are specified in a full and exact way. Formal logic provides an example of such a language, and, e.g. for the section, propositional logic, a semantic definition of truth can be precisely elaborated (in metalanguage) by a recursive statement of the truth-conditions for sentences in this section. By contrast, a semantic definition of truth cannot be constructed for the sentences of an everyday language; such a language is too 'rich' and 'untidy' and is subject to paradoxes like that of the Liar, the reason being that it is semantically closed containing within itself names of its own expressions and semantic notions such as 'true'.

Tarski's work is certainly valid as a metalogical description and formulation of the concept of truth that is *operational* in formal logic. It does not deal, however, with the nature of truth or with the ultimate reality of correspondence. Thus it is left to the philosophy of logic to move from the level of sentences to that of propositions, and to elucidate truth in the personal contexts of sepeech and knowledge.

Chapter-3
The Rigour and Range of Proof in Formal Logic

Chapter 3

INTRODUCTION: THE SIGNIFICANCE OF GÖDEL'S THEOREM; EVALUATING FORMAL LOGIC AS A BODY OF TRUTHS

In his historic paper, On Formally Undecidable Propositions of Principia Mathematica and Related Systems Kurt Gödel wrote:

> The development of mathematics in the direction of greater exactness has—as is well known—led to large tracts of it becoming formalized, so that proofs can be carried, out according to a few mechanical rules. The most comprehensive fromal systems yet set up are, on the one hand, the system of Principia Mathematica (PM) and, on the other, the axiom theory for set theory of Zermelo-Fraenkl (later extended by J. v. Neumann). These two systems are so extensive that all methods of proof used in mathematics today have been formalized in them, i.e. reduced to a few axioms and rules of inference. It may therefore be surmised that these axioms and rules of inference are also sufficient to decide *all* mathematical questions which can in any way at all be expressed formally in the systems concerned. It is shown below that this is not the case, and that in both the systems mentioned there are in fact relatively simple problems in the theory of ordinary whole numbers which cannot be decided from the axioms. This situation is not due in some way to the special nature of the systems set up but holds for a very extensive class of formal systems, including, in particular, all those arising from the addition of a finite number of axioms to the two systems mentioned...' (pp. 37-8 in Meltzer's translation; published by Oliver & Boyd, Edinburgh and London, 1962)

The discovery by the young Austrian mathematician that there are arithmetical propositions which are neither provable nor disprovable within their arithmetical system, was announced by him to the Vienna Academy of Sciences in 1930, and published in 1931. 'A relation (class) is called arithmetical,' he says, 'if it can be defined solely by means of the concepts + , . [addition and multiplication applied to natural numbers] and the logical constants ∨ , –, (x), =, Where (x) and = are to relate only to natural numbers. The concept of "arithmetical proposition" is defined in a corresponding way.' (Ibid., p. 63) The theorem belongs to metamathematics (Hilbert's name for the study of rigorous proof in mathematics and mathematical logic) and shows that there is an inherent characteristic incompleteness in formal mathematics.

In the light of this limitation of mathematics one can appreciate, properly, the fact that in metalogic one assesses formal logic with regard to possession of the following three qualities:

(1) the quality of neither containing nor admitting of inconsistency among its theses;

(2) the quality that every tautology expressible in its language can be brought into a relation of deducibility from its principles, i.e. from the axioms and rules of inference when logic is given an axiomatized format; from the Logical Argument Formulae when it is constructed on a natural deduction basis;

(3) the quality of being able to decide, with regard to every expression in its language, whether or not it is a tautology (or a logical contradiction or a contingent proposition).

A separate assessment is made of the two main sections of logic —propositional logic and predicate logic.

ASSESSING THE CONSISTENCY, COMPLETENESS AND DECIDABILITY OF PROPOSITIONAL LOGIC

(a) Our modern logic of propositions is a consistent system.

It is consistent in the strongest possible way because every proposition derived in it is inescapably a tautology. Thus not only are contradictions absent in it but minor inconsistencies and contingent propositions have not any place either. This can be easily shown because of the fact that a certain type of proof, explicit in its sequence, is demanded for every proposition that is derived.

In a natural deduction system proof is begun with an application (or applications) of the Rule of Assumptions. Formalized as a line of proof, such an application reads

1 (1) *p* A

i.e. on the assumption that *p* is true, it follows that *p* is true. Formalized for truth-table testing this is the obvious tautology, $p \mid\!- p$, or *Cpp*. Any other stage in the proof consists of the application of some LAF and can be formalized, for truth-table testing, as a conditional proposition whose truth-value is guaranteed by the fact that it does not express anything new other than what is contained in a movement of natural deduction which can never give rise to a false consequent from true antecedents. Thus the sequence of proof is at every stage tautology-preserving. (One could take each natural deduction movement in turn —each LAF —and display its tautology-preserving character.)

With regard to modern axiomatic systems of propositional logic, a proof of consistency is in principle the same. Any proposition is derived ultimately from axioms (truth-tabled tautologies) on the basis of explicit, simple, rules of inference: the tautologous quality of each minute derivation is evidenced by the simple, explicit, nature of the rule applied.

(b) Our modern logic of propositions is a complete system.

In, e.g. physical science, the prevailing theory which co-ordinates and organizes physical knowledge into a deductive system (e.g. relativity theory, today) is subject to the following assessment when a new discovery in physics is made: is the explanatory power of the theory such that the new discovery of law (made independently of the theory perhaps) can be presented as an implication of the theory —not only compatible with it but also deducible from it. If physical theory were able to guarantee that it could situate, within itself, any new discovery as simply another deducible proposition then it would be a complete system. (The reliability of the discovery is not at issue in this context of completeness.)

To say that our modern logic of propositions is complete is to say that it can provide a proof for every wff (in the language of propositional logic) which is genuinely tautologous —all such tautologies can be derived from the LAF's of a natural deduction format, and from the rules and axioms of an axiomatic format. (How one discovers the genuine tautologies is not at issue here.)

The technique of proof consists in trying to achieve, in the format of a thesis, that which is displayed, mechanically, in each line of a truth-table. If one takes the truth-table of any tautology, each line provides a particular set of values for the variables and displays at thee matrix point of the line that the expression as a whole has the value 1. Does this truth-table characteristic of a tautology enable us to capture for every tautology, the logical content of every line in its truth-table so that we can express and prove that content in the language and by the rules of our system? If so we can provide a proof for every tautology.

1. Let *P* be a metalogical variable used to express our problem: can propositional logic prove any tautology, *P*?

2. Let *p*, *q*, *r*, *s*, *t*... be the propositonal variables in *P*. Any assignment of values for *p*, *q*, *r*, *s*, *t* enables one to write down a set of propositons that (under the assignment made) are all true. Thus if $p = 0$, $q = 0$, $r = 1$, $S = 1$, $t = 0$, then a set of true propositions are $-p$, $-q$, r, s, $-t$ and I can symbolize this set w_1 w_2 w_3 w_4 w_5

3. Now under this assignment of values, the total proposition

p is either true or false. If true then (under the given assignment of values), $w_1\ w_2\ w_3\ w_4\ w_5$ imply it. If false then $w_1\ w_2\ w_3\ w_4\ w_5$ imply $-P$. Where P is a tautology it always has the value 1, under all assignments of values for the variables.

4. Thus the logical force or content of each line in the truth-table for a genuine tautology can be formalized as a sequent: $w_1 \ldots\ldots w_n \vdash P$. There can be 2^n sequents of the same pattern developed simply and solely from the range of truth possibilities that the variables in P have.

Each sequent comes into existence with its validity guaranted by two simple facts: (1) the wff's on the left of the therefore-indicator, $\vdash$, are simply and validly derived from some particular assignment of values to the variables (i.e. any assignment enables one to determine, immediately, a set of true wff's, $w_1 \ldots\ldots w_n$); (2) the wff on the right of the therefore-indicator is the tautology presented, and as a tautology is, of course, true under all assignments of values to the variables in it. Since each sequent corresponds to a different set of values for the variables and since the 2^n sequents completely map the range of possible assignments, it follows that in guaranteeing that these sequents are all true we are situating within our system of deductions not only P but also the tautologous quality of P.

(c) Our modern logic of propositions contains decision procedures for determining whether any given well-formed formula in its language is a tautology, a logical contradiction or a contingent proposition.
These procedures are:

(1) the truth-tables procedure;
(2) the normal forms procedure;
(3) the truth trees procedure.

We have seen in chapter 2 that each of these procedures is quite adequate for the function of decision. Accordingly, the system, propositional logic, is said to be *decidable.*

Conclusion. The rigour and range of proof in propositional logic is seen, on assessment, to be quite remarkable. This section of formal logic is a complete corpus of established truths: it possesses all those truths that are expressible in the language of propositional variables; only truths can feature as theses in it; and it has a decision procedure for determining with regard to any expression in its language, whether it is a tautology, a logical contradiction or a contingent proposition. It therefore provides a finished grammar of connectivity.

ASSESSING THE CONSISTENCY, COMPLETENESS AND DECIDABILITY OF PREDICATE LOGIC

The same type of proof is available for the *consistency* of predicate logic as for that of propositional logic. In its natural deduction format its theses are generated entirely from LAF's and inherit a logical soundness from nature; in its axiomatic format the simple rules of inference which determine derivations preserve the truth quality of axioms.

We have seen however that while *decision procedures* have been found for certain fragments of predicate logic, the system as a whole is not decidable. This does not merely signify that a decision procedure has not actually been found for it—in 1936 Alonzo Church proved that such a procedure could never be devised. This technical result is not surprising, humanly: in effect a decision procedure in predicate logic would trace out systematically every consequence of the assumption that the premisses and the contradictory of the conclusion are jointly consistent. If they are not, at least two of these consequences must be inconsistent, and must show up in the systematic unfolding of implications as two lines, one of which is the negation of the other. For if the proof can develop without terminating by inconsistency, there is a domain (D_w) (i.e. a domain which has a denumerable, or enumerably infinite number of members) in which a possible world can be described satisfying the assumption that the premisses and the contradictory of the conclusion are jointly consistent. However even when the systematic unfolding of implications is proceeding indefinitely, there may be no indication, mathematical or otherwise, about the indefinite process that inconsistency *cannot* appear. Thus in predicate logic where infinite instantiation is possible, while one could expect a decision procedure which would display *any valid* argument as being *valid,* one could not expect a general decision procedure which would display *any invalid* argument as *invalid.*

What is technically called the philosophy of conservatism emphasizes that the important quality of both logical proofs and decision procedures is that they conserve the quality of truth and validity, that they will never assess an invalid argument as valid. It is important to note also that a pragmatic response to Church's result has been the working out of decision procedures for various special cases in predicate logic. Some are, technically, of substantial interest and there are good lists given by W. Ackermann in his *Solvable Cases of the Decision Problem* (1954) and by A. Church in *Introduction to Mathematical Logic* (1956).

The absence of a mechanical decision procedure makes it more difficult to devise a proof for the *completeness* of predicate logic than for that of propositonal logic (where the truth table test is basic to the method of proving completeness). Kurt Gödel was the first to devise one (1930) and his method can be extended to both axiomatic and natural deduction presentations. The distinction between weak and strong completeness may be defined as follows in the context of axiomatization: a system is said to be weakly complete if its axiomatic basis is sufficient for the generation of the set of all its valid wff's; it is said to be strongly complete if its axiomatic basis cannot be made more powerful without inconsistency resulting.

Of course no system actually proves all the sequents and theorems that can be proved, for an indefinite number of substitutions is possible for variables and each selection could be proved and given a theorem or sequent number. In practice a system confines itself to the generalizations which are basic to all possible substitution work, adding only theorems and sequents which are of special metalogical interest. It is clear that a proof is not changed in sequence, structure or in grounds cited, when it is repeated for some substitution instance.

The assessment, then, of modern predicate logic shows it to be a consistent and complete system, lacking however a general decision procedure.

A SUMMARY ASSESSMENT OF LOGIC IN GENERAL

Both propositional and predicate logic have the characteristic of being consistent and complete systems. Thus they are completely competent to present logical truths in the format of deducibility. Since the system of predicate logic is not decidable, it follows that deducibility rather than decidability is the primary, form of logical certification.

In *The Development of Logic,* the authors (W. and M. Kneale) make the following observation:

> Under the influence of mistaken theories of logic philosophers have sometimes assumed that truisms of logic must all be certifiable as such by a simple procedure. Wittgenstein, for example, wrote:
>
> > 'Our fundamental principle is that every question which can be decided at all by logic can be decided off-hand....It is possible...to give at the outset a description of all "true" logical propositions. Hence there can *never* be surprises in logic...Proof in logic is only a mechanical expedient to facilitate the recognition of tautology, where it is complicated.' (*Tractatus Logico-Philosophicus,* 5.511, 6.125, 6.1251, 6.1262)
>
> And mathematicians for their part have sometimes thought that Frege's theory must be wrong because the problems of number theory are not all soluble by rules of thumb such as should in their opinion be sufficient for the settlement of all logical questions. In the paper in which he proved the incompletability of formal arithmetic Gödel

made clear for the first time that discovery of a universal decision procedure for general logic would be sufficient for a solution of some famous unsolved problems of number theory...In the context in which it was written this remark was not intended to suggest the unplausibility of finding a universal decision procedure for general logic. Within a few years the impossibility of such a discovery was proved by a development of Gödel's own technique.

THE CONCEPT OF PROOF IN LOGIC

The concept of *proof of A* which is operational in logical systems identifies it with a sequence of wff's the last of which is *A* and each of which is either a principle of the system (an axiom or a LAF) or derivable from previous wff's of the sequence according to the rules of inference of the system. In two-valued logic the process of derivation or deduction is presented in specific terms of preserving the value of truth: if the previous wff's of a sequence are true what is *proved* from them is also true: the truth of a conclusion is seen (evidenced) and necessitated by the pervasive presence of truth in the proof. The process of proof has the characteristic of preserving values of rationality, truth and tautologousness during the development of logical systems.

Chapter-4

A Discussion of Russell's Paradox and of the Grounds for Classal Thought and for Calculi of Classes

Chapter 4

RUSSELL'S PARADOX

To fall under a concept or defining property, to belong to a class, to be part of a concept's extension—these seem to be identical.

Take the concept, *class that does not belong to itself.* Examine the content and extension of this concept. Its extension is the class of those classes that do not belong to themselves. This itself is a class (a class of classes.) Does it belong to itself or not? If it does, then it does not fall under the concept whose extension it is, i.e. the concept, *class that does not belong to itself.* If it does not belong to itself, then it falls under the concept, *class that does not belong to itself,* while not being part of the concept's extension. The alternatives are exhaustive and the outcome in each case seems to be a contradiction (or to run counter to the expectancy of natural thought.)

Russell describes, very simply, the development of the paradox: 'it seemed to me that a class sometimes is, and sometimes is not, a member of itself. The class of teaspoons, for example, is not another teaspoon, but the class of things that are not teaspoons, for example, is not another teaspoons. There seemed to be instances which are not negative: for example the class of all classes is a class. The application of Cantor's argument [that there is no greatest cardinal number] led me to consider the classes that are not members of themselves; and these, it seemed, must form a class. I asked myself whether this class is a member of itself or not. If it is amember of itself, it must possess the defining property of the class, which is to be not a member of itself. If it is not a member of itself, it must not possess the defining property of the class, and therefore must be a member of itself. Thus each alternative leads to its opposite and there is a contradiction.

'At first I thought there must be some trivial error in my reasoning. I inspected each step under a logical microscope, but I could not discover anything wrong.' (*My Philosophical Development,* p. 76)

THE IMPACT OF RUSSELL'S PARADOX ON FREGE'S SYSTEM OF LOGIC AND MATHEMATICS

A primary aim of Frege's was to construct a language able to signify, exclusively, the forms (simple, complex and systematic) of thought—where thought denotes not psychic vitality but that which is signified by, or contained in, thought.This language would symbolize precisely that which is germane to exact proof, to the inferential process as such, for what we prove is not a sentence or the judgement it expresses but the thought content of these, i.e. that in them which can be understood by any mind and is the same for every mind—'objective thought'. He was not interested in concepts of particular objects or in proofs of particular empirical propositions, but wanted to formalize depth structures and depth processes of objective thought in a language that would disengage them from particular contexts and from the particular argumentative forces and consequences of object-language. While having no particular reference, the variables and constants of his language were able to determine definitely the truth conditions of all statements made in the language, so that these statements had two reference values, the True and the False. The true statements constituted Logic, the depth science of objective thought. With his language, syntax and grammar he was able to discover and formalize, substantially, both propositional and predicate logic.

In studying the foundations of Arithmetic (for him the theory of natural and real numbers), Frege came to believe that Arithmetic is reducible to Logic, that the very nature of conceptual thought gives rise to our thinking numerically as it does to our thinking logically; in present-day terms we might say that it lies totally within the impulse of conceptual thought and of natural deduction to think and reason numerically.

Frege's belief may be studied, philosophically, in the light of key concepts which appear in the arithmetical expansion of logical thought—'number', 'class', 'extension'. (In this study the significance of Russell's paradox can be very starkly appreciated); and technically, in the light of his formalization of Arithmetic:

For Frege, a concept symbolized in logic as a propositional function, gives rise to the notion of class, i.e. the set of things realizing this concept, possessing this defining property. A class can be fully described in the logical notation of predicate logic with identity. Classes are similar or dissimilar: two classes are similar if there is a way of coupling all the objects in one with all the objects in the other, one to one. The concept of number arises in response to the question: how many?—no matter what particular form an answer may take its basic conceptual content is 'just as many as are in this similar class'. How many people are there in the auditorium? 'Just as many as there are seats' answers the question numerically, i.e. by coupling the audience with a similar class. If I want to give the number more absolutely I will couple the audience with the set of *all* similar classes: this is what I do when I use a numeral (e.g. 1000) which names the set in question. *Numerals* then are class names; the cardinal *numbers,* designated by numerals, are classes—equivalence classes of concepts generated by the equivalence relation 'just as many as': the number of *Fs* is, in definition, the class of concepts G such that there are as many *Fs* as *Gs*.

Thus number is a property of classes; class and extension are an objective dimension of every concept; numbers can be apprehended as logical objects through the fact that whatever falls under a concept and therefore possesses the defining property of a class must be a member of that class, so that we can pass from a concept to its extension; numerical thought is constitutionally logical, i.e. in content, form and grammar it is totally logical; and any logical formalization of thought is implicity numerical, for the extension of a concept is so necessarily linked with its intension that whatever object falls under a concept must be part of its extension.

Technically, Frege offered confirmation for this philosophical position by presenting Arithmetic as an axiomatic theory whose notions and laws were entirely reducible to logical ones. (It is important to note that Frege did not hold the logistic thesis for the whole of mathematics but only for the theory of natural and real numbers: for him geometry was founded on synthetic *a priori* truths that could not be reduced to logic. And he did succeed in deriving, on the basis of his definitions, all the Peano axioms for the natural numbers and therefore in showing that all those arithmetical statements are analytic which do not require that every natural number has an immediate successor—i.e. that the number series be infinite.)

It is clear that Russell's paradox affected not only Frege's particular formalization of Arithmetic. ('It is a matter of my Axiom (V). I have never disguised from myself its lack of the self-evidence that belongs to the other axioms and that must properly be demanded of a logical law'—Appendix to *Grundgesetze der Arithmetik*), not only his belief that 'The basis of arithmetic lies deeper, it seems, than that of any of the empirical sciences, and even that of geometry' (*Grundlagen*, pp. 20-1), but also his whole philosophical conception of numerical thought. It was just before the publication of the second volume of the *Grundgesetze* (in 1903) that Russell communicated his paradox, and in the Preface Frege had written:

> The whole of the second part is really a test of my logical convictions. It is improbable that such an edifice could be erected on an unsound base...As a proof of the contrary, I can only admit the production by someone of an actual demonstration that upon other fundamental convictions a better and more durable edifice can be erected, or the demonstration by someone that my premisses lead to manifestly false conclusions. But nobody will be able to do that. (p. 147)

In his appendix on the paradox Frege immediately acknowledges its seriousness: 'Hardly anything more unfortunate can befall a scientific writer than to have one of the foundations of his edifice shaken after the work is finished.'

In the event, Frege was content with a technical escape from the paradox by stating a new criterion for equality in extension, modifying his fifth law to read 'Two concepts have equal extensions if and only if any object, which is not the extension of one of them, falls under one if and only if it falls under both.' It is likely that he came to see that with this weakened law the crucial theorem that the series of natural numbers is infinite was no longer valid in his axiomatization of arithmetic; and after his death Stanislaw Lesniewski showed that the modified law gave rise, itself, to contradiction. However, in his late years' he seems to have reached the conclusion that he had been mistaken in principle concerning the nature of numerical thought: 'In 1923 he became convinced that the whole project of founding arithmetic on logic was in error and that the theory of classes constituted the nub of the error: set theory was an intellectual aberration which had led him and others astray. Since mathematics still needed to be unified, geometry would have to be taken as the fundamental mathematical theory and analysis and even number theory derived from it: all mathematical truth was thus synthetic a *priori*. Frege began some work expounding this new philosophy of mathematics but he was unable to carry it far and published none of it.' (Article by Michael Dummett on Frege in *The Encyclopedia of Philosophy,* vol. 3, p. 227)

THE DEVELOPMENTAL INFLUENCE OF RUSSELL'S PARADOX WITHIN HIS OWN SYSTEM

Frege exemplifies a three-level semantic approach to meaning, dealing with it in co-ordinated terms of thought-language-reality. For him, object and concept (real 'thereness' and intelligible content) were fundamental terms for language analysis and for the exact expression or interpretation of logical and mathematical statements. The impact of Russell's paradox within the context of a two-level semantics (where it is the truth of *sentences, their* correspondence with reality that is *solely* focused) is very different and Russell himself exemplifies this difference. He also exemplified a belief in analysis which he described in later life as the strongest and most unshakeable prejudice in his philosophical method. The outcome of this dual commitment (to a two-level semantics and to analysis) was a kind of Russellian analysis called reduction which sought, by means of a strict linguistic rectitude, to eliminate paradoxes and to reach truth and certainty as an impersonal correspondence between what we say and the facts.

This meant, in the first place, reducing the number of primitive terms to a minimum, eliminating inferred entities and oblique talk. As a case in point, number is not a primitive term. Numbers, as Frege had shown, can be defined as classes of classes: 0 as the class of all empty classes; 1 as the class of all classes each of which is such that any member is identical with every other member; 2 as the class of all classes each of which is such that it includes a member not identical with another member and such that it includes a member not identical with another member and such that any member is identical with one or other of these. Russell comments (in *My philosophical Development,* p. 71) that thus 'we get rid of numbers as metaphysical entities. They become, in fact, merely linguistic conveniences with no more substantiality than belongs to "etc." or "i.e.". Kronecker, in philosophizing about mathematics, said that "God made the integers and the mathematicians made the rest of the mathematical apparatus." By this he meant that each integer had to have an independent being, but other kinds of numbers need not have. With the above definition of numbers this prerogative of the integers disappears and the primitive apparatus of the mathematician is reduced to such purely logical terms as *or*, *not*, *all* and *some*. This was my first experience of the usefulness of Occam's razor in diminishing the number of undefined terms and unproved propositions required in a given body of knowledge.' (Alan Wood points out that 'Russell's use of Occam's Razor was not only a means to an end but part of something which was a motive in itself, a passion which had almost as much force in Russell's mind as his passion for impersonal truth... it might variously be described as love of aesthetic elegance, love of unity, love of system, or profundity'. It was part of the inmost essence of his intellectual impulse.)

Another case in point of genuine primitive terms is the category of words that have the straightforward meaning of pointing to an object. These must be carefully distinguished from other words. In his theory of descriptions, he points out that the only primitive terms which have this straightforward meaning are names: these are logically structureless: they simply pick out what we are making predications about; they ary significant only because there is something they refer to and if there were not this something they would be empty noises, not words. The man who substitutes a description (e.g. 'the only satellite of the earth' for a name ('the moon') is no longer, linguistically, in direct contact with the world, he is speaking about a complex of concepts and a missing *referent* cannot be replaced by the *sense* of concepts. Fully analysed, the sentence '*the golden mountain does not exist*' is seen to be without a logical subject: it concerns the propositional function 'X is golden and a mountain' and says that this is false for all values of X. Thus the paradox of talking about a golden mountain although no golden mountain exists disappears when we see that while a name cannot occur significantly in a proposition unless there is something that it names, a description may contribute to the meaning of a sentence without having any meaning at all in isolation—it is an incomplete symbol whose use is defined within the context of the entire sentence.

From the very beginning Russell felt that the source of his paradox lay in treating 'class' as the name of an object. It is interesting to recall here Wittgenstein's last meeting with Frege: 'as we were waiting at the station for my train, I said to him "Don't you ever find any difficulty in your theory that numbers are objects?" He replied "Sometimes I seem to see a difficulty—but then again I *don't* see it.'" Russell, however, came to the conclusion that classes are merely a convenience in discourse. In *My Philosophical Development* he explains the development of his view:

> Let. us start with a homely illustration [of what is meant by 'class']. Suppose, at the end of dinner, your host offers you a choice of three different sweets, urging you to have any one or two or all three, as you may wish. How many courses of conduct are open to you? You may refuse all of them. That is one choice. You may take one of them. This is possible in three different ways and therefore gives you three more choices.You may choose two of them. This again is possible in three ways. Or you may choose all three, which gives you one final possibility.The total number of possibilities is thus eight, i.e. 2^3.It is easy to generalize this procedure. Suppose you have *n* objects before you and you wish to know how many ways there are of choosing none or some or all of the *n*. You will find that the number of ways is 2^n. To put it in logical language: a class of *n* terms has 2^n sub-classes. This proposition is still true when *n* is infinite. What Cantor proved was that even in this case, 2^n is greater than *n*. Applying this, as I did, to all the things in the universe, one arrives at the conclusion that there are more classes of things than there are things. It follows that classes are not 'things'. But, as no one quite knows what the word 'thing' means in this statement, it is not very easy to state at all exactly what it is that has been proved...
>
> I should now phrase the matter somewhat differently. I should say that, given any propositional function, say *fx*, there is a certain range of values of *x* for which this function is 'significant'—i.e. either true or false. If *a* is in this range, then *fa* is a proposition which is either true or false. In addition to substituting a constant for the variable

> x, there are two other things that may be done with a propositional function: one is to assert that it is always true; and the other that it is sometimes true. The propositional function, 'if x is human, x is mortal' is always true; the propostional function 'x is human' is sometimes true. There are thus three things that can be done with a propositional function: the first is to substitute a constant for the variable; the second is to assert all values of the function; and the third is to assert some values or at least one value. The propositional function itself is only an expression. It does not assert or deny anything. A class, equally, is only an expression. It is only a convenient way of talking about the values of the variable for which the function is true.(pp.81-2)

Russell believed that his paradox had arisen precisely because classes and individuals had been put on the one level and remained wholly convinced all his life that some form of a doctrine of types was essential to a solution. The basic idea of such a doctrine would be to distinguish various levels of predicates. A predicate holds for individuals, but we cannot meaningfully assert that a predicate of predicates does or does not hold for an individuals. In terms of functions, his hierarchy of types was 'individuals, one-place functions of individuals (that correspond to properties), two-place functions of individuals (that correspond to two-term relations)... functions of functions of individuals...and so on'. (Ibid., p. 77) He realized later that in his early theory of types he was defining categories of entities not syntactical categories of signs, and indeed, a consistently formulated doctrine of syntactical categories was first worked out by Lesniewski and the Polish logistic school'. (Ibid.,p. 79) But it is quite clear that his theory provided, in principle, a rule and a reason which eliminated a major cause of paradoxes. Further, as a ground for condemning the kind of reflexive self-reference that is in such paradoxes as The Liar, he introduced a distinction of orders within each type thus obtaining what came to be known as the ramified theory of types.

Reviewing in 1959 the development of his thought, Russel noted that he had come to conceive the science of logic as being grounded in language: 'I no longer think that the laws of logic are laws of things; on the contrary, I now regard them as purely linguistic.' (*My philosophical Development,* p. 102)

CLASS TERMS IN THE HISTORY OF TRADITIONAL PHILOSOPHY AND LOGIC—THE PROBLEM OF UNIVERSALS

To describe our world and our life we use terms such as wood, glass, steel, sky, sea, air, large, small, coloured, black, hot, cold, hard, soft; living, dead, growing, eating, running; angry, pleasant, intelligent, conscientious, etc. We feel that these physical, biological and psychological words are true of individual things and people, but they also have distinctive properties of their own: they are, themselves, classal and universal in meaning and are applied indefinitely to vast ranges of individuals. The question arises: what (if anything) corresponds in reality to the classal, universal features of words? This is the traditional problem of universals.

In its basic formulation it is mainly a logical problem, but it opens on to three departments of philosophy—Metaphysics, Psychology and Epistemology. It leads directly to the more particular and metaphysical question: what precisely is the structure of reality? and rival metaphysical systems have often tested their strength on the general problem of universals. It gives rise also to a psychological question: is there really a universal idea, a unit of cognition higher than sense? We speak of concepts and ideas, and describe them as universal and abstract, but on empirical enquiry are they reducible to sense-impressions and sense-imagery? Finally, an epistemological question emerges: concepts are supposed to disclose and signify real objects: how can universal concepts constitute objective knowledge of individual things?

The problem of universals has been discussed in various ways throughout the histroy of Western philosophy. A classic text in Porphyry's third-century *Introduction to the Categories of Aristotle* formulated the Greek problem for medieval logicians (Boethius' sixth-century translation of Porphyry being one of the main logical works in early medieval libraries).

> Mox de generibus ac speciebus illud, sive subsistant, sive in solis nudisque intellectibus posita sint, sive subsistentia corporalia sint an incorporalia, et utrum separata a sensibilibus an in sensibilibus posita et circa haec consistentia sint, dicere recusabo; altissimum enim negotium est hujusmodi et majoris egens inquistitionis.
>
> As for genus and species, I beg to be excused from discussing at present the question whether they exist in reality or have their place simply and solely in thoughts, and if they exist, whether they are corporeal or incorporeal, and whether they are separable or exist only in sensible things and dependent upon them. For such a study is very deep and requires another and larger inquiry. (As translated in Kneale's *The Development of Logic,* p. 196)

The universal term is *unum—versus—alia,* 'one related to many', a term that can be predicated of many subjects. Porphyry does not speak of universals as such but of 'genera' and 'species' these being the two main members of the predicables, the traditional five-fold division of universal predicate terms—genus, species, differentia, proprium, accident. His choice brings out the fact that the traditional problem was to a great extent a problem of the structure of reality: do essences, natures, types exist? have these words a foundation in reality and if so what is the foundation? His choice also reminds us that traditional philosophy has debated the logical problem mainly in the context of predication rather than in the logico-mathematical context where the issue is the validity of class as such, and of names for collectivities. It is this latter issue which is the more central since the time of Russell's paradox.

The various traditional theories are as follows:

Nominalism: For the nominalist the general term or class

name is a purely linguistic phenomenon. It does not derive from a higher level of cognition than sense and it is not founded on the reality of types or essences in nature. Thinking of, and referring to, things in groups or bundles is completely reducible to a skill in the use of linguistic signs for individuals.

In general, nominalists have tended to operate a two-level semantics and, philosophically, a Sensist approach, eliminating belief in genuinely abstract ideas and in a distinctive knowledge and higher insight given by the processes of human understanding. Berkeley and Hume exemplify the traditional nominalist rejection of abstract ideas. Selecting Locke as a typical exponent and defender of them, Berkeley argues that it is psychologically impossible to frame an abstract idea:

> To be plain, I own myself able to abstract in one sense, as when I consider some particular parts or qualities separated from others, with which though they are united in some object, yet it is possible they may really exist without them. But I deny that i can abstract one from another, or conceive separately, those qualities which it is impossible should exist so separated; or that I can frame a general notion by abstracting from particulars in the manner aforesaid [i.e. Lockean]. (*Treatise Concerning the Principles of Human Knowledge,* para. 10)
>
> ...the idea of man that, I frame to myself, must be either of a white, or a black, or a tawny, a straight or a crooked, a tall, or a low, or a middle-sized man. I cannot by any effort of thought conceive the abstract idea above described...
>
> ... wherein 'tis true, there's included colour, because there is no man but has some colour, but then it can be neither white, nor black, nor any particular colour; because there is no one particular colour wherein all men partake. So likewise there is included stature, but then 'tis neither tall stature nor low stature, nor yet middle stature, but something abstracted from all these..(Ibid., paras.10 and 9)

The so-called abstract idea is really a particular idea used by the mind 'to represent or stand for all other particular ideas of the same sort.' (Ibid., para. 12) Hume carries Berkeley's theory further, explaining how a particular idea 'is applied beyond the limits of its real nature as if it were universal':

> Abstract ideas are therefore in themselves individual, however they may become general in their representation. The image in the mind is only that of a particular object, though the application of it in our reasoning be the same, as if it were universal... The word raises up an individual idea, along with a certain custom; and that custom produces any other individual one, for which we may have occasion... For this is one of the most extraordinary circumstances in the present affair, that after the mind has produced an individual idea, upon which we reason, the attendant custom, revived by the general or abstract term, readily suggests any other individual, if by chance we form any reasoning, that agrees not with it. Thus should we mention the word, triangle, and form the idea of a particular equilateral one to correspond to it, and should we afterwards assert, *that the three angles of a triangle are equal to each other,* the other individuals of a scalenum and isoceles, which we overlooked at first, immediately crowd in upon us, and make us perceive the falsehood of this proposition, though it be true with relation to that idea, which we had formed. (*Treatise of Human Nature,* Book I, part 1, § 7)

In so far as a nominalist holds that generality attaches to words he is vulnerable to the type-token distinction. All occurrences of the word 'man' are individual and in speaking of the *same* word we are moving from tokens to types; there seems no reason why generality should not be extended to other categories besides words. On a last analysis, traditional nominalism tends to analyse generality linguistically and on the basis of a skill we develop in dealing with a world of individuals. It adheres strictly (and in a doctrinaire fashion) to a two-level semantic approach.

Conceptualism: For the conceptualist, human thought is a higher level of cognition than sense and is constituted by ideas with a genuinely general signification. Abstraction is a phenomenon of thought and universal, classal ideas are natural mental facts, anterior to, and independent of, conventional verbal expression. This reduction of the universal to thought is total (as the reduction to language was total for the nominalist): to exist outside the mind is to be singular, and the classal, universal properties of ideas are not realized in singular things.

In the Platonic dialogue, *Parmenides,* Socrates appears as a very young man expounding to the great Parmenides and Zeno his theory that individual sensible things participate in *forms.* Parmenides is critical and Socrates is led to make various suggestions as to the nature of the forms. One suggestion is that a form is really a thought and therefore is not in things at all, but in our minds. Parmenides replies that thought is always a thought of some extramental object and further if forms are thoughts the things that participate in them must be thoughts also. Thus for the first time in history something like a doctrine of conceptualism was formulated only to be promptly rejected.

It is the medieval philosopher and logician, William of Occam, who gives the most complete version of this view (his school were later called nominalists, terminists, moderns because they were following a new modern and anti-realist way of interpreting Aristotle). For him any form of *concrete* universality, of *concrete* classal stratification, is unthinkable; 'every positive thing existing outside the soul is by that very fact singular'. Universality is a phenomenon of signification *only;* the universal is a predicate or meaning self-producing in thought under the natural action of similar objects on sense and a community of sense-intuitions; it is ncessary for thought and communication: 'the intellection, by which I understand man, is the natural sign of man, just as groaning is the sign of sickness, of sadness or orpain and such a sign can stand for men in mental propositions, just as a word can stand for things in vocal propositions'. (*Summa Logicae,* 1, 15 Bohner's edition, p. 48) Occam feels that he was the first philosopher who did not attribute *any reality at all* to universality in things. (Sentences, 1, 2, 7, B)

Realism: Forms of realism go beyond both nominalism and conceptualism in asserting some king of formal correspondence between what is *meant,* in language and thought, and what really *is* so.

In the Ultra-realism of Plato there is a world directly and formally corresponding to the nature and properties of thought; logical properties are also properties of things; the *modus mentis* and *modus rei* are identical in a World of Ideas in comparison with which our present sensible environment is a shadow, opaque, world.

In the Middle Ages the theory of Ultra-realism was widely held in various technical forms from the ninth to the twelfth century, e.g. by Adelhard of Bath, William of Champeaux, William of Auvergne. Moderate Realism slowly took shape with growing opposition to Ultra-realism but it was not formally propounded until the middle of the twelfth century. With Abelard (1079-1142) it was firmly established and became incorporated into Scholasticism. Contact with the works of Aristotle and with his Arabian commentator, Avicenna (980-1037), led to the full development of the theory in the following century. Thomas Aquinas gave it a full exposition mainly in his De Ente et Essentia.

Any statement of Moderate Realism amounts to a commentary on the medieval formula: *Univer salia sunt formaliter in mente, fundamentaliter autem in rebus ipsis* (Universals exist formally only in the mind, but they have a foundation in reality itself). There are as many human natures (e.g.) as there are individual men. In each individual, human nature is individualized and therefore rendered exclusive and incommunicable; it exists in reality only as that which a particular unique individual is. But one and the same concept is knowledge of all these individuals; through the concept we grasp the essence not only of the individual present here and now, but of every individual of his class. Thus while human nature exists in reality individualized and therefore incommunicable, it exists in the mind unindividualized, as the content of a concept, as that which a concept means. As abstracted the essence is not characterized by the incommunicability and exclusiveness of the individual; universality is a characteristic of it and it is predicable of many.

A material thing is a complex, sensible, intelligible entity. Intelligible aspects (e.g. being of this or that type) are just as real and as factual as sensible aspects (e.g. shape, size, movement). Thus in virtue of a common intelligibility, individual men and animals are in real relations of specific or generic identity. Confined to the intelligible aspects of things, concepts cannot provide a knowledge of singular objects in their singularity but they do provide a synthetic knowledge of a theoretically indefinite range of objects.

Moderate realism naturally tends to make predication a central topic (how universal meanings can be properly referred to real individuals). Medieval theory provides a complete doctrine here: The subject-term is simply spoken of as designating the object about which we are making the predication. This object is called the supposit of predication. Thus in the sentence: men are mortal, *men* is the subject-term, the supposit of predication are the real men signified by the term. It is the logical function of a subject-term to designate the supposit of predication. This may be done by means of a term like 'this' or 'that' accompanied by a gesture (e.g.) this is a hospital) or by means of a term which classifies the supposit (e.g. hospitals are necessary) or which connotes some of its attributes (the very young patients are difficult) In the first case the supposit is taken at the level of perception without any formal conceptualization; in the other cases what before were predicates are used as explanatory and descriptive features of the supposit. In some sentences it may be quite difficult to determine the supposit, e.g. in impersonal statements such as: it is fine.

The predicate term is spoken of as signifying the nature or a less fundamental feature attributed to the subject. It signifies this nature or quality in a state of total abstraction. That is to say (1) it does *not* signify the nature or quality in a state of formal abstraction, as isolated from supposits. We do not say 'Socrates is redness' or 'Socrates is humanity'. A term cannot function as predicate if it connotes a formality, i.e. a form considered in isolation and independence of supposits. (2) It signifies a nature or quality as realized in supposits which however are left undetermined. This state of abstraction is called total abstraction.The nature or quality is thought of not in isolation but as characterizing a concrete whole or *totum* (which, however, is not in any way determined). In English, adjectives like *red, human* and substantives *man, horse,* fulfil this logical requirement for the predicate-term. Both are abstract terms by total abstraction, strictly speaking, although they are often described as concrete to contrast them with terms like *redness, humanity,* which are abstract terms by formal abstraction.

The medieval analysis of predication itself distinguishes an *identity* that is affirmed and an *attribution* that is thereby made. In 'Socrates is a red thing the copula ('is') identifies the being concretely, designated by the subject-term ('Socrates') as a supposit indeterminately referred to by the predicate (which in traditional logic, as we have seen, signifies a quality, e.g. red, as realized in supposits which however are left undetermined).

In and through that identification an attribution is also made. Aquinas says that it is the *natura absoluta* which is attributed. This is a very technical term and doctrine which Aquinas derived from Avicenna (the Arabian translator and commentator of Aristotle) through Albertus Magnus. He distinguishes three ways in which an essence or intelligible structure can be considered or attributed. It can be considered as individualized *hic et nunc* (determinately therefore); and it can be considered as conceptualized. In predication it is not attributed in either of these two ways. When I say Socrates is a man I do not *attribute* to Socrates anything that accrues to human nature from its being individualized in him. If I did so, that which I attribute to him could not be attributed to other individuals—the predicate *man* would be exclusive to him. Neither do I attribute to Socrates anything that accrues to human nature from its conceptual mode of existence. If I did so, the individual Socrates would be declared to be the species man, to have the *ratio specier*.

What is *attributed* therefore to the supposit is neither the essence (i.e. intelligible structure) as conceptualized nor as determinately individualized, but according to its content or constitutive notes viewed absolutely or *secundem se.* The essence so taken is termed the *natura absoluta.* Aquinas says (*De Ente et Essentia,* ch. IV): 'Haec natura est quae praedicatur de omnibus individuis.'

Summary statement concerning the traditional theories, Nominalism, Conceptualism and Realism. It is evident that in the traditional problem of universals, the problem of generality is restricted predominantly to the names of objects and their qualities. Through wittgenstein's advocacy of 'family resemblance' instead of 'something in common', and through the developement of semantics (pointing out, e.g. the generality that wouds like 'and', 'if . . . then', 'either . . . or', etc. have through syntactical function) the terms and scope of the problem have changed considerably today.

PERSPECTIVE ON RUSSELL'S PARADOX

The role and use of the concept, class, in contemporary mathematics. It is generally accepted in mathematics that the term, *set,* is an undefined term, the concept of set being one of the most primitive and fundamental concepts underlying mathematical structures.

Russell's paradox and others—the Cantor, Burali–Forti and Zermelo–Konig ones—concern the possibility of certain questionable sets; they showed that not only is an intuitive notion of set not precise enough for use in strict logical derivation but that, also, it is open to these paradoxes. While Russell's theory of types made a contribution to fundamental logical theory providing a new, refined, logical intuition, Zermelo attempted simply to give better 'definition' to set by subjecting it to axioms which do not allow the introduction of the paradoxical sets. The aim of this approach, technically described as axiomatic set theory, is to provide a derivation for all the theorems that mathematicians need. 'Admittedly, the consistency of the system remains unproved, and a new paradox may crop up in the theory. We can only check that the arguments leading to the known paradoxes cannot be reproduced in the system. In view of Gödel's theorem (1931), the very notion of consistency proof for set theory raises profound difficulties. After Zermelo, axiomatic set theory was developed by A. A. Fraenkel, Thoralf Skolem, and John von Neumann in the 1920s, by Paul Bernays and Kurt Gödel in the late 1930s, and by many others since then. It has become a lively and wide domain of investigation, and a return to a naive, intuitive view of sets seems impossible.' (*Encyclopedia of Philosophy,* vol. 5; article on Logical paradoxes by John van Heijenoort, p. 49)

In subjecting the notion of set to the control of axioms on the basis of our experience of paradox and impossibility, axiomatic set theory seems to agree, in principle, with traditional moderate realism that universals have a foundation in reality and their extensive use in theory must therefore be guided by reality testing. Reality controls deemed necessary to govern classal thought may be formally embodied either in axioms or in a 'definition'of set.

Stanislaw Lesniewski (1886-1939) and mereology, the theory of concrete totalities. Professor Lejewski of Manchester (a disciple of Lesniewski) writes:

Lesniewski's discovery in 1911 of Jan Lukasiewicz's

monograph on the principle of contradiction in Aristotle... was a turning point in his philosophical career. From this book Lesniewski first learned of symbolic logic, of Bertrand Russell's work and of the antinomy of the class of all classes that are not elements of themselves. The problem of antinomies immediately fascinated him and for many years absorbed a large part of his interest. His persistent efforts to solve this problem eventually resulted in the construction of a system of the foundations of mathematics distinguished by originality, comprehensiveness and elegance.

Analysis of the Russellian antinomy convinced Lesniewski that we should distinguish between the distributive and the collective interpretations of class expressions. The expression 'A is an element of the class of b's' in which the term 'element of' and 'the class of' are used distributively, means simply that A is a b. If, however, we interpret the terms 'element of' and the 'class of' collectively [i.e. as concrete totalities], then our original expression means that A is a part (proper of improper) of the whole consisting of b's, that is that A is part of the object that has the following two properties: (1) every b is a part of it, and (2) every part of it has a common part with a b. According to Lesniewski the presuppositions of the Russellian antinomy appear to be true because we fail to distinguish between the distributive and collective interpretations. Once the distinction is made it is evident that on either interpretation some of the presuppositions on which the antinomy hinges turn out to be false. Lesniewski developed his ideas concerning the collective interpretation of class expressions by constructing a deductive theory, first outlined in Polish in 1916. At that time Lesniewski mistrusted symbolic language and formulated his theorems and gave proofs of them in ordinary language. Thus, his theory, which he subsequently termed 'mereology'... does not resemble a formal calculus but reads rather like Euclid. Among the various systems of mereology [after the Greek word for

> 'part': *meros*] the one based on 'element of' as the only undefined term, with 'the class of' introduced by definition, appears to have been most popular with Lesniewski and his pupils. (*Encyclopedia of Philosophy,* vol. 4, p. 441)

No antinomies occur in this theory and it can in many cases be applied in place of the traditional calculus of classes. Lesniewski uses the word class but the word refers not to abstract classes but to concrete collective totalities ('concrete heaps' Quine called them); it is not only material things that form a merological whole: if there are purely spiritual beings they too form a concrete collective totality and may be designated as one object. Lesniewski's theory describes objects in terms of the concepts, *part* and *whole,* and he referred to it himself as a doctrine of part-whole relations.

Guido Küng points out:

> In 1926 Tarski drew Lesniewski's attention to the similarity existing between his mereology and Whitehead's theory of events. Whitehead too refers to part-relations; one event can be part of another; two events can overlap. In the United States, mereology is known as the 'calculus of individuals'—a designation that is etymologically somewhat paradoxical, since the objects of mereology are anything but indivisible *individua.* It was developed there independently of Lesniewski by N. Goodman and H. S. Leonard around 1930. [It is possible that Whitehead's ideas partly inspired the work: he was teaching at Harvard at the time, with Leonard working under him.] J. H. Woodger, the English biologist, constructed his own, similar theory and applied it to biology...It is not suprising that interest in mereology should have developed independently in different parts of the world. this is readily explained by the nominalistic trend in contemporary philosophy [the theory of classes makes explicit reference to abstract objects]...Unfortunately Lesniewski's work, the first in the field of mereology and the most detailed and precise, remained largely unknown outside Poland until 1937, when

> Tarski brought it to a wider public. Lesniewski's theory is being developed further by B. Sobocinski and C. Lejewski. (*Ontology and the Logistic Analysis of Language,* p. 107)

It is relevant to note that for Lesniewski a theory should develop and formalize knowledge of the truth. Its axioms should be true propositions and its rules of inference should be intuitively valid ones. 'He consequently described himself as a confirmed intuitionist who at the same time was a radical formalist [insisting on subjecting any intuitively sound theory to the process of formalization] and a better characterization of this standpoint could hardly be given.' (C. Lejewski in an article, 'On Lesniewski's Ontology', *Ratio,* vol.1, no. 2, December 1958) Thus his mereology, even more than axiomatic set theory, subjects itself to the control of experience.

It may be helpful to remark here on Geach's work, *Reference and Generality.* It discusses various kinds of expressions with which, it seems, we can refer to any given individual: a proper name, a general term, a many worded description, a phrase with 'some' or 'every', an indefinite pronoun like 'something', 'everything' or 'the same', or a pronoun looking back to an antecendent of one of these kinds. In discussing the claims of these expressions to be referring expressions, he notes that there are two quite distinct relations which are frequently not grasped as distinct, namely the relation of a name to the thing named and the relation of a predicate to what it is true of. Lesniewski had noted, similarly, that class or set terminology (generated by the operation of an abstraction or collective functor) was needed to name any collection as a concrete individual, whereas such terminology used distributively in predication was dispensable: the distributive use could be expressed without abstraction (collective) operators by means of the copula together with other functors and defined constants. Accordingly, he emphasized the distinction between the distributive and collective use of class expressions.

For Frege, Russell and most modern logicians, class terms like 'man' are not in the syntactic category of names. It is interesting to hear Geach who favours the opposite ('simple and natural view'of Aristotle) say:

> ...thanks to Russell and Frege, most of the logical insights that were lost by Aristotle's Fall have been recovered; but not, to my mind, quite all of them...What we still have not got is a formal theory that recognizes the status of some general terms as names without blurring the distinction between names and predicables. Success in stating such a theory would be paradise Regained. (*A History of the Corruptions of Logic:* an inaugural lecture delivered before the University of Leeds, January 1968)

Formal solutions to the paradoxes. In his *Foundations of Mathematics* (1925), F. P. Ramsay divided paradoxes into two groups: syntactic paradoxes (e.g. those of Russell and Burali-Forti) involve only syntactic and mathematical notions, semantic paradoxes (e.g. the Liar paradox, and those of Berry and Richard) are not due to any fault in logic but to a vagueness, ambiguity or confusion that centres on the distinction between a word or phrase and its meaning. Such a fundamental division, widely used for many years, is no longer acceptable.

It is true to say that, in practice, paradoxes which cannot be handled by a simple theory of types (assuming a hierarchy of parts of speech in one's basic language) are now generally dealt with by assuming a hierarchy of languages—a basic language, a metalanguage for describing and evaluating the meaning and truth of expressions in our basic language, a metametalanguage for discussing expressions in our metalanguage and so on. In general the nonsense of paradoxes is traced to some failure in linguistic rectitude which demands that we acknowledge the natural stratifications within lanugage and between languages.

John van Heijenoort sums up the situation:

> Any given paradox rests on a number of definitions, assumptions and arguments, and we can solve it by questioning any of these. That is why the literature on

> paradoxes is so rich and abounds with so many solutions. That is also why there is no one problem of the paradoxes. For the important paradoxes, the question is not of solving them by any means but of solving them by means that enlarge and strengthen our logical intuitions. It is to find, among the sometimes too numerous solutions, the one that fits our logic most smoothly and perhaps, to some extent, to adapt our logic to this solution. (*Encyclopedia of Philosophy,* vol.5,p. 51)

The history of paradoxes and of their solutions underlines the value, for logic, of a distinction between expressive and descriptive thought. There is a distinction between *meaning* and *intelligibility.* Physical things (e.g. the table) are intelligible. So are the ink marks on this page but they also *say* something, are meaningful, significant; so also as I think about the world, not only am I informed but I judge and assert it to be as I think it—I *know* it:my thought is knowledge. Paradox is always possible in the media of meaningful speech, writing and thought for these are humanly constituted. It has always been an objective and function of logic to be so developed that paradoxes would be logically ungrammatical.

However, there are many forms of thought. In thought, in writing, in speech we may be expressive rather than descriptive or objective—e.g. we may express questions, commands, prayers, exhortations; we may express classes that cannot possibly be—whether classes that do not belong to themselves or classes that do belong to themselves. Logic, however, has shown itself to be concerned not with what reason *can express* but with what reason *must accept* as being possible. It is concerned with what can be *said* as distinct from what can be expressed; its contexts are language and thought as mediating knowledge.

Traditional logic was an abstractive logic and its theory of universals was a theory of descriptive universals (its universals are the universals of a vernacular object-language). Modern logic is constructive and a distinction between expressive and descriptive universals is demanded in the practice and in the definition of this purer kind of logic. Russell's paradox shows this.

It is interesting to note that modern logic is not an absolutely pure logic: while propositional logic gives a *priori* laws of all possible worlds, predicate logic provides only the depth grammar of thought about a universe with at least one individual in it. Such thought is, of its objective nature, classal and numerical and so the calculus of classes and arithmetic seem to qualify, with predicate logic, to be part of its depth grammar. Thus it is possible to argue that the logistic thesis is correct only because logic as yet is not pure enough.

Chapter-5

The Language of Formal Logic

Chapter 5

INTRODUCTION

The language employed by Formal Logic is a special artificial one. There are many advantages in departing from the use of vernacular languages. The latter are object-languages but logic needs a second-order or meta-language. Again vernacular words are constantly acquiring new nuances of meaning and new idiomatic uses; scientific work requires greater fixity of meaning. Finally built into vernacular words is a whole code of directions for pronunciation; the alphabet is a phonetic code, vernacular words are phonograms or phonographs. Thus a person is able to pronounce a vernacular word before he learns to associate the appropriate meaning with it. It is important that a vernacular language should facilitate oral communication. It is not necessary that a scientific language do so and great economy and conciseness is achieved by devising a language which consists of ideograms, i.e. signs which stand directly for concepts. The mathematical symbol '×' exemplifies this: it stands directly for a mathematical idea, we learn to associate a certain sound or pronunciation with it; on the other hand seeing the corresponding vernacular word, 'multiplied by', we can immediately pronounce it without knowing what meaning to associate with it.

For the purpose of doing complex calculations quickly it is important not only that one's language be non-vernacular, but also that it be very simple visually. A multiplication sum that is simple with Arabic numerals (e.g. 87 × 96) is very difficult with Roman ones (LXXXVII × XCVI). Operations performed in Formal Logic have a great affinity with mathematical calculation; as a consequence the artificial languages developed by logicians have been very simple.

At the present day two important notations used are the Lukasiewicz system and the Peano-Russell system. The former was invented and employed by the Polish logician, Lukasiewicz, since 1929; the latter was a modification by Russell of the symbolism of the Italian logician, Peano and goes back to 1910 when the *Principia Mathematica* by Bertrand Russell and A.N. Whitehead was published.

At the end of the chapter a table will display and correlate symbols of the main notations. For the present it will be convenient to use the Lukasiewicz system. Like any logical language it can be analysed into variables and constants.

THE UTILITY OF VARIABLES

Using variables a logician can isolate, for study, the basic structure of an argument. In other words variables accomplish for him, in the world of meaning, what scientific equipment accomplishes for the physicist or chemist, in the physical world. It was through his invention and use of variables that Aristotle became the founder of Formal Logic.

Take the following argument:

If all living things can reproduce their kind
And if the virus is a living thing
Then the virus can reproduce its kind.

This is an argument in biology. By using the familiar variables *M, P, S* we can abstract the generic structure of this discourse from its specific context; or, in other words, we can generalise its structure to the utmost as follows:

If all *M* is *P*
And if all *S* is *M*
Then all *S* is *P*.

This generic or generalized structure is still intelligible and meaningful, but its specific content or matter has been emptied out. We are focusing the original discourse on biology in its basic or generic intelligibility, drained of all particular reference; as such it is seen to have a valid structure, to be a syllogism in Barbara.

The variables used here (*M, P, S*) were substituted for terms, i.e. for the subjects and predicates of the propositions constituting the argument. The section of Formal Logic in which the variables used always stand for terms is called Terminal Logic. In Lukasiewicz's notation, variables are denoted by small latin letters, and the initial ones of the alphabet *a, b, c, d*...are used to denote term-variables of the Aristotelian logic: *Aab* means All *A* is *b; Eab* means No *a is b; lab* means some a is b: and *Oab* means some *a* is not *b*.(The capital letters *A, E, I* and *O* are used in their traditional senses, signifying quantity and quality.) When these symbols are substituted in the above discourse on biology it reads: If *Abc* and if *Aab* then *Aac*.

In the case of some arguments the only way of displaying basic structure is to use variables that stand not for terms but for whole (unanalysed) sentences. A person may reason as follows: 'If the army revolted, there would have been bloodshed; there has not been bloodshed, therefore the army has not revolted.' This argument connects up, conditionally, the sentences 'the army revolted' and 'there has been bloodshed'. The way to display its structure is to substitute variables for these sentences. Lukasiewicz denotes such (sentential) variables by the small letters *p, q, r, s*.... Using two of these the generic form of the argument is isolated as follows: 'If *p, q;* but not *q*, therefore not *p*.' The section of Formal Logic in which the variables used always stand for whole sentences or propositions is called Propositional Logic or Sentential Logic (or the Logic of Propositions, the Logic of Sentences). The Stoics founded this section and in modern times Frege is responsible for its immense development.

The logician needs a third kind of variable to deal with arguments that centre around relationships. 'If Smith is the teacher of Jones, then Jones is the pupil of Smith.' To isolate the generic structure of this argument we need to substitute variables not only for Smith and Jones but also for the particular relationship between them: 'If *X* is *R* of *Y*, then *Y* is *R*-converse of *X*.' The section of Formal Logic which studies generic structures of discourse where there are variables standing of relations is called the Logic of Relations. It was pioneered by Augustus de Morgan but nowadays is developed as part of Predicate Logic and Class Calculus. Lukasiewicz's notation does not cover it.

CONSTANTS

It is a matter of empirical fact not of logic that, e.g. 'animal life depends on oxygen'. But it is a matter of logic, not of empirical fact, that 'if all living things are dependent on oxygen, and if animals are living things, then animals are dependent on oxygen'. If that discourse comes under questioning it won't be relevant to investigate the biological facts (none are asserted) but the significance of the words *If...and if...then.* These are formative, organizing words with fixed meanings, giving basic structure to the discourse. They are an example of logical *constants* (*operators, functors, connectives* are also used to name these words). Other familiar vernacular constants are: *and; either...or, not both; it is not the case that.*

Constants are obviously a very important part of logical language. The particular constants used in any system must be presented and defined very exactly. In Lukasiewicz's system constants are denoted by capital letters—*N, K, A, D, C* being the main ones used. He says: 'The principle of my notation is to write the functors before the arguments [an argument is an expression determined by a functor, e.g. *p* is an argument in the expression *Np*]. In this way I can avoid brackets.' (*Aristotle's Syllogistic,* p. 78)

It is tempting to associate each of these capital letters with a vernacular phrase, e.g. *N* with 'it is not the case that', *K* with 'and', *A* with 'either...or', *D* with 'not both', *C* with 'if...then'. The underlying assumption is that the meanings are identical. This is not always the case and it is an important theoretical fact that the artificial symbols were not created simply to follow directions of reference in the vernacular. Thus it is important to note how each constant is defined. The technique used is a very exact one: it consists in showing the effect or influence a constant or functor has on the propositional variables it modifies or connects. By drawing up truth-tables the variables are seen in all the possible truth-values they can have; the resulting, net, truth-value of the complex expression measures the force of the logical constant in the expression.

Thus take the expression *Np* which has one variable (*N* is said to be a monadic functor, having only one argument), *p* is a propositional variable and has two possible values, true and alse. Where *p* is true, the expression as a whole (*Np*) is false; where *p* is False, the expression as a whole is true. These results are determined by the meaning of the logical constant *N*; they measure and present that meaning very exactly. Thus with the number 1 signifying true, and the number 0 signifying false, *Np* is defined technically as follows (the value of the whole expression being put under the constant):

N	*P*
0	1
1	0

Obviously *N* has the very same truth-table as the vernacular negative, 'it is not the case that...'

In the expression *Kpq,* there are two variables and *K* is said to be a dyadic functor, connecting two arguments. The possible combined values of the variables are

p	*q*
1	1
1	0
0	1
0	0

(These values are given in a standard order: 11, 10, 01, 00). The resulting values of the expression as a whole, given under *K,* are:

K	p	q
1	1	1
0	1	0
0	0	1
0	0	0

The values under *K* (1000) form the matrix line of the truth-table. Such is the meaning of *K* that the expression as a whole is true only when *p* and *q* are both true. Obviously *K* has the force of conjunction like the vernacular 'and'. Its technical definition is the matrix line of the truth-table: 1000.

The truth-tables for the other constants are as follows:

A	p	q
1	1	1
1	1	0
1	0	1
0	0	0

D	p	q
0	1	1
1	1	0
1	0	1
1	0	0

C	p	q
1	1	1
0	1	0
1	0	1
1	0	0

It is evident that the constant *A* (1110) corresponds to the vernacular *'either...or'* in the simple alternative force of these words where the alternatives are not presented as mutually exclusive; also that *D* (0111) corresponds to 'not both'. However, the disadvantages of associating vernacular meanings with the symbols of Formal Logic is brought out in the case of *C*. It is frequently translated as 'if...then'. Now, a truth table for 'if...then' would read as follows (with the value of the expression as a whole in the last column):

p	q	If p then q
1	1	1
1	0	0
0	1	here the expression as a whole does not seem to qualify for either value
0	0	" " " " " " " "

Thus *C* (1011) and 'if...then' (10—) simply do not have the same truth-tables and are not equivalent.

If one insists on translating *C* as 'if...then' formidable

paradoxes develop. In the truth-table for *C*, whenever *p* has the value 0 (false) the total proposition (*Cpq*) is true; whenever *q* has the value 1 the total proposition is also true. If *p* and *q* are identified as the antecedent and consequent, respectively, of an 'if...then' proposition then according to our truth table a conditional with a false antecedent is always true as is also any conditional with a true consequent (any sentence, *q*, follows from a false sentence, *p;* and a true sentence *q* follows from any sentence, *p*). Thus the proposition, 'If the moon is made of green cheese then the earth is flat', is true because the moon is not made of green cheese; and the proposition, 'If 2 + 2 = 4 then today is Monday', is true when today is Monday, regardless of any other fact.

These are called the paradoxes of material implication (verum sequitur ad quodlibet; ex falso sequitur quodlibet) because the vernacular word, implication, is still frequently retained to denote the significance of *C*, the qualification *material* being added to indicate that the connection asserted between *p* and q is not one of consequence but of simple material concurrence—that *C* signifies the lowest common denominator in the various vernacular uses of the words, *if...then.*

The fundamental solution to the paradoxes lies, however, in pointing out that *C* is a symbol in Formal Logic and is not properly presented as a shorthand equivalent of any vernacular expression. What fact is it employed to signify? It is a binary propositional constant or connective, i.e. it connects two propositional variables (*p* and *q*). Now the possible combined truth-values of these variables are 11, 10, 01, 00; and it is possible to have 16 different connectives each resulting in a different matrix line for the proposition as a whole:

From the viewpoint of Formal Logic there are 16 possible logical constants, each exercising a different connecting force on *p* and *q*, as defined in a special matrix line. Since *p* and *q*, are variables applicable to any entities which have propositional form, no connection or relevance of meaning is asserted or can

Value of variables		Possible matrix lines (with the symbol definedby each line)															
p	*q*	*V*	*A*	*B*	*C*	*D*	*E*	*F*	*G*	*H*	*I*	*J*	*K*	*L*	*M*	*X*	*O*
1	1	1	1	1	1	0	1	0	0	1	1	0	1	0	0	0	0
1	0	1	1	1	0	1	0	0	1	0	1	1	0	1	0	0	0
0	1	1	1	0	1	1	0	1	0	1	0	1	0	0	1	0	0
0	0	1	0	1	1	1	1	1	1	0	0	0	0	0	0	1	0

be assumed in their joint use—their only known value is that each must be true or false and that together they have a limited combined set of values. With such variables a constant can only construct a truth-functional expression, i.e. one whose meaning is confined to truth-values and whose truth is therefore determined by the particular truth-values of its constituents. In social communication, however, one's connectives are not merely truth-functional: one expects a relevance in meaning between the propositions one connects in, e.g. an 'if...then' statement.Such a presumption would not be in keeping with the use of genuine variables whose simple function it is to formalize any and all entities that are propositions.

The symbols *A, C, D, E, K* denote constants which are very useful in Formal Logic (*J* is the symbol for the important relation of contradiction). To what extent they may be equivalent to vernacular words is a matter not for Formal Logic but for Applied Logic.

WELL-FORMED FORMULAE (wff's)

There are rules for the formation of complex expressions from variables and constants. The principle of Lukasiewicz's notation is 'to write the functors before the arguments' whether the argument be simply a variable (e.g. *Np*) or variables (e.g. Cqp) or an expression consisting of varibles and a miondic functor (e.g. *ANpq*) or a complex expression consisting of variables and other functors, monadic or dyadic, etc. (e.g. *CCpqKNqNp*). (We shall see that in working out truth-tables one proceeds leftwards from the variables and simplest arguments to the constant of widest force.)

An expression is a wff in propositional logic if and only if

(1) it is a *p, q, r or s; or*

(2) it is a two-unit expression in which the first unit is a monadic functor (in practice *N* is the only one used) and the second unit is a wff; or

(3) it is a three-unit expression in which the first unit is a dyadic functor (e.g. *C, A, K, E, D),* and the second and third units are wff's.

Thus the expression *p* is a wff; so is the expression *Np*; so therefore are the expressions *NNp* and *NNNp*. We an see whether any complex expression is or is not well-formed by underlining, from the left, every constituent wff that consists of two or more letters; the expression as a whole is a wff if and only if it gets underlined by one line. Thus

NCAKpqrs is a wff.

but

ANCpNqrNs is not a wff: *Ns* is outside the scope of the main functor *A*.

EQUIVALENT EXPRESSIONS

Expressions are said to be equivalent when their truth-tables are identical, i.e. when they have the same variables and are true or false together for all the values of these variables. (*E* is the symbol for the constant, equivalence, and the matrix line of *Epq* is 1001.)

The following are examples of equivalent expressions:

C p q	*A N p q*	*D p N q*
1 1 1	1 0 1 1	1 1 0 1
0 1 0	0 0 1 0	0 1 1 0
1 0 1	1 1 0 1	1 0 0 1
1 0 0	1 1 0 0	1 0 1 0

The matrix line of the two latter expressions, appearing under the dyadic functors *A* and *D,* is the same as that of the first expression (1 0 1 1). Thus these expressions have a common definition; any one of them may be substituted for any other in processes of logical derivation for their value (truth or falsity) is the same.

Theoretically, it would be possible to so translate all expressions in Propositional Logic that besides the variables only one symbol would be needed, *D* (called also Sheffer's functor). But what would be gained by this economy in basic symbols would be lost in the cumbersome lengthy appearance of formulae. Logical language must try to achieve both economy in its symbols and a basic readability in its formulae.

THE MAIN NOTATIONS USED IN PROPOSITIONAL LOGIC

In their *Dictionary of Symbols of Mathematical Logic,* R. Feys and F.B. Fitch correlate (p. 31) the symbols used by Russell in the *Principia Mathematica* (henceforth PM), by Hilbert and Ackermann in *Principles of Mathematical Logic* and Hilbert & Bernays in *Grundlagen der Mathematik* (HA and HB), by Lukasiewicz (L), by Hermes-Scholz (HS) and by some other authors:

English equivalent	PM	HA HB	L	HS	Other notations
not p	$\sim p$	p	Np	p	p–p, $\neg p$
p and q	$p.q$	$p \; \& \; q$	Kpq	$p \vee q$	
p or q	$p \vee q$	$p \vee q$	Apq	$p \vee q$	$p + q$
if p then q	$p \supset q$	$p \rightarrow q$	Cpq	$p \rightarrow q$	
p if q	$p \subset q$		Bpq	$p \leftarrow q$	
p if and only if q	$p \cong q$	$p \sim q$	Epq	$p \leftrightarrow q$	

The authors observe that the notation under HA, HB is used also by Gentzen, while that under HS appears in numerous publications by members of the school of Munster. Polish logicians frequently use Lukasiewicz's notation, of course. 'Notations related to those given under HA and HS are used, e.g. by Tarski, Beth and also by Kleene, but the latter uses Heyting's negation sign' (Ibid., p. 32) (Heyting symbolizes not—p as $\neg p$).

Chapter-6

Logical Truth and Methods of Deciding What is Logically True

Chapter 6

THE NATURE OF LOGICAL TRUTH

Take this syllogistic sentence: '*If* all men are mortal and *if* Socrates is a man, *then* Socrates is mortal.' To decide whether this sentence is true or false, you do not study the *natural truth* of the constituent propositions. The sentence does not say that these are true; it says that the words 'if and if then' are true. You find that these words are true in Virtue of the form of the sentence (it is a first figure form, mood Barbara) and independently of the content.

By using variables let us get rid of any particular content from the above syllogism: *If MaP and if SaM then SaP.* This sentence is true because of its form and independently of any particular content it may have. Such truth is called formal or logical truth. It is concerned with the truth of the words 'if and if then', with the presence of implication which these words signify and which the syllogism claims is present. It must be distinguished from natural truth, which is the truth of statements about natural facts, about the natural world.

When it is *said* that in the syllogism logic is not concerned with truth, what is *meant* is that logic is not concerned with *the natural truth* of the constituent propositions (with the mortality of men, the humanity of Socrates in the example given earlier). It is very much concerned with logical truth (the word *validity* is used as a synonym for logical truth). One and the same sentence may claim to be true both logically and naturally—e.g. 'All men are mortal, but Socrates is a man; therefore Socrates is mortal.' The word, *therefore,* signifies the logical claim that implication is present; but in addition the premisses and conclusion are *asserted* to be true. Logic does not deal with propositions as personal assertions. Thus it won't formulate the syllogism as a pattern of personal inference but exclusively as a pattern of implication (*If* all men are mortal *and if* Socrates is a man, *then* Socrates is mortal).

EXAMPLES OF SENTENCES WHOSE CLAIM IS TO LOGICAL TRUTH

Sentences which express valid forms of immediate inference are logical truths, e.g. (a) those based on relationships in the Square of Opposition as: 'If *SaP* then *SiP*' 'if *Sop* is true then *Sap* is false' (b) those expressing converses, obverses, contrapositives and inverses as: 'If *SaP then PiS*' 'If *SaP* then *SeP*'.

Coming to mediate inference there are 24 valid moods of *the simple categorical syllogism (including* 4 weakened moods not mentioned in the mnemonic Barbara, Celarent). The 24 sentences which express these moods are true in virtue of their form and express logical truth, e.g. If *PeM* and if *SaM* then *SeP* (Cesare). These 24 sentences do not express any natural truth, they express the fact of implication or involvement.

Similarly, the sentences which express valid forms of other varieties of the syllogism express logical truth.

The above are examples treated already in the preparatory section of this course. They belong to Terminal Logic where the variables signify terms. In Propositional Logic where the variables signify propositions, the following sentence, e.g. expresses logical truth: 'If it is the case both that if *p* is true *q* is true and that *p* is true, then *q* is true.' This sentence is true independently of content, of any particular propositions substituted for *p* and *q*. Finally, in Relational Logic, the proposition expressing converse relationships has formal or logical truth, e.g. 'If *X* is *R* of *Y*, then *Y* is *R*—converse of *X*.'

ON FINDING A DECISION PROCEDURE FOR LOGICAL TRUTH IN PROPOSITIONAL LOGIC

We have seen that a sentence may be a statement about natural facts and be either true or false naturally, in virtue of its content. Or it may be a statement about the presence of implication and be true or false logically, in virtue of its form, independently of its content. (It may also be a statement claiming both natural and logical truth.) By what criterion can we determine whether a sentence claiming logical truth is actually true or false, logically? We are concerned at present with sentences whose variables, *pqrs,* stand for propositions.

Wittgenstein used the concept of tautology to clarify the idea of logical truth and through him truth-tables were accepted as an important method (always applicable in propositional logic) for determining logical truth or falsity. The relationship between truth tables and logical truth may be explained as follows:

1. A proposition expressing logical truth is always complex (it must have room for the presence of implication).

2. Given a complex proposition with *n* constituent propositions, if the truth of the complex proposition is completely determined by the truth of the constituent ones, then it is said to be a truth-function of *n* propositions. There is always a rule determining its truth from the truth or falsity of the constituents. The following are examples of truth-functions of two propositions, denoted by the variables *p and* q, with their truth-tables (the numerals indicate the order in which the columns should be filled):

3	1	2
C	*p*	*q*
1	1	1
0	1	0
1	0	1
1	0	0

7	6	5	1	3	2	4
C	*K*	*C*	*p*	*q*	*p*	*q*
1	1	1	1	1	1	1
1	0	0	1	0	1	0
1	0	1	0	1	0	1
1	0	1	0	0	0	0

7	5	1	3	6	2	4
K	*D*	*p*	*q*	*K*	*p*	*q*
0	0	1	1	1	1	1
0	1	1	0	0	1	0
0	1	0	1	0	0	1
0	1	0	0	0	0	0

The matrix-line in each case is the first column; in the first example it is 1 0 1 1, in the second 1 1 1 1, in the third 0 0 0 0.

3. Among the various truth-functions of the *n* propositions we have referred to, that proposition which has the truth-value 'true' for every possible combination of truth-values in the *n* propositions is said to be the *tautology* of the *n* propositions. It is clear that what it expresses is true independently of the content of its variable constituents; it is a *logical truth* or *logical law*. It is the business of logic to detect tautologies. The second example above (*CKCpqpq*) is a tautology or logical truth, its matrix line being 1 1 1 1. The first example (*Cpq*) is true for some of the combined values of its variables but not for all of them: its matrix line is 1 0 1 1 and it is called a *contingent proposition*. The third example (*KDpqKpq*) is not true for any of the combined values of its variables: its matrix line is 0 0 0 0 and it is described as *logically false or* as a *logical contradiction.*

DRAWING UP TRUTH-TABLES: SOME TECHNICAL DETAILS

The order in which values are given to the variables is governed by rule. According as there are one, two or three variables, the order is as follows:

If there are *n* variables, the column under the *m*th variable should contain 2^{m-1} sets of 2^{n-m} 1's followed by 2^{n-m} 0's (where *m* is the numerical ranking of the variable, first, second or third, etc.). A truth function of *n* variables needs 2^n rows across

p	*p*	*q*	*p*	*q*	*r*
1	1	1	1	1	1
0	1	0	1	1	0
	0	1	1	0	1
	0	0	1	0	0
			0	1	1
			0	1	0
			0	0	1
			0	0	0

to provide for all combined values (the 2 denotes the values possible in Two-Value Logic, truth and falsity).

In evaluating the expression as a whole for each of the combined values of the variables, one fills in the values for the most elementary parts first under the relevant constant or functor. In Lukasiewicz's system this means moving from right to left. The table on p. 74 recalls the values of basic expressions.

When one is simply concerned with deciding whether an expression is or is not a logical law, and the number of variables makes the full truth-table procedure too laborious, one may use a shorter, *reductio ad absurdum,* type of procedure. If the expression is a logical law, then the matrix line of its table must be a series of 1's. Making the assumption that an 0 is included in its matrix line and working downwards from this fact to consequent values for the elementary parts of the total expression, we may find that one of these values contradicts the definition of one of the constants (e.g. that *C* 1 1 would have the value 0). This would show that 0 could not occur in the matrix line and therefore that the expression is a logical

Values of Basic Expressions

Expression (the numbers here are the values of the variables)	Value	*Expression* (the numbers here are the values of the variables	Value
N 1	0	*K* 1 1	1
N 0	1	*K* 1 0	0
A 1 1	1	*K* 0 1	0
A 1 0	1	*K* 0 0	0
A 0 1	1	*E* 1 1	1
A 0 0	0	*E* 1 0	0
D 1 1	0	0 *E* 0	1
D 1 0	1	*E* 0 0	1
D 0 1	1	*C* 1 1	1
D 0 0	1	*C* 1 0	0
		C 0 1	1
		C 0 0	1

law. If, on the other hand, the assumption does not involve the violation of any basic rule or definition, then the matrix line, which has all possible values, must include an 0 and so the expression is not a logical law.

TESTING THE VALIDITY OF ARGUMENTS (IN PROPOSITIONAL LOGIC) BY THE TRUTH-TABLE METHOD

An argument may be formulated as an 'if...then' statement, with the cumulative evidence as antecedent and the conclusion as consequent. Testing its validity may be treated as a process of discovering whether the antecedent may be true and yet the conclusion be false. At first sight, it does not seem possible to apply a test based on truth-tables, as an 'if...then' statement does not seem to qualify for evaluation in the cases where its antecedent is false. However, the vernacular 'if...then' and the symbol *C* agree partially in their truth-tables, namely in the cases where the antecedent is true; further a *C* proposition is never false or invalid (but always true) when its antecedent is false. Thus, since we are simply trying to discover whether the conclusion may be false when the antecedent is true, the extra values in the *C*-truth-tables would not affect a test for invalidity. This is the pragmatic justification for symbolizing arguments as *C* statements so as to make them amenble to evaluation by truth-tables. The matrix line of a valid argument should consist of 1's, since only a true antecedent with a false consequent will give rise to an 0.

Example: 'If the cost of living rises or the balance of payments improves, then salary increases will be granted. But no salary increases will be granted. Therefore the balance of payments will not improve.' Symbolizing 'the cost of living will rise' as *p*, 'the balance of payments will improve' as *q*, and 'salary increases will be granted' as *r*, the total expression may be formulated as: *CKCApqrNrNq*. Its truth table is:

11	10	9	8	1	2	4	7	5	6	3
C	*K*	*C*	*A*	*p*	*q*	*r*	*N*	*r*	*N*	*q*
1	0	1	1	1	1	1	0	1	0	1
1	0	0	1	1	1	0	1	0	0	1
1	0	1	1	1	0	1	0	1	1	0
1	0	0	1	1	0	0	1	0	1	0
1	0	1	1	0	1	1	0	1	0	1
1	0	0	1	0	1	0	1	0	0	1
1	0	1	0	0	0	1	0	1	1	0
1	1	1	0	0	0	0	1	0	1	0

(The numerals indicate the order in which the columns should be filled.) The matrix line (under *C*, on the left) does not include an 0, and so the argument is not invalid.

DECISION PROCEDURES (FOR PROPOSITIONAL LOGIC) OTHER THAN THAT OF TRUTH-TABLES.

Truth-tables furnish an effective procedure, in Propositional logic, for deciding whether any sentence is true or any argument is valid. This decision can be made for a sentence or argument, chosen quite arbitrarily, without the need of relating it to any other proposition or displaying it as deducvible from other propositions. In other words, the method is mechanical. There are two other mechanical decision procedures (a) the normal form procedure and (b) the trees procedure. In outlining these procedures it is convenient at times to depart from the Polish notation in using '*V*', instead of 'A' '.' instead of '*K*', '—' instead of '*N*' and '→' instead of '*C*'.

(a) *The normal form procedure:* This procedure is based on the fact that with regard to two contradictions, *p* and –*p*, both of them can never be true together, and one or other of them must be true. Because of the latter fact a *conjunctive* chain of expressions *each* of which has the form *pV* –*p* (with or without other alternatives) is definitely a tautology; and because of the former fact a *disjunctive* chain of expressions *each* of which has the form, *p*.–*p* (with or without other conjuncts in the atom), is definitely a chain of propositions none of which can ever be true and so is a logical contradiction.

From this basis it is possible to construct fully a decision procedure. Beginning with definitions:

An *atomic expression* is either a propositional variable or the negation of some propositional variable, e.g. *p, –q*.

An *elementary disjunction* is an expression of the form ($A_1 \vee A_2 \vee ... A_n$) where $A_1 ... A_n$ are atomic expressions.

An *elementary disconjunction* is an expression of the form (A_1 A_2 ...A_n) where $A_1...A_n$ are atomic expressions.

A *conjunctive Normal Form* (CNF) is an expression of the form (B_1 B_2... $\vee$ B_n) where $B_1...B_n$ are elementary disjunctions.

A *Disjunctive Normal Form* (DNF) is an expression of the form ($B_1 \vee B_2 ... \vee B_n$) where $B_1...B_n$ are elementary conjunctions.

Now it is possible to reduce every wff in propositional logic to a CNF and to a DNF. the basic reason is that the constants are a systematic set of symbols and the force of all operators can receive an equivalent expression in CN terms and in DN terms. Thus even in the most complex formula equivalent replacements can be made, systematically,until the whole formula has the required normal format. For such systematic replacements the following equivalences are very useful:

EKppp
EAppp
EKpqKqp
EApqAqp
EKpKqrKKpqr
EApAqrAApqr
ENNpp
ECpqANpq
EEpqKCpqCqp
ENKpqANpNq
ENApqKNpNq
EApKqrKApqApr
EKpAqrAKpqKpr

When a complex expression is simplified down to a CNF an inspection of the atomic expressions shows whether or not it is a conjunctive chain of elementary disjunctions each of which must always be true (on the basis of containing, among the alternatives, two contradictories). If so it is a tautology. If not it may be a logical contradiction or a contingent proposition. Simplified down to a DNF an inspection of the atomic expressions shows whether or not it is a disjunctive chain of elementary conjunctions none of which can ever be true (on the basis of containing, among the conjuncts, two contradictories). If so it is a logical contradiction. If not (since we already know it is not a tautology) it must be a contingent proposition.

Thus with this method we can decide, independently of truth-tables, whether any given wff in propositional logic is a tautology, a logical contradiction or a contingent proposition.

(b) *The method of truth trees:* It derives from Beth's method of semantic tableaux and Hintikka's method of model sets and is based on the fact that if an argument is valid no case can be cited in which the premisses are true along with the contradictory of the conclusion. By means of branch-lines the method diagrams the various ways in which the constituent propositions of an argument can be made true. As soon as contradictories are discovered on a branch-line it is closed (it cannot be cited in support of a possibility that the premisses and contradictory of the conclusion may be simultaneously true). If all the branch-lines are closed the argument is valid. In *Formal Logic: Its Scope and Limits* Richard Jeffrey gives an excellent presentation.

Applying the method to the simple argument: If $A \rightarrow -B$ and if $-C \rightarrow A$, then $B \rightarrow C$, we first list the premisses and the contradictory of the conclusion. Then we write down the various ways in which the contradictory of the conclusion, i.e.$-(B \rightarrow C)$, may be made true namely by B being true or C being false. Next on lines branching from C we put the conditions which can make the first premiss true, namely by A being false or –

B being true (i.e. *B* being false). The diagram now reads:

Line 1. $A \rightarrow -B$
Line 2. $-C \rightarrow A$
Line 3. $-(B \rightarrow C)$
Line 4. B
Line 5. $-C$
Line 6. $-A$ $-B$
×

The branch line with $-B$ can now be closed because it has a contradictory on the main line (i.e. *B*). Closure is indicated by placing an × under $-B$. Now on lines branching from $-A$ (which is the only open branch line left) we put the conditions which can make the second premiss true:

Line 6. $-A$
Line 7. C A
× ×

Each of these branch lines must be closed because *C* is in contradiction with –C (Lines 5) and *A* is in contradiction with $-A$ (Line 6).

Thus the diagram displays the fact that no instance can be cited in which the premisses and the contradictory of the conclusion are simultaneously true. Since an argument can always be formulated as a statement of material implication ths decision procedure may be described as deciding both the validity of arguments and the logical truth of statements.

DECISION PROCEDURES IN SECTIONS OF LOGIC OTHER THAN PROPOSITIONAL LOGIC

Propositional Logic is the basic section of Formal Logic: its variables stand for whole sentences and its truth can be used in other sections of Logic where the internal structure of propositions is analysed. Thus the tautology *CKCpqpq* holds no matter what kind of propositions are substituted for *p* and *q*. However, while the truths of Propositional Logic can be imported into e.g. Terminal Logic, the latter discovers logical truths that are quite outside the reach of the former. Thus *CKpqr* is a contingent proposition: if one does not look within the internal structure of three propositions (*p*, *q*, *r*) there is nothing to indicate that a logical truth could have this form. But if the three propositions happen to be internally structured as follows: *MaP, SaM, SaP*, then the whole expression is seen, in Terminal Logic, to be logically true and is described in traditional terms as a valid syllogism. If the three propositions were structured *MoP, SaM, SaP,* the whole expression would, logically, be invalid because of the fallacy of an undistributed middle.

Thus other sections of Formal Logic not only use the truths of Propositional Logic but have the function also of discovering other logical truths. The problem is that where variables do not stand for whole unanalysed propositions a truth-table test is not applicable and indeed it does not seem possible to devise a *mechanical* test for displaying logical truth in *all* sections of logic.

Chapter-7
Logic and Deductive Systems

Chapter 7

INTRODUCTION

Logic is concerned with:

(a) defining the nature, elements and structuring of a deductive system. There are two main types, axiomatic systems and natural deduction systems;

(b) formulating logical truths into a deductive system;

(c) defining the relationship between its own deductive system and others: do the propositions of Logic function elsewhere as, e.g. axioms or rules of inference?

THE NATURE OF A DEDUCTIVE SYSTEM

On what general conditions is an explanatory system of concepts and propositions (such as a human science) possible? Aristotle asked that question and answered it as follows: On condition (a) that every term need not be resolved into simpler terms and meanings, i.e. that there are indefinables, primitive terms and concepts in human experience which cannot be humanly defined and need not be defined; (b) that every proposition need not be proved, i.e. that there are propositions which are indemonstrable, whose meaning guarantees their truth, which cannot be proved and need not be proved. Aristotle pointed out that if actually there are not such terms and propositions, then human science as an explanatory system of propositions about the real world is not possible.

We are not concerned here with the empirical value of particular primitive terms and propositions, or with the claim that this or that system of propositions may make to be true knowledge of the world, but with the organizational fact that system is impossible if there is an infinite regress in the certification of meanings and implications.

For about 2000 years Euclid's Geometry was regarded as the model of logical organization, consisting firstly of a set of underived propositions: definitions, postulates and axioms (general and geometrical), and secondly of a systematic series of derived propositions or theorems. However, a rigorous study of Euclid beginning in the last century revealed very important logical deficiencies, such as the following:

(1) Euclid begins with definitions; what one really needs to begin with is indefinables, a geometrical alphabet and rules for constructing definitions from it.

(2) Euclid does not distinguish between the kind of definition which simply says 'this is my name or symbol for this entity' and the kind of formula which gives a description of the entity. The former is an appellation, the latter a description.

(3) Euclid separates postulates and axioms but he does not distinguish between them sharply. Some of his axioms are not really self-evident, and his postulates were generally presented as safe assumptions.

(4) Theorems are supposed to be derived exclusively on the basis of the definitions, postulates and axioms. But in fact that is often not so. Diagrams which appear to be only aids to the imagination may provide spatial intuitions without which one could not be satisfied with the deducibility of the theorem. Thus in the first proposition of Euclid, describing two circles of radius *AB*, one with *A* as centre, the other with *B*, the existence of a point of intersection is exhibited in the diagram, not proved. Again, sometimes a theorem requires a postulate that does not feature in the original set—e.g. the argument for his twenty-ninth proposition assumes that through a point outside a straight line there passes only a single line parallel to that straight line.

This rigorous study of Euclid's Geometry and the desire to perfect its structure gave rise to the broader question: what is required, logically, for any system of propositions to be fully and perfectly organized? At first it was assumed that every system would be axiomatic in character, i.e. that the deductive apparatus must always consist of axioms as well as rules of inference. Indeed the whole study used to be called Axiomatics. But by 1934 Gerhard Gentzen and Stanislaw Jaskowski had developed an alternative procedure to the axiomatic one: it dispenses with axioms, using rules of inference alone and is known as natural deduction. Thus a general study of deductive systems must take account now not only of axiomatic systems but also of natural deduction systems. Further, it is no longer assumed that the only acceptable way of presenting the propositions of Logic itself is in an axiomatic system. In this respect contemporary Logic seems to be moving away from Frege and Russell in whose systems deductive behaviour was controlled by axioms and rules; many authors hold today that it would be best to concentrate the deductive power of a system in rules alone.

THE ELEMENTS AND STRUCTURE OF AN AXIOMATIC SYSTEM

In this logical study we are not concerned with the material or natural truth of propositions but with their organization into a system. We are concerned (1) that there be an explicit distinction between expressions and propositions that are underived and those that are derived; (2) that rules for constructing well-formed expressions and propositions be explicit; (3) that rules for deriving propositions be explicit also.

In detail, the following rules must be observed in the construction of an axiomatic system:

1. The primitive language or underived symbols of the system, together with rules for constructing complex expressions from them,must be clearly set out. Expressions that conform to these rules are called well-formed expressions; the rules are called formation rules. Included in the formation rules are rules of definition in virtue of which one can state that an expression is equivalent to some other one.

2. The postulates of the system must be set out clearly and fully. In axiomatics all underived propositions are classified as postulates i.e. they are not presented as truths, and thus there is not any distinction made between axioms and postulates. The postulates of a system are the propositions from which we deduce the others. An economical selection is called a set. The requirements for a postulate are that it be (a) *coherent,* entirely expressible in the language of the system; (b) *contributive,* i.e. give rise to implications; (c) *consistent,* i.e. not be incompatible with any other proposition of the system; and (d) *independent,* i.e. not be implied by other postulates, jointly or singly taken. A proposition derived within the system is called a theorem.

Thus in an axiomatic system there are no mere facts, i.e. facts which cananot be known from anything else and do not entail anything else.

3. The rules of inference must be set out fully. These are rules which determine when a proposition can be said to be a consequence of other propositions. If the rule relates simply to the mechanical transformation of expressions (e.g. by the substitution of equivalent expressions), the consequence is said to be syntactic; if the rule is based on meaning then the consequence is said to be semantic. These are the rules which determine when a deduction is properly constructed.

4. The definitions or fundamental equivalences used in the system must be set out and accord with the formation rules for expressions.

The rest of the system consists in proceeding by successive stages to all the possible theorems, every step being shown and its validity certified by a reference to the relevant rule of inference used. In modern systems the whole deduction proceeds in a formalistic manner, i.e. the rules of inference are such that attention can be completely focused on the form of the symbols (not on any content of meaning they may have or be given later) and propositions be derived with the eye as in mathematical calculation. When a system is worked out completely, at a syntactic or formalistic level, it may be found applicable to more than one context in life or science. Thus two axiomatic systems dealing with different sets of objects may be isomorphic, i.e. be simply two interpretations of the same primitive language, postulates, rules of inferences and definitions. This is a feature not only of mathematical systems in particular but in general of all axiomatic systems:

> 'Mathematics is a science in which we never know what we are talking about nor whether what we are saying is true': this well known sally of Russell's which occurred to him in reflecting on axiomatized mathematics, holds equally well for axiomatics in general. Similarly, it is really towards axiomatics that this other sally of Poincare's is directed: 'Mathematics is the art of giving the same name to different things.' (*Axiomatics* by Robert Blanche, p. 31)

Indeed, formalized logic has been used in areas as distant from argument as electrical switching circuits and computers. It is frequently possible to master a system in itself and to distinguish it from various interpretations or projections of it.

NATURAL DEDUCTION SYSTEMS

In presenting an organized body of knowledge in any area, the axiomatic approach takes an initial grip on the reality we seek to know. Such a grip is furnished by the axioms or fundamental truths, and from there a theoretic process provides other truths in the form of implications. In contrast, a natural deduction system takes its first grip not on *what* is known, but on the *rational quality* of all human knowledge. It begins by formalizing movement in which reason is acting under the impulse of its own nature. Each of these movements is a natural deduction: its guarantee is the nature of reason and it is presented as acceptable to any person who is not prepared to abdicate his reason.

Any formalization of a natural deduction may be called a logical argument formula (LAF). It is evident that if one can reduce arguments to LAF's one has a method of showing their validity. It will also emerge that one can not only prove the validity of arguments but also the truth of all the propositions that feature in the systems of propositional and predicate logic.

To the ordinary conventional symbols a natural deduction system adds a symbol which indicates, positionally, assumption and derivative. It is of the form, |– , and is often called 'the therefore indicator'. The assumption(s) may be put to the left of |– and the derivative to the right (this has advantages for the printer); or the assumption(s) may be situated above the horizontal line and the derivative beneath. For the moment, we will continue to use the Polish symbols.

The following are the main LAF's. Most of them are named after the connectives *K, A, C, N* according as a connective features in the premiss but not the conclusion (e.g. 'K-out', 'K eliminated'), or is introduced by the conclusion (e.g. 'K-in', 'K introduced').

Ki (K-in)

(1)	*p*	*A*
(2)	*q*	*A*
3.	*Kpq*	1, 2, *Ki*

Ko (K-out)

(1)	*Kpq*	*A*
(2)	*p*	1, *Ko*

The right hand column gives the reason for each line: *p* and *q* are assumptions (a rule of assumptions justifies the introduction of any proposition at any stage in a proof); the reasons for line (3), *Kpq,* are the premisses (1) and (2) and a natural deduction formalized as the rule of inference *Ki*.

Ai (A-in)

(1)	*p*	*A*
(2)	*Apq*	1, *Ai*

(Given *p*, a proposition combining *p* and any other

Ao (A-out)

(1)	*AKqp*	*Kqr*	*A*
(2)	(2.1)	*Kqp*	*A*
	(2.2)	*q*	2.1, *Ko*
(3)	(3.1)	*Kqr*	*A*

alternative proposition is derivable.)

(3.2) | *q* 3.1, *Ko*
(4) q 1, 2, 3, *Ao*

In *Ao*, items (2) and (3) are themselves composite or tail items, sequences. Item (1) is called simply a well formed formula (wff). It is important to note the force of the word, *formula.* One can use symbols as a kind of shorthand to represent sentences; used in this way symbols indicate both content and form. However, when I use a symbol, p, to indicate the presence of the kind of entity that has propositional form, then an act of understanding of form underlies my use of the symbol and I am formalizing sentences not merely representing them. In *Ao* the natural deduction is based on the fact that each of the alternatives has the same derivative, *q*.

Ci (C-in)

(1) | (1.1) | *p* *A*
(1.2) | *Apq* 1.1, *Ai*
(2) *CpApq* 1, *Ci*

Co (C-out)

(1) | *Cpq* *A*
(2) | *p* *A*
(3) | *q* 1, 2, *Co*

In *Ci*, *p* which is an assumption in (1) becomes the antecedent of the wff, *CpApq*. This latter formula does not require *p* as assumption: its truth-table shows that it is true for all values of *p* and q. Thus although *CpApq* is reached by a *method* of supposition, any assumption made is discharged in the process and *CpApq* can be asserted, absolutely, as a wff that is true. Thus it is not impossible for the method of natural deduction to establish absolute truth; the only question is the extent of its capacity here.

Ni (N-in)

(1) | (1.1) | *KqKpNp* *A*
(1.2) | *KpNp* 1.1,*Ko*
(2) *NKqKpNp* 1,*Ni*

(1) | (1.1) *KrKsNr* *A*
(1.2) *r* 1.1, *Ko*
(1.3) KsNr 1.1, *Ko*
(1.4) *Nr* 1.3, *Ko*
(1.5) *KrNr* 1.2, 1.4, *Ki*
(2) *NKrKsNr* 1, *Ni*

No (N-out)

```
(1) | (1.1) | NCKpqp                    A
    | (1.2) | (1.2.1)Kpq |  A
    |       |            |----------
    |       | (1.2.2)p   |  1.2.1,   Ko
    | (1.3) | CKpqp                   1.2,  Ci
    |       |------------------
    | (1.4) | KCKpqpNCKpqp            1.3, 1.1, Ki
    |-----------
(2) | CKpqp                           1,  No
```

In these LAF's, an assumption leads to a formal contradiction (the conjunction of a proposition and its negation); thus by natural deduction the negation of the assumption is derivable.

Rep (Repetition) *Double Negation (DN)*

```
(1) | p A           (1) | KpAsr A            (1) | p  A            (1) | NNp A
    |------             |------                  |--------            |----
(2) | p  1,rep      (2) | KpAsr  1, rep      (2) | NNp 1,DN        (2) | p
1,DN
```

This importance of being able to repeat a proposition at various stages in our reasoning, reminds us that circular argumentation is unsound only if it claims to be providing new information and fails to acknowledge the repetition. Repetition can advance a reasoning process: the legitimacy of our repetition of *p* derives from the fact that it is already a proposition in our system (by assumption or derivation). With regard to negation, a double application of this operation is intuitively, self-nullifying.

What constitutes proof in a natural deduction system? A proof is a complete sequence of items each of which has a good reason. Items are of two kinds: (1) single wff's and (2) a sequence of items, called a tail item.

(1) With regard to a single wff, it will be either above or below the horizontal line in a |–. If it is above, a good reason is that it has the status of an hypothesis (we are assuming it in order

to see what is deducible from it: we can write *hyp* or *A* at the right hand side to indicate this). If it is below, then in order to provide a good reason we must be able to present it as the last item in an LAF, indicating two things: firstly, the kind of LAF of which this wff is being thought of as the last item and, secondly, which preceding items are being presented as the preceding items of this LAF. The basis of this is that the LAF's are such that any argument that can be formalized by one of them is a valid argument (the last item, the conclusion, actually does follow from the premisses).

(2) With regard to a tail item, it has a good reason if each of its constituent items has a good reason. Some of these constituent items may themselves be sequences, but ultimately all the sequences resolve into items that are wff's. Thus eventually we can always decide whether the whole tail item has a good reason.

Thus in a natural deduction system an argument is valid when it can be formalized by an AF that corresponds to a proof in that system. It is evident that such a system is potentially a rich and powerful source of proof.

What exactly is proved in a natural deduction system? It establishes two kinds of conclusion really: (1) *sequents* (a sequent being a whole complex of items including the assumptions); and (2) *theorems* (*theorem* has a specialised meaning here and connotes the conclusion of a provable sequent which in the process of being reached by the method of supposition becomes logically independent of the actual suppositions. The LAF, *Ci*, is a rich source:

1	1.1	*p*	*hyp*	
	1.2	*Apq*	1.1,	*Ai*
2	*CpApq*		1,	*Ci*

(We may take advantage of theorems and their substitution instances to shorten proofs by a rule for theorem introduction, just as it is practical to have a rule for using sequents already proved.)

Are truth-tables useful in natural deduction systems? As an adequate mechanical decision procedure in propositional logic, the truth-table method reaches the same results as the process of natural deduction or the axiomatic process. The relative simplicity of this area permits a mechanical procedure to be adequate and it can be useful in many ways and equally in all systems. However, natural deduction systems differ in their reliance on truth-tables. One kind relies completely on rules of inference to control the use and behaviour of logical constants. An example is in *Logic: Techniques of Formal Reasoning* by Donald Kalish and Richard Montague (New York, 1964; chs. 1 and 2). The second kind uses truth-table definitions for the connectives and the notion of tautological-implication. An example is in *Introduction* to *Logic* by Patrick Suppes (Princeton, N.J. 1957; ch. 2).

RELATING THE AXIOMATIC AND THE NATURAL DEDUCTION APPROACHES TO THE SCIENCE OF LOGIC ITSELF

In 1934 Carnap noted *(Logische Syntax der Sprache)* that for every logical axiom there is an equivalent inference rule and therefore that the choice of formulating a logical fact as an axiom or rule of inference is an issue of practice rather than of principle. Putting the words 'can be asserted' before a law translates it into a rule, i.e., into a declaration of *something that can be done* rather than a declaration of *what is so*. The equivalence of *P* and *Q* can be translated into a rule by saying one can be substituted for the other; the implication of *P* and *Q* is similarly translated by saying that if *Q* is asserted *P* can be asserted. Thus the same logical content and power can be built into both an axiomatic system and a natural deduction one.

Both techniques are frequently used nowadays. It is a matter for metalogic to study their comparative suitability within logic. The following chapters which present a precis of the main sections of formal logic will exemplify both techniques. It is important to remember that formalized logic is unique as a formal system. Every other system (e.g. geometry) presupposes a logic that governs the derivation of its theorems from its axioms; this logic brings to the system not extra premisses but rules of inference. Thus logic is a formalizing principle in other systems.

The main sections of standard two-value logic are Propositional Logic and Predicate Logic. The former is the logic of the interconnection of propositions, the latter is generated from their internal structure. (*Sentence* is the name of the verbal structure; *proposition* is the name of the meaning contained in this structure. In his practical work, which resembles mathematical calculation, the logician is immediately concerned with the verbal structure; accordingly, propositional logic is often called *Sentential Logic,* or *The Logic of Sentences,* or *Sentential Calculus* or *The Calculus of Sentences.* Predicate logic gives rise to a Class Calculus or a Calculus of Classes. Later we shall note the difference between a logic and the calculus associated with it.)

Modal Logic and Many-Valued Logic are sections of logic which are called non-standard because they do not work within the simple true-false framework.

Chapter-8

A Precis of Propositional Logic

Chapter 8

In Propositional Logic, truth-tables furnish an effective procedure for deciding whether any sentence is true or any argument is valid. Thus it is not necessary to organize this section into a system of propositions: the propositions can be shown, separately, to be tautologies and do not need the credential of deducibility within a system.

This chapter will (1) present a limited, selected list of tautologies in Propositional Logic; (2) indicate how these tautologies can be formalized into an axiomatic system; and (3) survey the classic axiomatic systems that have been constructed.

A SELECTED LIST OF TAUTOLOGIES OR LAWS IN PROPOSITIONAL LOGIC

(a) *First principles of traditional logic*

Epp	(Principle of Identity)
NKpNp or DpNp	(Principle of Non-Contradiction)
ApNp	(Principle of Excluded Middle)

(b) *Tautologies in which the variables are equiform*

Epp	Principle of Identity
ENNpp	Principle of Double Negation
ENNNpNp	Principle of Triple Negation
ENpDpp	Reduction of Negation
EAppp	Ist law of Tautology
EKppp	2nd law of Tautology

c) *Tautologies which analyse the meaning of the A functor*

EApqCNpq	
EApqDNpNq	Reduction of Alternation
EApqNKNpNq'	De Morgan's 3rd Law
EApqCCpqq	

EApqAqp	Commutative Law of the Sum.
EApAqrAApqr	Associative Law of the Sum
EApKqrKApqApr	Distributive Law of the Sum
EApApqApq	1st law of Simplification of the Sum
EApKpqp	2nd law of Simplification of the Sum
ENApqKNpNq	De Morgan's 1st Law

(d) *Tautologies which analyse the meaning of the C functor*

ECpqANpq	
ECpqDpNq	Reduction of Implication
ECpqNKpNq	
ECpqEpKpq	
ECpqEqApq	
ECpqCNqNp	Law of Simple Contraposition
ECpNqCqNp	2nd Law of Simple Contraposition
ECNpqCNqp	3rd Law of Simple Contraposition
ECpCqrCqCpr	Law of Simple Commutation
ECKpqrCpCqr	1st Law of Exportation
ECKpqrCqCpr	2nd Law of Exportation
ECpCpqCpq	
ECKpqrCKNrqNp	1st Law of Syllogistic Contraposition
ECKpqrCKpNrNq	2nd Law of Syllogistic Contraposition
ENCpqKpNq	

(e) *Tautologies which present the C functor in an evidence-conclusion format*

CpCqp	1st Paradoxical law ('Verum sequitur ad quodlibet')
CNpCpq	2nd Paradoxical law ('Ex falso sequitur quodlibet')
CCpNpNp	1st Reductio ad absurdum
CpCNpq	
CKpNpNp	2nd Reductio ad absurdum

CpApq	Law of the new factor
CKpqp	1st law of the a *fortiori*
CKpqq	2nd law of the a *fortiori*
CKpqCpq	
CEpqCpq	

(f) *Tautologies which analyse the meaning of the D functor*

EDpqANpNq	
EDpqCpNq	
EDpqNKpq	
EDpqDqp	Commutation of Exclusion
EDpqNp	Reduction of Negation
ENDpqKpq	

(g) *Tautologies which analyse the meaning of the K functor*

EKpqNANpNq	De Morgan's 4th Law
EKpqNCpNq	
EKpqNDpq	Reduction of Conjunction
EKpqKqp	Commutative Law of the Product
EKpKqrKKpqr	Associative Law of the Product
EKpAqrAKpqKpr	Distributive Law of the Product
EKpApqp	1st Law of Simplifying the Product
EKpKpqKpq	2nd Law of Simplifying the Product
ENKpqANpNq	De Morgan's 2nd Law
ENKpqDpq	

(h) *Tautologies which analyse the meaning of the E functor*

EEpqAKpqKNpNq	
EEpqKCpqCpq	
EEpqEqp	Commutative Law of Equivalence
EEpEqrEEpqr	Associative Law of Equivalence
EEpqENpNq	Inversion of Equivalence
EEpqENqNp	1st Contraposition of Equivalence
EENpqENqp	2nd Contraposition ofEquivalence
EEpNqEqNp	3rd Contraposition of Equivalence

(i)Tautologies which have the format of models for general syllogistic inference

CCqrCCpqCpr
CCpqCCqrCpr
CCpqCCqrCCrsCps
CCpqCCqrCCrsCCstCpt
CKCpqCqrCpr
CKKCpqCqrCrsCps
CKLKKCpqCqrCrsCstCpt
CCpqCArpArq

(j)Tautologies which have the format of models for syllogistic inference of the hypothetical kind

CpCCpqq	Modus ponendo ponens 1°
CKCpqpq	Modus ponendo ponens 2°
CKCpNqpNq	
CKCNpqNpq	
CKCNpNqNpNq	
CNqCCpqNp	Modus tollendo tollens 1°
CKCpqNqNp	Modus tollendo tollens 2°
CKCpNqqNp	
CKCNpqNqp	
CKCNpNqqp	
CKCpqCprCpKqr	Law of multiplying the consequent
CpCqKpq	
CKCpqCrsCKprKqs	Multiplication of both sides
CKCpqCrsCAprAqs	Addition of both sides
CKCpr?CqrCApqr	1st constructive dilemma
CKCprCNprr	2nd constructive dilemma
CKNqNrCCpAqrNp	1st destructive dilemma
CKCpKqrKNqNrNp	2nd destructive dilemma
CKCpqCpNqNp	3rd reductio ad absurdum

(k)*Tautologies which have the format of models for syllogistic inference of the disjunctive and copulative kind*

CNpCApqq	Modus tollendo ponens 1°

CNqCApqp
CKApqNpq Modus toller to ponens 2°
CKApqNqp
CKApNqNpNq
CKANpqpq
CKANpNqpNq
CpCDpqNq Modus ponendo tollens °
CqCDpqNp
CpCNKpqNq
CKDpqpNq Modus ponendo tollens 2°
CKDpNqpq
CKDNpqNpNq.
CKDNpNqNpq

AN AXIOMATIC SYSTEM OF THE TAUTOLOGIES OF PROPOSITIONAL LOGIC

The work of formalizing Propositional Logic, begun by Frege & Peano was completed by Russell & Whitehead in the *Principia Mathematica.* Subsequently, the five axioms used in the PM were reduced to four by Hilbert, to three by Lukasiewicz, to one by Nicod. The problem of the 'single, sufficient and shortest' axiom continued to be investigated by Lukasiewicz and his school. In 1925 Alfred Tarski provided a fifty-three lettered axiom; in 1933 Sobocinski provided a twenty-seven letter one; this was shortened soon after-wards by Lukasiewicz to twenty-five letters, and again by Lukasiewicz, in 1936, to twenty-three letters. The shortest one was proposed in 1955 by C.A. Meredith, an Irish associate of Lukasiewicz, and contains 21 letters:

CCCCCpqCNrNsrtCCtpCsp

The following system is that of Hilbert-Ackerman, as modified by Bochenski through incorporating Lukasiewicz's method of deduction. The proof preceding each theorem is expressed in a single probative verse or derivational line, and it employs special symbolism. Before presenting the system as a whole it may be helpful to anticipate two of the early theorems which will be proved and to analyse the derivational lines which precede them:

1.44 $r/Nr \times 1.23\ p/r,\ q/p \times 1.23\ p/r = 1.51$

1.51 *CCpqCCrpCrq*

Here the theorem proved is 1.51. The derivational line reads: 'Take the expression 1.44; for "*r*"substitute "*Nr*"; apply the expression 1.23 (a definition) after substituting "*r*" for "*p*" and "*p*" for "*q*"; apply the same definition 1.23 again but this time substitute "*r*" for "*p*"; and one will thus obtain the theorem to be proved 1.51.' (Bochenski's *A Precis of Mathematical Logic,* p. 31).

1.51 $p/App,\ q/p,\ r/p = C\ 1.41 - C1.42\ q/p - 1.52$

1.52 *Cpp*

Here the theorem proved is 1.52. The derivational line reads: 'Take the expression 1.51; for "*p*" substitute "*App*", for "*q*" substitute "*p*", for "*r*" substitute "*p*"; this will result in an expression composed of (1) *C* followed by an expression equiform with 1.41; (2) *C* followed by an expression equiform with 1.42 after "*p*" is substituted for "*q*"; (3) the theorem 1.52 (which by a double application of the rule of detachment can now be stated separately, i.e. since the whole sentence is a law of the system, and 1.41 and 1.42 are also laws, then 1.52 is also a law)."

The foundations and early theorems of Hilbert–Ackerman's system, as modified and presented by Bochenski, are as follows:

1.1 *Primitive Terms, Rule of Definition and Rules of Formation*

1.11 Primitive terms; '*D*'—dyadic functor; '*p*', '*q*', '*r*', '*s*'—sentential variables.

1.12 Rule of Definition: A new term can be introduced into the system by formulating a group of terms, called the 'definition', and consisting of: (1) an expression which contains the new term and in which all the others are terms of the system; (2) '='; (3) an expression which contains only primitive terms or terms already defined.

1.13 Rules of Formation: (1) a variable is a sentence; (2) a group of terms consisting of '*N*' followed by one sentence is a sentence; (3) a group of terms consisting of 'A', 'C', 'D', 'E' or 'K' followed by two sentences is a sentence.

1.2 *Definitions*

1.21 *NP = Dpp*

1.22 *Apq = DNpNq*

1.23 *Cpq = ANpq*

1.24 *Kpq = NANpNq*

1.25 *Epq = KCpqCqp*

1.3 Rules of Deduction

1.31 Rule of Substitution: A sentence may be substituted for a variable, but the same sentence must be substituted for all equiform occurrences of variable in the expression.

1.32 Rule of substitution by definition: A definition may be substituted for the expression which it defines in a sentence, and reciprocally, without being substituted for all equiform occurrences of that expression.

1.33 Rule of detachment: If a sentence consisting of '*C*' followed by two sentences is a law of the system, and if a sentence equiform with the first of these sentences is a law of the system, a sentence equiform with the second can be posited as a law of the system.

1.4 *Axioms*

1.41 *CAppp*

1.42 *CpApq*

1.43 *CApqAqp*

1.44 *CCpqCArpArq*

1.5 *Deduction of Theorems*

1.44 *r/Nr* × 1.23 *p/r, q/p* × 1.23 *p/r* = 1.51

1.51 *CCpqCCrpCrq*

1.51 *p/App, q/p, r/p* = *C* 1.41 – *C* 1.42 *q/p* – 1.52

1.52 *Cpp*
1.52 × 1.23 *q/p* = 1.53
1.53 *ANpp*
1.43 *p/Np q\p = C 1.53 - 1.54*
1.54 *ApNNNp*
1.54 *p/Np* × 1.23 *q/NNp* = 1.55
1.55 *CpNNp*
1.44 *p/Np, q/NNNp, r/p = C* 1.55 *p/Np, – C* 1.54–1.56
1.56 *ApNNNp*
1.43 *q/NNNp,* × 1.23 *p/NNp, q/p = C* 1.56 – 1.57
1.57 *CNNpp*
1.44 *q/NNp, r/Nq = C* 1.55 – 1.58
1.58 *CANqpANqNNp*
1.51 *p/ANqNNp, q/ANNpNq, r/ANqp = C* 1.43 *p/Nq, q/NNp – C* 1.58 – 1.59
1.59 *CANqpANNpNq*
1.59 *p/q, q/p* × 1.23 × 1.23 *p/Nq, q/Np* = 1.60
1.60 *CCpqCNqNp*
1.41 *p/Np* × 1.23 *q/Np* = 1.61
1.61 *CCpNpNp*
1.51 p/Apq, q/Aqp, r/p = C 1.43 – C 1.42 – 1.62
1.62 *CpAqp*
1.62 *q/Nq × 1.23 p/q, q/p* = 1.63
1.63 *CpCqp*
1.63 *q/Np* = 1.64
1.64 *CpCNpp*
1.44 *p/r, q/Apr, r/q* = C 1.62 *p/r, q/p* – 1.65
1.65 *CAqrAqApr*
1.44 *p/Aqr q/AqApr, r.p = C 1.65 – 1.66*
1.66 *CApAqrApAqApr*
1.51 *p/ApAqApr, q/AAqAprp, r/ApAqr* = C 1.43 *q/AqApr – C* 1.66 – 1.67
1.67 *CApAqrAAqAprp*
1.51 p/Apr, q/AqApr, r/p = C 1.62 p/Apr – C 1.42

r/r – 1.68

1.68 *CpAqApr*
1.44 *q/AqApr, r/AqApr* = *C* 1.68 – 1.69

1.69 *CAAqAprpAAqAprAqApr*
1.51 *p/AAqAprAqApr, q/AqApr, r/AAqAprp* = *C* 1.41 *p/AqApr* – *C* 1.69 – 1.70

1.70 *CAAqAprpAqApr*
1.51 *p/AAqAprp, q/AqApr, r/ApAqr* = *C* 1.70 – *C* 1.67 – 1.71

1.71 *CApAqrAqApr*
1.44 *p/Aqr, q/Arq, r/p* = *C 1.43 p/q, q/r* = 1.72

1.72. *CApAqrApArq*
1.51 *p/ApArq, q/ArApq* = *C* 1.71 *q/r, r/q* – *C* 1.72 – 1.73

1.73 *CApAqrArApq*
1.51 *p/ArApq, q/AApqr, r/ApAqr* = *C* 1.43 *p/r, q/Apq* – *C* 1.73 – 1.74

1.74 *CApAqrAApqr*
1.51 *p/AqApr, q/AqArp, r/ApAqr* = *C* 1.72 *p/q, q/p* – *C* 1.71 – 1.75

1.75 *CApAqrAqArp*
1.51 *pArApq, q/ArAqp, r/ApAqr* = *C* 1.72 *p/r, q/p, r/q* – *C* 1.73 – 1.76

1.76 *CApAqrArAqp*

A SURVEY OF CLASSIC AXIOMATIZATIONS OF PROPOSITIONAL LOGIC

This survey is based on the detailed systematic presentation in *Notions De Logique Formelle* by Professor Dopp (Appendix 1. p. 261 seq.). The axiomatic systems are classified according to the nature of the functors used in their sets of axioms, and they are further varied according to the number of axioms needed:

1. *Systems using the five operators C, N, K, A, E* (→, ~, ∨, ↔ *in the Peano-Russell notation)*:

(a)Having 15 axioms:

Hilbert-Bernays, 1934
Hermes-Scholz, 1952

(b)Having 10 axioms:

Moh Shaw-Kwei, 1957 (two different systems)

(c)Having 9 axioms:

Jaskowski

(d)Having 5 axioms:

Moh Shaw-Kwei, 1957

2.*Systems using the four functors C, N, K, A:*

(a)Having 12 axioms:

Heyting, 1930
S. Kanger, 1955

(b)Having 10 axioms:

Tarski, 1952

3.*Systems using the three functors C, N, K:*

(a)Having 5 axioms:

Porte, 1958 (three different systems)

(b)Having 4 axioms:

Porte, 1958

(c)Having 3 axioms:

Rosser, 1953

4.*Systems using the three functors C, N, A:*

(a)Having 7 axioms:

Jaskowski, 1948

5.*Systems using the two functors C, N:*

(a)Having 7 axioms:

Russell, 1906

(b)Having 6 axioms:

Frege, 1879
Hilbert, 1922
Moh Shaw-Kwei,1957 (two different systems)

(c)Having 5 axioms:

Curry

(d)Having 4 axioms:

Curry

Tarski, 1930
Porte, 1958

(e)Having 3 axioms

Lukasiewicz, 1924
Lukasiewicz, 1929
Lukasiewicz, 1930
Sobocinski, 1953
Arai, 1965
Mendelson

(f)Having 1 axiom:

Lukasiewicz (two different systems)

Meredith, 1953
Lukasiewicz-Tarski, 1930
Tanaka, 1966

6. *Systems using the two functors C, A:*

(a)Having 6 axioms:

Jaskowski, 1948

(b)Having 5 axioms:

Russell and Whitehead, 1910

(c)Having 4 axioms:

Hilbert-Ackerman, 1928

(d)Having 3 axioms:

Rasiowa, 1949
Meredith, 1951

(e)Having 1 axiom:

Meredith, 1953

7.*Systems using the two functors N, A:*

(a)Having 5 axioms:

Reichenbach, 1953

(b)Having 3 axioms:

Rose, 1949

8.*Systems using the two functors N, K:*

(a)Having 4 axioms:

Sobocinski, 1939
Sobocinski, 1962

9.*Systems using only the functor D:*
(a)Having 1 axiom:

Nicod, 1918
Lukasiewicz, 1925
Wajsberg, 1931
Lukasiewicz, 1931

10.*Systems which include a propositional constant, which symbolizes a proposition that is (necessarily) false:*
(a)Having 11 axioms:

Schutte, 1960

(b)Having 5 axioms:

Peirce, 1885

(c)Having 4 axioms:

Wajsberg, 1937

(d) Having 3 axioms:

Church, 1951

(e)Having 2 axioms:

Rose, 1951

(f)Having 1 axiom:

Lukasiewicz-Meredith, 1953 (two different axioms, each with 6 variables)

Meredith, 1953 (two different axioms the first with 5 variables, the second with 6)

Chapter-9

Predicate Logic

Chapter 9

INTRODUCTION

In propositional logic variables stand for whole, unanalysed propositions; these are the atoms out of which complex, molecular propositions are constructed through the operation of connectives such as *K, C, A,* etc. A variable such as *p, q* or *r* is used to signify any entity that has propositional form, whatever its internal structure. Thus propositional logic is only suited for dealing with arguments whose logical force derives completely from the connectives, *K, C, A,* etc. It cannot evaluate the following argument, for instance: 'If everything that can reproduce its kind, is living; and if a virus can reproduce its kind, then it follows that a virus is living.' Translated into the language of propositional logic this sequence of three different propositions reads 'If *p* and if *q,* then *r.*' Such a reading does not credit the argument with any logical force. However, if we use the traditional symbols *S, P* and *M* for the subject of the conclusion, the predicate of the conclusion and the term common to both premisses we display the basic and compelling force of the argument:

If all *M* is *P*;
and if all *S* is *M*,
____
then all *S* is *P*

Obviously there is room for a section of logic which expresses the internal structure of atomic propositions and studies the operation and the laws of predication. This is broadly the function of Predicate Logic.

THE LANGUAGE OF PREDICATE LOGIC

It consists of

1. *proper names:* frequently the initial letter of the proper name is used, e.g. '*v*' for 'Voltaire';

2. *arbitrary names:* they designate individuals also but only those arbitrarily chosen. The letters '*a*', '*b*', '*c*', '*d*' will be used for such individuals which are designated not in their individuality but only in so far as they are typical cases;

3. *individual variables:* the letter '*x*', '*y*', '*z*' will be used as variables for the individuals of any universe of discourse;

4. *predicate letters:* the initial capitals of the predicate words will be used as such letters; otherwise '*F*', '*G*', '*H*', '*I*'. Followed by one name they signify a *property;* followed by two or more names they signify a *relation.* Thus *Fx* signifies that *x* has the property *F; Fxy* signifies that *x* has the relation *F* to *y*.

5. *quantifiers:* (*x*) is the symbol of universal quantification; thus (*x*)*Fx* can be read: 'for every value of *x* (or take any object *x*) *x* is *F*.'

(*Ex*) is the existential quantifier and (*Ex*)*Fx* means that 'an object *x* can be found such that *x* is *F* or 'there exists some object *x* such that *x* is *F*

6. *the connectives of propositional logic:* instead of using the Polish notation, we will use a notation that is basically Peano-Russell:

'–' instead of '*N*'
'≡' instead of '*E*'
'∨' instead of '*A*'
'→' instead of '*C*'
'|' instead of '*D*'
'.' instead of '*K*'

7. *A class designating symbol:* '*x*' signifies 'the *xs* such that...'

8. *A symbol representing identity:* '=' is this symbol; when it is included predicate logic or calculus (PL or PC) is called predicate

logic or calculus with identity (PLI or PCI). This symbol is a predicate letter although it has a fixed meaning, and by convention is placed between its terms. It appears in complex expressions in just the way *F* and *G* appear.

The above simple formal language has great expressive power, as can be seen from the following translations:

Voltaire is a Frenchman who smiles: $Fv.\ Sv$
There is a Frenchman who smiles: $(Ex)\ (Fx.\ Sx)$
All Frenchmen smile: $(x)\ (Fx \rightarrow Sx)$

(A universal propositions expressed in the form of a material implication governed by the universal quantifier: Russell called this formal implication.)

Some Frenchmen smile: $(Ex)\ (Fx.\ Sx)$

(A particular proposition is expressed in the form of a simple conjunction–not a material implication–governed by the existential quantifier; the truth of an existential proposition is not implied by the truth of the corresponding universal.)

No Frenchmen smile: $(x)\ (Fx \rightarrow -\ Sx)$

Some Frenchmen do not smile: $(Ex)\ (Fx.\ -Sx)$
The class of cats who smile: $(x)\ (Cx.\ Sx)$
John does not like any strangers: $(x)\ (Sx \rightarrow -\ Ljx)$
Valid conclusions are those which are implied by the premisses: $(x)\ (Cx.\ Vx \rightarrow Ix)$
Only valid conclusions are implied by the premisses: $(x)\ (Ix \rightarrow Cx.\ Vx)$

Following Euclid if we can prove that an arbitrarily selected triangle has the property *F* (i.e. if we can prove *Fa*), then we can soundly conclude that all triangles have *F* (i.e. that $(x)\ Fx$).

There are exactly two Frenchmen who smile:

$(Ex)\ (Ey)\ [(Fx.\ Sx)\ .\ (Fy\ .\ Sy)\ .\ -(x = y)\ .\ (z)\ [(Fz\ .\ Sz) \rightarrow ((z = x) \vee (z = y))]]$

'There exists an *x* and there exists a *y* such that *x* is a Frenchman and smiles and *y* is a Frenchman and smiles, and

x and y are not the same person; and for every value of z, if z is a Frenchman and smiles he is either x or y.'

Thus through use of the identity symbol we can make exact numerical statements in predicate calculus—'at least one thing', 'at most one thing', 'one thing', 'two things', 'three things' and so on through the number series.

DISCOVERING TRUTHS IN PREDICATE LOGIC

In the section on propositional logic we used the mechanical method of truth-tables to discover the logical truths (tautologies, laws) of that area; in addition, selecting a few of these simple truths as a set of axioms we systematically deduced the rest. We can establish also that our axiomatic system is both consistent and complete (see later section on Metalogic).

Predicate logic does not possess a mechanical decision procedure. On the other hand it has this enormous advantage that for every law of propositional logic one can formulate analogous laws in predicate logic by simply substituting wff's from predicate logic for the propositional variables p, q, r, s, prefixing the universal quantifier if individuals variables are used. Thus from the law $p \equiv p$, one can form the analogous law $(x)\ Fx \equiv Fx$; we could also form the law $Fa \equiv Fa$, using the individual constant a and omitting the quantifier. One can discover a vast number of logical laws, simple and complex in this way; the only limit is the range of laws within propositional logic itself and the scope of substitution for the propositional variables.

How are the laws which are not analogous discovered and established? Of course both the axiomatic and the natural deduction approach employ procedures which are techniques of discovery. We have seen axiomatic techniques in operation in the area of propositional logic, and one well known axiomatic system of predicate logic is that presented by Hilbert and Ackermann in their *Principles of Mathematical logic.* Here we will indicate how the same range of logical truth can be discovered from the natural deducation approach.

To the LAF's of propositional logic four further ones are added concerning the quantifiers:

U-in

(1)	*Fa*	*A*
(2)	(*x*) (*Fx*)	*1, U-in*

U-out

(1)	(*x*) *Fx*	*A*
(2)	*Fa*	*1, U-out*

('*a*'being an arbitrary name)

also

(1)	(*x*) *Fx*	*A*
(2)	*Fi*	*1, U-out*

(where '*i*' is a proper name)

U-in is based on the logical force of a typical case having the predicate *F*. It is not because the individual designated by *a* is arbitrarily chosen that we can generalize from it but because it is designated and used not in its individuality but only in so far as it is a typical case. Arbitrary choice as such does not guarantee that the individual chosen will be used only in so far as it is typical; however it is an acknowledgement that *any* individual can be used in this way, and some proofs in Euclidean Geometry are familiar examples of this usage. Formal logic is not concerned with the practical difficulties of defining the typical case but with the fact that on the assumption that a typical case, as such, has a predicate *F*, then it follows by natural deduction that this predicate belongs to every individual of the type. *U-out* accepts that any instantiation of a universal predication holds.

E-in

(1)	*Fa*	*A*
(2)	(*Ex*) *Fx*	*1, E-in*

E-out

(1)	*Ex* (*Fx*)		*A*
(2)	2.1	*Ga*	*A*(*G* signifies properties that constitute the type.)
	2.2	P	*any expression that*

follows from 2.1.

(3) | P 1, 2, *E*-out

also

(1) | Fi A

(2) | $(Ex)\ Fx$ 1, *E*-in

(where '*i*' is a proper name).

E-in accepts that any single case of a predication entitles the derivation of an existential proposition; *E*-out is based on the fact that an existential proposition is a finite or infinite disjunction (A_1 or A_2 or A_3 or A_n has F) and what is shown to be true of each and every disjunct or of a typical disjunct, a, is therefore derivable from the existential proposition. The fact that *E*-out, like *U*-in, can be based on the logical force of a typical case does not render it redundant: a function of propositional logic is to determine the conditions, if any, on which an existential assumption can give rise to a natural deduction process.

There are two rules concerning identity in proofs: *I*-in allows us to introduce, at any time and as a matter of transparent logical truth not as an assumption, $t = t$; in virtue of the rule *I*-out, given that $t = s$ we are allowed to transform a statement containing occurrences of t into a statement which replaces one or more occurrence of t by s.

Finally ~~to~~ expedite and shorten proof there is a rule of theorem introduction (*TI*), allowing us to introduce, at any stage. a theorem already proved or any substitution instance of it; and there is a rule of sequent introduction (*SI*) enabling us to do the same with regard to sequents and their substitution-instances.

The complete list of LAF's and rules which constitute our apparatus for discovering logical truth is given in the following table. Assumptions are placed for convenience to the left of the therefore indicator |–, and the derived propositions to its right; in some cases there are no assumptions for, as we have seen, the method of supposition can lead to a conclusion where truth is displayed as free from the initial suppositions. The LAF's from propositional logic are the same as those formulated in chapter 3 in the Polish notation.

Table of LAF's and rules used in a natural deduction system of Predicate Logic

A rule of assumptions (A) entitles us to introduce any proposition at any stage in a proof)

1. *p. q* |– *p. q*	Symbolized as *Ki*(*K*-in)
2. *p. q* |– *p*	" " *Ko* (*K*-out)
3. *p* |– *p*∨*q*	" " *Ai*
4. (*q. p*) ∨ (*q. r*) |– *q*	" " *Ao*
5. |– *p* → (*p*∨*q*)	" " *Ci*
6. *p* → *q.p* |– *q*	" " *Co*
7. |– – (*r.* (*s.* – *r*))	" " *Ni*
8. |– ((*p. q*) → *p*)	" " *No*
9. *q* |– *p*	" " *Rep.*(Repetition)
10. *p* |– – – *p*	" " *DN* (double negation)
11. *Fa* |– (*x*) *Fx*	" " *Ui*
12. *x* (*Fx*)|– *Fa* also (*x*) *Fx* |– *Fm*	" " *Uo*
13. *Fa*|–(*Ex*) *Fx* also *Fm* |– (*Ex*) *Fx*	" " *Ei*
14. *Ex* (*Fx*), *Fa* → *p* |– *p*	" " *Eo*
15. *t* = *t*	" " *Iit*(Identity appears as a line in the proof)
16.Given that t s. we are allowed to transform a statement containing occurrences of t |*P(t)*|into a statement which replaces one or more occurrences of *t* / *y s* |*P(s)*|.	Symblized as *Io* (Identity is used in the production of a line in the proof, and disappears on use).
17. Rule of Theorem Introduction, allowing us to introduce any theorem already proved and any substitution instance of it.	Symbolized as *Ti*
18. Rule of Sequent Introduction, allowing us to introduce any sequent already proved and any substitution instance of it.	" " *Si*

This table constitutes an apparatus for discovering proofs (and therefore truths) in predicate logic: we can construct sequences, the last item being a conclusion, the other items the basis on which it is derived and *all* items having a good reason: being justified by a rule such as that of assumptions, or theorem introduction, etc. or by an LAF such as *Ki* or *Ko*, etc. Thus, directly, the table provides us with the means of displaying a fundamental basis on which logical truths or valid sequents can be justified; it does not provide us with a direct means of discovering and displaying invalidity. By contrast the method of truth-tables is a procedure that within propositional logic displays both validity and invalidity and can always be applied.

Truth discovery by natural deduction is a matter of strategy. Can the table of LAF's and rules be used to supply a justification (proof) for saying that this proposition (*p*) is derivable from certain assumptions; or that this other proposition (*q*) can be derived by the method of supposition and also shown to be true independently of any initial supposition made. Through practise and experience one must develop a sensitivity as to what LAF, and rules are likely to be helpful in discovering, constructing and formalizing derivations.

PRACTICE IN DERIVATION BY THE METHOD OF SUPPOSITION—A SAMPLING OF LOGICAL LAWS IN PREDICATE LOGIC WITH THEIR PROOFS

The law is stated first. Each line of the proof is numbered serially; the number is placed to the immediate left of the expression and is in brackets (e.g. (1), (2)). Each line must have a good reason; this reason may be, e.g. the rule of assumptions, or that this line is derivable from earlier ones by one of the LAF rules; whatever the reason be it is given in the column on the right, e.g. *A* (this line is an assumption); 1, 2 *Ki* (this line is derived from 1 and 2 on the basis of the LAF, *Ki*). On the extreme left there is a column giving the assumptions required for each line. If a line is there through use of the rule of assumptions, then it depends on itself as an assumption and accordingly we put its own number in the left-hand column; if it is there by derivation we must pool the assumptions required for its premisses (this is easily done as the right-hand column gives us the serial numbers of the premisses, and the left-hand column at each number gives us the relevant assumptions). Thus taking the following line

1, 2, 3 (6) *P* 2, 3 *Ko*

we may read it as follows: the expression, *P,* is line 6 in the proof; it is derived by *Ko* from lines 2 and 3; the assumptions on which it rests are lines 1, 2 and 3. It is well to recall that in the application of *Ci*, the new conditional has as its antecedent an expression which was an assumption; it is not an assumption for the new conditional and does not appear in the column of assumptions for the new conditional; it is called the discharged assumption. Thus in the application of *Ci* the number of assumptions is reduced by one and a *Ci* proposition derived by the method of assumptions may have no assumptions. Such a proposition is called a theorem. A sample example is $\vdash (p \, . \, q) \rightarrow p$. Its proof is

1 (1) $p \, . \, q$	*A*
1 (2) p	1, *Ko*
(3) $(p \, . \, q) \rightarrow p$	1, 2, *Ci*

A similar discharging of assumptions occurs in the application of *Ni* and *No.* If on the assumption of a proposition *p* (positive or negative) a formal contradiction is derived from it then the negation of *p* follows by natural deduction; and $-p$ is implied by the formal contradiction not by the proposition *p* which has been used in the *method* of supposition but is now discharged *evidentially* as an assumption. A simple example is $\vdash - -$ (r. (s. – r)). Its proof is

1 (1) r. (s. – r)	A
1 (2) r	1, *Ko*
1 (3) $s. - r$	1, *Ko*
1 (4) $- r$	3, *Ko*

1	(5) $r. - r$	2, 4, *Ki*
1	(6) $(r. (s. - r)) \to r. - r$	1, 5, *Ci*
	(7) $- (r. (s. - r))$	6, *Ni*

Of course if there are assumptions involved in the derivation of the formal contradiction then the conclusion will rest on these. An example is the proof of the logical law p → q, p → – q |– – p:

1	(1) $p \to q$	*A*
2	(2) $p \to - q$	*A*
3	(3) p	*A*
1, 3	(4) q	1, 3, *Co*
2, 3	(5) $- q$	2, 3, *Co*
1, 2, 3	(6) $q. - q$	4, 5, *Ki*
1, 2	(7) $p \to (q. - q)$	3, 6, *Ci*
1, 2	(8) $- p$	7, *Ni*

–p rests on 1 and 2 as assumptions; 3 is discharged as an assumption although its supposition has been useful in the process of discovering 8.

What are basic guidelines in the technique of proof-discovery? The nature of the quantifier (e.g. *U*) and of the main connective (e.g. *C*) in the desired conclusion invite the use of those LAF's which succeed in introducing such a quantifier (e.g. *Ui*) and such a connective (e.g. *Ci*). Similarly the quantifier (e.g. *E*) and the connective (e.g. ∨) in an assumption we are given invite us to consider LAF's which reach derivations on the basis of such a quantifier (e.g. *Eo*) or such a connective (e.g. *Ao*). In the proof of theorems we rely heavily on *Ci*, *Ni* and *No*. At times with the help of *Ni* or *No* it is easiest to reach a desired proposition through the rejection of its contradictory. The repetition of a proposition already in our sequence with a good reason, and the operation of double negation on it, can facilitate proof work; and such work is shortened by use of rules permitting the economy of theorem and sequent introduction. Finally, immense technical advantages are gained by the use of the typical case (symbolized by the arbitrary name) to prove a universal or to replace it; in the latter eventuality one is enabled to use procedures from propositional logic which would be inapplicable with quantifiers present.

The following are examples of proofs for some valid sequents and some true theorems (in these proofs where there is more than one assumption, a comma is used to separate them):

Proof of (*x*) *Fx* → *Gx,* (*x*) *Gx* → *Hx* |– (*x*) *Fx* → *Hx*

1	(1) (x) *Fx* → *Gx*	*A*
2	(2) (x) *Gx* → *Hx*	*A*
1	(3) *Fa* → *Ga*	1, *Uo*
2	(4) *Ga* → *Ha*	2, *Uo*
	(5) ((p→q).(q.r))→ (p → r)	*SI* (from propositional logic)
	(6)((*Fa*→*Ga*).(*Ga*→*Ha*)→(*Fa*→*Ha*)	5, *p* | *Fa,q* | *Ga,r* | *Ha*
1,2	(7) (*Fa* → *Ga*) . (*Ga* → *Ha*)	3, 4, *Ki*
1,2	(8) *Fa* → *Ha*	6, 7, *Co*
1,2	(9) (*x*) *Fx* → *Hx*	8, *Ui*

Proof of Fm. Gm |– *Hm* →*Gm*

1	(1) *Fm. Gm*	*A*
2	(2) *Hm*	*A*
1	(3) *Gm*	1, *Ko*
1	(4) *Hm*→*Gm*	2, 3, *Ci*

This is one of the paradoxes of material implication: in virtue of the meaning of →, *Gm* established in the domain of the assumption *Fm. Gm* is materially implied by any other assumption. There is a good reason for each of the lines (2), (3) and (4) so this sequence constitutes a proof. The more familiar format of the paradox of material implication is, of course, that a true proposition is implied by any proposition.

Proof of *Fa* / *Ga,* – *Ga* |– – *Fa*

1	(1) *Fa* → *Ga*	*A*
2	(2) – *Ga*	*A*

3	(3) Fa	A
1,3	(4) Ga	1, 3, Co
1,2,3	(5) Ga . – Ga	4, 2, Ki
1, 2	(6) $Fa \rightarrow (Ga$. – $Ga)$	3, 5, Ci
1, 2	(7) – Fa	6, Ni

(In the domain of the assumptions (1) and (2), *Fa* involves a formal contradiction and so can be negated by the rule *Ni*)

Proof of (Fm → Gm) . Hm, – Hm |– – p

1	(1) $(Fm \rightarrow Gm)$. Hm	A
2	(2) – Hm	A
3	(3) p	A
1	(4) Hm	1, Ko
1,2	(5) Hm . – Hm	4, 2, Ki
1,2	(6) $p \rightarrow (Hm$. – $Hm)$	3, 5, Ci
1,2	(7) – p	6 Ni.

The negation of any proposition, p, follows from assumptions that posit both *Hm* and *–Hm*.

Proof of –(Fm . –Gm) |– Fm → Gm

1	(1) – (Fm . – Gm)	A
2	(2) Fm	A
3	(3) – Gm	A
2,3	(4) Fm . – Gm	2, 3, Ki
1,2,3	(5) $(Fm$. – $Gm)$. – $(Fm$.– $Gm)$	4, 1, Ki
1,2	(6) –$Gm \rightarrow ((Fm$.–$Gm)$.–$(Fm$.–$Gm))$	3, 5, Ci
1,2	(7) – – Gm	6, Ni
1,2	(8) Gm	7, DN
1	(9) $Fm \rightarrow Gm$.	2, 8, Ci

Proof of Fm → Gm, Fm ∨ (Hm . Gm) |– Gm

1	(1) $Fm \rightarrow Gm$	A
2	(2) $Fm \vee (Hm$. $Gm)$	A
3	(3) Fm	A

1,3	(4) *Gm*	1, 3, *Co*
5	(5) *Hm . Gm*	*A*
5	(6) *Gm*	5, *Ko*
1	(7) *Fm* → *Gm*	3, 4, *Ci*
	(8) (Hm . Gm) → Gm	5, 6, *Ci*
1,2	(9) *Gm*	2, 7, 8, *Ao*

In applying *Ao* to the disjunction assumed at line 2, we take each disjunct in turn and assume it (lines 3 and 5). If the required conclusion can be demonstrated to be derivable from each disjunct then we may present it as derivable from the assumption of the disjunction as a whole. However, any extra assumption used in the course of this demonstration must either be eliminated (the assumptions on which the final conclusion is based (accordingly, the assumption madeat line 1 is requisite).

Proof of (*x*) *Fx* |– (*Ex*) *Fx*

1	*(1)* *(x)* Fx	A
1	(2) *Fa*	1, *Uo*
1	(3) (*Ex*) *Fx*	2, *Ei*

Proof of (*x*) (*Fx* → *Gx*), (*Ex*) *Fx* |– (*Ex*) *Gx*

1	(1) (*x*) *Fx* → *Gx*	*A*
2	(2) (*Ex*) *Fx*	*A*
3	(3) *Fa*	*A*
1	(4) *Fa* → *Ga*	1, *Uo*
1,3	(5) *Ga*	4, 3, *Co*
1,3	(6) (*Ex*) *Gx*	5, *Ei*
1,2	(7) (*Ex*) *Gx*	2,3,6,*Eo*

The desired conclusion is reached at line (6) but not on the desired assumptions.However, having shown that the conclusion follows from the assumed existence (line 3) of *any* typical demonstration instance with the property *F*, we know by the rule of *Eo* that this conclusion is therefore secure provided that *some* object can be found which has *F*. Thus assumption (3) is discharged and replaced by assumption (2).

Proof of (*x*) *Fx* → *Gx* |– (*Ex*) *Fx* → (*Ex*) *Gx*

1	*(1)* (x) Fx → Gx	A
2	*(2)* (Ex) Fx	A
3	(3) *Fa*	*A*
1	(4) *Fa* → *Ga*	1, *Uo*
1,3	(5) *Ga*	3, 4, *Co*
1,3	(6) (*Ex*) *Gx*	5, *Ei*
1,2	(7) (*Ex*) *Gx*	2,3,6, *Eo*
1	(8) (*Ex*)*Fx*→(*Ex*)*Gx*	2, 7, *Ci*

This proof simply needs to conditionalize the previous proof: what was an assumption in the latter has now the role of antecedent in a conclusion.

Proof of |– (*x*) (*p* . *Fx*) → (*p* . (*x*) *Fx*)

1	*(1)* (x) (p . Fx)	A
2	(2) *p* . *Fa*	*Uo*
2	(3) *p*	2, *Ko*
1	(4) *Fa*	2, *Ko*
1	(5) (*x*) *Fx*	4, *Ui*
1	(6) *p* . (*x*) *Fx*	3, 5, *Ki*
	(7) (*x*) (*p*. *Fx*) → *p* . (*x*) *Fx*	1, 6, *Ci*

Conditionalizing (6) results in line (1) no longer having the role of an assumption: it appears in line (7) as an antecedent materially implying line (6). Thus line (7) does not depend on any assumption—it is a *theorem* in the distinctive sense this term has in a system of natural deduction.

Proof that (*x*) (*Fx* → *Gx*) |– (*x*) (*Ey*) (*Fx* . *Hxy*) → (*Ey*) (*Gy* . *Hxy*)

1	*(1)* (x) Fx → Gx	A
2	(2) (*Ey*) (*Fy* . *Hay*)	*A*
3	(3) *Fb* . *Hab*	*A*
3	(4) *Fb*	3, *Ko*
3	(5) *Hab*	3, *Ko*
1	(6) *Fb* → *Gb*	1, *Uo*
1,3	(7) *Gb*	4, 6, *Co*

1,3	(8) $Gb \,.\, Hab$	7, 5, *Ki*
1,3	(9) $(Ey)\,(Gy.Hay)$	8, *Ei*
1,2	(10) $(Ey)\,(Gy.Hay)$	2, 3, 9, *Eo*
1	(11) $(Ey)\,(Fy.Hay) \rightarrow (Ey)(Gy.Hay)$	2, 10, *Ci*
1	(12) $(x)\,(Ey)\,(Fy.Hxy) \rightarrow (Ey)(Gy.Hxy)$	11, *Ui*

Introducing the universal quantifier (x), line (12) simply universalizes line (11).

Proof of $\vdash (x)\,(x = x)$

(1) $a = a$	Ii
(2) $(x)\,(x = x)$	*1*, Ui

Rule *Ii* permits us to introduce an identity and it does not rest on any assumptions. Thus in this proof there is no column of assumptions.

Proof of $(a = b), (b = c) \vdash (a = c)$

1	(1) $(a = b)\,.\,(b = c)$	*A*
1	(2) $a = b$	1, *Ko*
1	(3) $b = c$	1, *Ko*
1	(4) $a = c$	2, 3, *Io* (since $a = b$, we can substitute a for b in (3).)

Proof of $Fa \vdash (Ex)\,(x = a\,.\,Fx)$

1	(1) Fa	*A*
	(2) $a = a$	*Ii*
1	(3) $(a = a)\,.\,Fa$	1, 2, *Ki*
1	(4) $(Ex)\,((x = a)\,.\,Fx)$	3, *Ei*

Proof of $(Ex)\,Fx.\,(Ey)\,Fy\,.\,-(x = y) \vdash -((Ex)\,Fx\,.\,(Ey)\,Fy) \rightarrow (x = y)$

1	(1) $(Ex)\,Fx\,.\,(Ey)\,Fy\,.\,-(x = y)$	*A*
1	(2) $(Ex)\,Fx\,.\,(Ey)\,Fy$	1, *Ko*
1	(3) $-(x = y)$	1, *Ko*
4	(4) $((Ex)\,Fx\,.\,(Ey)\,Fy) \rightarrow (x = y)$	*A*
1,4	(5) $x = y$	4, 2, *Co*

1,4 (6) $(x = y) . - (x = y)$ 5, 3, *Ki*
1,4 (7) $((Ex)Fx.(Ey)\ Fy \rightarrow (x = y)) \rightarrow (x = y).-(x=y)$ 4, 6, *Ci*
1 (8) $- (((Ex)\ Fx\ .\ (Ey)\ Fy) \rightarrow (x = y))$ 7, *Ni*

This law says that if at least two objects have *F*, it is not the case that at most one object has F. This indicates how predicate Calculus with Identity (*PCI*) extends itself naturally into a calculus of numerical quantifiers.

THE RANGE OF LOGICAL LAWS IN PREDICATE LOGIC

Some analogous laws

$(x)\ Fx \vee Fx \ |- (x)\ Fx$ $[(p \vee p) \rightarrow p]$
$(x)\ Fx\ .\ Gx \ |- (x)\ Fx$ $[(p\ .\ q) \rightarrow p]$
$(Ex)\ Fx \ |- (Ex)\ Fx$ $[p \rightarrow p]$
$- (Ex)\ Fx \ |- - (Ex)\ (Fx\ .\ Gx)$ $[- p \rightarrow - (p\ .\ q)\ ]$
$(x)\ Fx \rightarrow Gx -| \ |- - (Ex)\ (Fx\ .\ - Gx)$ $[p \rightarrow q \equiv - (.-q)]$
$(x)\ (-Fx.-Gx) -| \ |- - (Ex)(Fx \vee Gx)$ $[- p.- q \equiv -(p\ .\ q)]$
$(x)\ (-Fx \vee - Gx) -| \ |- - (Ex)\ (Fx\ .\ Gx)$ $[- p \vee -q \equiv -(p\ .\ q)]$
$(x)\ Fx\ .\ Gx \ |- (x)\ Fx \vee Gx$ $[(p\ .\ q) \rightarrow (p \vee q)]$
$(x)\ Fx \rightarrow Gx \ |- (x) - Gx \rightarrow - Fx$ $[p \rightarrow q) \rightarrow (-q \rightarrow -p)]$
$(x)\ Fx \rightarrow Gx, (x) - Gx \ |- (x) - Fx$ (modus tollendo tollens)
$(x)\ Fx \rightarrow Gx, (x)\ Fx \ |- (x)\ Gx$ (modus ponendo ponens)
$(x)\ (Fx \rightarrow Gx)\ .\ (x)\ (Fx \rightarrow Hx) \ |- (x)\ Fx \rightarrow (Gx\ .\ Hx)$ $[((p\ .\ q)\ .\ (p \rightarrow q) \rightarrow p \rightarrow (q\ .\ r)]$

In *Principia Mathematica* the chief purpose of the propositions which are numbered *10 is 'to extend to formal implications (i.e. to propositions of the form (*x*)...) as many as possible of the propositions proved previously for material implications, i.e. for propositions of the form $p \supset q$.' (*Principia Mathematica,* Vol. 1, p. 138)

Some laws governing the movement of quantifiers

$(x)\ Fx.Gx \dashv\vdash (x)\ Fx.(x)\ Gx$

$(Ex)\ Fx.Gx \vdash (Ex)\ Fx\ .\ (Ex)\ Gx$ (The converse conditional does not hold.)

$(x)\ Fx \vee (x)\ Gx \vdash (x)\ Fx \vee Gx$

$(Ex)Fx \vee Gx \dashv\vdash (Ex)\ Fx \vee (Ex)\ Gx$

$(x)Fx \rightarrow Gx \vdash (x)Fx \rightarrow (x)\ Gx$

$(x)\ Fx \rightarrow Gx \vdash (Ex)\ Fx \rightarrow (Ex)Gx$

$(x)\ (y)\ Fxy \dashv\vdash (y)\ (x)\ Fxy$ (The order of universal quantifiers does not affect meaning.)

$(Ex)(Ey)Fxy \dashv\vdash (Ey)(Ex)Fxy$ (The order of existential quantifiers does not affect meaning.)

$(Ex)\ (y)\ \mathrm{Fxy} \vdash (y)\ (\mathrm{Ex})\ \mathrm{Fxy}$ (where quantifiers are mixed the order can affect meaning;here the converse conditional does not hold.Taking *F* as signifying the relation of '*father of*' in the domain of people: if there exists an *X* such that for every value of *Y*, *X* is the father of *Y*—i.e. *X* is the father of everybody—then it follows that for every value of *Y* there exists a person *X* who is his father. But it does not follow *e converso* that if any person *Y* is child of *some* father, that there is one person who is father of everybody.)

Some laws expressing the relation between universal and existential quantifiers

$$(x)\ Fx\ \dashv\vdash -(Ex) - Fx$$
$$(Ex)\ Fx\ \dashv\vdash -(x) - Fx$$
$$(x) - Fx\ \dashv\vdash -(Ex)\ Fx$$
$$(Ex) - Fx\ \dashv\vdash -(x)\ Fx$$

An indefinite number of more complicated laws follow from the above, e.g.:

$$(x) - (Fx\ .\ Gx)\ \dashv\vdash -(Ex)\ (Fx\ .\ Gx)$$
$$(x) - (Fx \vee Gx)\ \dashv\vdash -(Ex)\ (Fx \vee Gx)$$
$$(x) - (Fx\ .\ - G..)\ \dashv\vdash -(Ex)\ (Fx.\ - Gx)$$

The following laws draw our attention to the fact that predicate calculus presupposes that any universe with which it deals is non-empty, i.e. that there is at least one thing in it corresponding to the variable *x*:

$$(x)\ Fx \rightarrow (Ex)\ Fx$$
$$(x) - Fx \rightarrow (Ex) - Fx$$

However predicate calculus does not presuppose that any *particular predicate* is verified in the universe of discourse, and (as we shall see in discussing the integration of the Aristotelian syllogistic into modern logic) it does not include $(x)\ (Fx \rightarrow Gx) \rightarrow (Ex)\ (Fx\ .\ Gx)$ among its logical truths.

As a calculus of quantifiers there is no essential reason why predicate calculus should restrict itself to the universal and existential quantifiers although it actually does so. It could be extended to include the numerical quantifiers: (there is at least one *x* such that...), (at most one *x* such that...), (exactly one *x* such that...), (at least two *x*'s such that...), etc. This possible extension invites consideration of the relationship between logic and mathematics.

Some laws governing multiple quantification:

(While presenting some laws governing the movement of

quantifiers it was noted that when all the quantifiers are universal, or all are existential their order does not affect meaning. Where quantifiers are mixed, the order can affect meaning.)

(*x*) (*y*) *Fxy* –| |– (*y*) (*x*) *Fxy*
(*Ex*) (*Ey*) *Fxy* –| |– (*Ey*) (*Ex*) *Fxy*
(*Ex*) (*y*) *Fxy* |– (*y*) (*Ex*) *Fxy* (the converse conditional does not hold)
(*x*) (*y*) *Fxy* |– (*x*) (*Ey*) *Fxy*
(*x*) (*y*) *Fxy* |– (*Ex*) (*Ey*) *Fxy*
(*x*) (*y*) (*Fxy*→ *Gxy*) |– (*x*) (*y*) *Fxy* → (*x*) (*y*) *Gxy*
(*x*) (*y*) (*Gxy*→*Hxy*), (*Ex*) (*Ey*) (*Fxy*.*Gxy*) |– (*Ex*) (*Ey*)(*Fxy*.*Hxy*)
(*x*) (*y*) *Fxy* –| |– – (*Ex*) (*Ey*) – *Fxy*
(*x*) (*y*) – *Fxy* –| |– – (*Ex*) (*Ey*) *Fxy*
(*Ex*) (*Ey*) *Fxy* –| |– – (*x*) (*y*) – *Fxy*
(*Ex*) (*Ey*) – *Fxy* –| |– – (*x*) (*y*) *Fxy*

Some laws governing instantiation

(*x*) *Fx* –| |– (*y*) *Fy*

(Both sentences express the same proposition, that everything has *F*. Thus this law makes the point that a universal holds for any instantiation. The instantiation here may be described as ambiguous expressed as it is through the use of a second variable. Similarly, (*Ex*) ix –| |– (*Ey*) *Fy* is a law.)

Fm, (*x*) *Fx* → *Gx* |– *Gm*
–Gm, (*x*) *Fx* → *Gx* |– – *Fm*
Fm, (*x*) *Fx* →– *Gx* |– – *Gm*

(Here *m* is used as a proper name and the instantiation is singular.)

(*x*) *Fx* –| |– *Fa*
Fa |– (*Ex*) *Fx*

(Here *a* is an arbitrary name and the instantiation is typical. We can argue from the universal to the typical instance, and the typical instance justifies both a universal and an existential derivative.)

Some laws which combine predicate and propositional variables

$$(x)\ p\ .\ Fx\ -|\ |-\ p.\ (x)\ Fx$$
$$(x)\ p \vee Fx\ -|\ |-\ p \vee (x)\ \mathrm{Fx}$$
$$(x)\ p \rightarrow Fx\ -|\ |-\ p \rightarrow (x)\ Fx$$
$$(Ex)\ p \rightarrow Fx\ -|\ |-\ p \rightarrow (Ex)\ Fx$$
$$(x)\ (Fx \rightarrow p)\ -|\ |-\ (Ex)\ Fx \rightarrow p$$

(Note that the quantifier, (*x*), governs the whole expression while the existential quantifier only governs an antecedent. The law may be read: 'Taking any *x*, if when *x* is *F* the proposition *p* is the case, then if an object *x* can be found such that it is *F* this materially implies that *p* is the case. And conversely, if an object *x* can be found which being *F* this materially implies that *p* is the case, then for every value of *x*: whre x is *F* the proposition *p* is the case.)

$$(Ex)\ (p \rightarrow Fx)\ -|\ \ |-\ p \rightarrow (Ex)\ Fx$$

Some laws concerning identity

$$|-\ (x)\ (x = x)$$
$$|-\ (x)\ (y)\ (x = y) \rightarrow (y = x)$$
$$|-\ (x)\ (y)\ (z)\ ((x = y\ .\ y = z) \rightarrow (x = z))$$
$$Fa\ -|\ |-\ (Ex)\ (x = a\ .\ Fx)$$

Some laws presenting expressions that are interderivable (and therefore equivalent)

$$(x)\ Fx \rightarrow Gx\ -|\ \ |-\ -\ (Fx\ .\ -\ Gx)$$
$$(x)\ Fx\ -|\ \ |-\ (y)\ Fy$$
$$(Ex)\ Fx\ -|\ \ |-\ (Ey)\ Fy$$
$$(x)\ p\ -|\ \ |-\ p$$
$$(Ex)\ p\ -|\ \ |-\ p$$
$$(Ex)\ (Ey)\ (Fx\ .\ -\ Fy)\ -|\ \ |-\ (Ex)\ Fx\ .\ (Ex)\ -\ Fx$$
$$(x)\ (y)\ Fx \rightarrow Fy\ -|\ \ |-\ (x)\ Fx \vee (Ey)\ -\ Fy$$

THE LAWS OF DYADIC, TRIADIC...*n*-ADIC PREDICATES INTERPRETED AS A LOGICAL THEORY OF RELATIONS

A propositional form with two free variables, such as $F(x, y)$, expresses a relation between the things x and y and may be translated explicitly and equivalently into an expression of the form xRy (read the thing x has a relation R to the thing y'). The negative $\sim F(x, y)$ can be similarly translated $\sim xRy$. The above expressions with R may be considered as generalizations of propositional forms with two free variables. Where there are three, four...*n* free variables the symbolization is $R(x_1, x_2, x_3)$, $R(x_1, x_2, x_3, x_4)$, $R(x_1 \ldots x_n)$.

Thus, technically speaking, what is called a logical theory of relations develops simply as the construction, in predicate logic, of complex expressions with more than one free variable or argument place. The tautologies discovered in this way are valued, interpretatively, as a theory of relations. Indeed, since these tautologies are predications made about ordered groups or sets of two, three, four...*n* members, it is felt that their predicates are properly and exactly conceived and symbolized as relations which generate and constitute sets of ordered dyads, triads, tetrads, etc. However, one might also argue that the abstract uninterpreted value of this part of predicate logic is being neglected, that this reflects the central position which class and set have occupied in the history of mathematical logic since Boole, and that here there may be a lapse from constructive, formalist logic into the more abstractive approach of earlier logics.

Some of the tautologies in question have already been noted in this chapter in the course of giving a sample of laws governing multiple quantification. Here we will not compile a more extensive list but rather will give such a summary account of the general nature, types and properties of relations, as is useful to the logician in interpreting many-termed predicates as relations. It is clear that such an account will apply to relations of all kinds, both those that are realized in the physical world and those that exist only in the mind, both those that are logical in their nature and those that are not. The terminology used will be rather like that of contemporary mathematics but in some respects will be slightly different; attention will be drawn to differences.

Two-term predicates or dyadic relations. The theory of dyadic relations is the only part of the logic of relations that has been developed. De Morgan and Peirce were pioneers, their calculus of relations being completed by the German logician E. Schroder (1841-1902).

In *xRy, x* is a predecessor with respect to the dyadic relation *R*, and *y* is a successor with respect to *R*. The class of all predecessors is known as the domain of R, the class of all successors as the counter-domain (converse domain or range). The domain and converse domain together make up the field of a relation. Relations of the First Order are those which hold between individuals; relations of the Second Order are those which hold between classes or between relations of the First Order. The relation of, e.g. membership is mixed since its predecessor is an individual and its successor a class.

A relation *R* is *reflexive* in the class *K* if every element of that class has the relation *R* to itself, i.e. if *xRx*. If that condition never holds *R* is *irreflexive*; if it may or may not hold, *R* is *non-reflexive.* Thus 'equal to' is reflexive; 'taller than' is irreflexive; 'admires' is non-reflexive: it simply allows of the case of self-admirations, *aRa*.

R is *symmetrical* when it always fulfils the condition: if *xRy* then *yRx*; where the condition of symmetry never holds (If *xRy* then ~*yRx*, as, e.g. in 'being parent of') the relationship is *asymmetrical;* if it may or may not hold (as, e.g. in 'likes', 'fears') the relation is *non-symmetrical.*

The necessary and sufficient condition for R being transitive is that if *xRy* and *yRz* then *xRz* (as in 'taller', 'older'). An *intransitive* relation does not allow of this condition being fulfilled (e.g. 'father of'); a *non-transitive* relation admits of, but does not require, this transferability (e.g. 'admires'). A transitive relation is such that relating two terms to a mean it also relates these terms to each other. Accordingly it gives rise to important deductive possibilities.

The interdependencies between reflexivity, symmetry and transitivity may be listed as follows (for non-empty relations):

1. If a relation is transitive and symmetrical, it is reflexive.
2. If a relation is transitive and asymmetrical, it is irreflexive.
3. If a relation is transitive and irreflexive, it is asymmetrical.
4. If a relation is asymmetrical, it is irreflexive.
5. If a relation is symmetrical and irreflexive, it is either intransitive or non-transitive.
6. If a relation is symmetrical and reflexive, it is either transitive or non-transitive.

R is said to be *connected* in the class K (i.e. to be a principle of order) if for any two elements x and y in the class, either xRy or yRx. Where both conditions are fulfilled at the same time, the relation is still connected. Connexity is very important in the creation of serial order: any relation that is transitive, asymmetrical and connected is a serial relation (e.g. 'left of' and 'right of' with regard to points on a line are connected relations), and any system ordered by a serial relation is a series, e.g. the system of natural numbers, the calendar. 'Ancestor of' is not a connected relation: the field of this relation is of those who are either ancestors or descendants, and picking any two individuals it is not true that some one of the two must be the ancestor of the other.

The relation of identity is reflexive, symmetrical and transitive; that of diversity is irreflexive, symmetrical, non-transitive and connected. The relation of inclusion between classes is reflexive and transitive; it is non-symmetrical (i.e. neither symmetrical nor asymmetrical) and it is not connected; the relation of membership in a class, on the other hand, is irreflexive, intransitive and asymmetrical. Thus the properties of membership are very different from those of class inclusion.

Some broad categories of relation are as follows:

(a) Relations that have the three properties of being reflexive, symmetrical and transitive are an important category. There is no universally accepted term for this category, 'equivalence' and 'identity' denoting examples rather than the category as such. Mathematicians, however, do designate the category by the term, equivalence relation; identity for them is a particular example of an equivalence relation. Numerous other examples may be cited, e.g. congruence (from Geometry), equally old, synonymous.

(b) Relations that are asymmetrical, transitive, connected (and consequently irreflexive) are a common class also—an example being the relation of 'less than' in the class of distinct numbers. They are often described as 'ordering', i.e. as establishing a serial order in their class. (Mathematicians reserve 'order relation' for a closely allied class of relations typified by 'less than or equal to'.)

(c) Functional relations form a category which consists of relations whose terms fall into a one-one, or one-many correspondence. 'Being a twin brother', is an example of a one-one relation: each person who is a twin of any other person is a twin of no other, and the other has no twin brother but this one—there is a one-to-one correlation between the terms (denoted by the variable x) of the domain of this relation (xRy) and the terms of its converse domain (denoted by the variable y). Thus the necessary and sufficient conditions for a one-one relation are that if xRy and if xRz then $z = y$; and at the same time, if xRy and if wRy, then $w = x$. A one-many relation holds between a single term in the domain and more than one term in the converse domain; these latter terms are not in the same relationship with any other term of the domain so that if xRy and if wRy, then $w = x$. The relation of a perfect square to its roots is an example of a one-many relation: as a square 9 correlates with both 3 and –3 as roots. (In this context 'many' means simply 'more than one'.)

In a functional relation x is always single-valued. Corresponding to any value for y there is a unique value for x: thus if xRy and if wRy then $w = x$. In the formula xRy, x is said to be the variable for function values, and y the variable for argument values. (Mathematicians, however, use domain for the argument values and the counter domain for the function values.) A unique value of the function corresponds to every value of the argument: this fact is symbolized $x = R$ (y) or in familiar mathematical symbols $x = f(y)$ which means 'x is that value of the function f which corresponds to (or is correlated with) the argument value y.' It is the defining characteristic of a functional relation that for any value of y it admits of only one value for x. In the vernacular to indicate the functional character of a relation, we insert the word 'the': e.g. we say 'x is the father of y' indicating that for every person y there exists but one person x who is the father of y; the formula $x = f(y)$ has the same force as the word 'the'.

The force of the word *function* in the context of functional relation may be brought out simply as follows: Since $9 = (-3)^2$, it is possible to correlate the value 9 to the value –3, i.e. we can assert in general that 9 is a function of –3, that $9 = f(-3)$. Specifically we can go on to say that 9 is predecessor in the relationship of being the square of –3, i.e. that it is the unique domain value of the relation (or function) of 'being square of' with respect to the argument value, –3. The number 9 is also predecessor in the relationship of being the square of 3. This is a one-many relationship therefore. In a one-one relation or biunique function not only is there a unique domain value x correlated to every converse domain value y, but also conversely only one converse domain value y, corresponds to any domain value x.

In elementary and in higher mathematical reasoning functional relations are of great importance; in applied mathematics too one frequently tries to analyse dependencies into functional relations. And in general there is an obvious value in trying to discover functions which establish one-to-one, or one-many, correspondences between the elements of separate classes, i.e. which map one class on another.

Many relations are not functional. Being a subject of the king is a many-one relation; being smaller than is a many-many relation. In neither case is the domain value unique, so the relation is not functional. (There used to be a wider meaning of the term, function; in the formula $x^2 + y^2 = 25$, where $y = 4$ the formula is valid for both $x = 3$ and $x = -3$; thus correlated with one number, y, are two numbers, x; the function was sometimes called a two-valued function and there could be many-valued functions. In the logic of relations, however, the efficacy of a function consists in correlating any argument value with a unique domain value.)

The converse of a one–many relation is many–one, e.g. 'The king rules the people' converts into 'the people are subject to the king'—the converse relation is substituted and domain and converse domain are interchanged. The converse of a one-one relation is one-one, of a many-one is one-many and of a many-many is many-many.

Many-termed predicates (n-adic relations). The most fundamental property of a relation is that of always forming dyads, triads, tetrads, etc. All other properties presuppose this one of degree. As well as two-termed or binary relations one also meets frequently with three-termed (ternary) relations and in general with many-termed ones. Some relations, e.g. 'among' and superlatives like 'least of', 'greatest of' have no definite degree but are simply more than dyadic: they are generally called *polyadic relations* (this term however has more than one usage). In geometry one speaks of a point B lying between A and C; in arithmetic of a number being the sum of two others; in algebra of the ratio $x : y : z : t$. Although many-termed relations play an important part in the various sciences, any detailed study of them has been within the mathematical discipline known as the theory of sets. The logic of relations focuses two-termed relations. However, relations of a higher degree than dyadic can be defined and treated as dyadic—as, e.g. the relation of a dyad to an individual, of a dyad to another dyad, of a triad (already reduced to dyadic form) to an individual, etc. Thus any function of three variables, $T(x, y, z)$ can be treated as a function of two variables, the couple (x, y) and z or the couple (y, z) and x. Hence the theory of dyadic relations is a general theory.

A later chapter will treat of that part of the theory of relations which focuses them in extension as, e.g the class of couples (x, y) such that xRy. This extensional part of the theory (the calculus of relations) is worked out, again, within an extensional study of predicates in general, the class calculus. Thus the logical theory of relations is constructed, intensionally,. within Predicate Logic and, extensionally, within Class Calculus; for the reason, it does not feature as prominently or as fundamentally in contemporary formal logic as early mathematical logicians, like De Morgan, felt it would.

HAS PREDICATE LOGIC A DECISION PROCEDURE FOR DETERMINING WHETHER ANY WELL-FORMED FORMULA IN ITS LANGUAGE IS A TAUTOLOGY

We have seen that the sole assumption made by modern Predicate Logic is that the universe with which it deals is non-empty—it may be finite or infinite but there is at least one individual in it. Thus a decision procedure for the whole of Predicate Logic would be a mechanical and automatic way of deciding, in a finite number of steps, whether any given wff (in the language of Predicate Logic) was true under all interpretations in all non-empty universes, finite or infinite. In 1936,on the basis of the work of Kurt Godel, Alonzo Church went on to prove the impossibility of discovering such a decision procedure. However, decision procedures have been found for certain fragments of quantificational logic—most importantly various ones have been found (independently, by many authors) for monadic-predicate formulae. The following one combines, in essence, the techniques of the Normal Form and Truth Trees procedures used in Propositional Logic.

It is based on the principle that an argument (expressed in the language of predicate logic) is valid only if the premisses and the negation of the conclusion cannot be jointly true in any non-empty universe. A positive search is conducted for a universe of which they could be a joint and true description, on the basis of (a) simplifying the truth functional structure of the argument, making it totally explicit in terms of '–', 'v' and '.'; (b) simplifying the atomic quantificational statements to instantiations that are systematically mapped on to the positive integer series 1, 2, 3... When contradictory predications occur among the instantiations, the proof of possibility (for a universe described jointly by the premisses and the negation of the conclusion) is said to be blocked; if it is clear that it must always be blocked in the search, then the universe sought is an impossibility and the original argument has been shown to be valid.

A set of rules must be drawn up governing the whole process of simplification and evaluation. In *Modern Deductive Logic,* Robert Ackermann gives the following rules for simplifying truth-functional structure and evaluating arguments in propositional logic:

Rule 1 $p \cdot q \vdash p$ Cs_1(conjunctive simplification$_1$)
Rule 2 $p \cdot q \vdash q$ Cs_2(conjunctive simplification$_2$)
Rule 3 $-(-p) \vdash p$ *DN*(double negation)
Rule 4 $-(p \cdot q) \vdash -p \vee -q$ DM_1 (De Morgan Rules$_1$)
Rule 5 $-(-p \cdot q) \vdash p \vee -q$ DM_2 (De Morgan Rules$_2$)
Rule 6 $-(p \cdot -q) \vdash -p \vee q$ DM_3 (De Morgan Rules$_3$)
Rule 7 $-(-p \cdot -q) \vdash p \vee q$ DM_4 (De Morgan Rules$_4$)
Rule 8 $-(p \vee q) \vdash -p \cdot -q$ DM_5 (De Morgan Rules$_5$)
Rule 9 $-(-p \vee q) \vdash p \cdot -q$ DM_6 (De Morgan Rules$_6$)
Rule 10 $-(p \vee -q) \vdash -p \cdot q$ DM_7 (De Morgan Rules$_7$)
Rule 11 $-(-p \vee -q) \vdash p \cdot q$ DM_8 (De Morgan Rules$_8$)

(By using the 8 De Morgan Rules we can simplify any negation of a conjunctive or disjunctive propositional form.)

Rule 12 $p\ q, -p \vdash q$ DS_1 (disjunctive syllogism$_1$)

Rule 13 $p \vee q, -q \vdash p$ — DS_2 (disjunctive syllogism$_2$)
Rule 14 $-p \vee q, p \vdash q$ — DS_3 (disjunctive syllogism$_3$)
Rule 15 $p \vee -q, q \vdash p$ — DS_4 (disjunctive syllogism$_4$)

(By application of these rules, any of the two expressions appearing on the left-hand side of a sequence can be simplified into the simple variable on the right-hand side.)

Rules 16 and 17: These are auxiliary rules of proof applying to the case when, with regard to a disjunctive proposition appearing in the argument, we do not know which disjunct is true. They are called auxiliary rules *D* and *DS* and entitle us to try each disjunct in turn to see whether in both cases the proof is blocked or whether in both cases it is not blocked. In the former case it is clear that our search for the possible universe is totally blocked by the disjunctive proposition (we have tried both its disjuncts). In the latter case, it is clear that the disjunctive proposition is not blocking the proof; indeed blocking does not occur if contradiction arises only through one disjunct and not through the other.

Rule D is the rule we cite when we are trying the first disjunct within our proof; the new line of proof is prefixed with an asterisk to remind us that it is a guess. Rule *DS* is the rule we cite when we are trying the remaining disjunct after the first disjunct has blocked the proof; we draw a line through each of the lines connected with the first disjunct and do not prefix an asterisk to the new line of proof as it expresses the only remaining sense in which the disjunctive proposition has to be considered.

Thus taking an argument which formalizes in propositional logic as $(-p \,.\, -q) \vee (p \,.\, -q), -p \vee r \vdash -q$, we write down the two premisses and the contradictory of the conclusion and proceed to see whether they constitute a description of a possible universe:

(1) $(-p \,.\, -q) \vee (p \,.\, -q)$
(2) $-p \vee r$

(3) q Contradictory of original conlusion

~~*(4) p (2) D~~

~~*(5) p (2) CS_2~~

~~*(6) $-p$ (2) CS_2~~

(The proof blocks at this stage with –q at (6) contradicting q at (3). Therefore erase lines (5) and (6) and try the remaining disjunct of (1), using the numbers 5 & 6 for the new lines.)

~~(5) p . q (1) *DS*~~

~~(6) q (5) CS_2~~

(Again the proof blocks: now we have tried both disjuncts of (1) under the first disjunct of (2). Since the proof blocks we can erase line 4 and all subsequent lines. We must try now the second disjunct of (2) using the number 4 for the new line.)

(4) r (2) *DS*

~~(5) (p . q) (1) *D*~~

~~(6) q (5) CS_2~~

(The proof blocks here with $-q$ at (6) and q at (3). Erase lines (5) and (6). Try the second disjunct of (1).)

(5) p . $-q$ (1) *DS*

(6) $-q$ (5) CS_2

(Again the proof blocks and since each of the two disjuncts in (1) has been used with each of the two disjuncts in (2), this final blocking of proof shows that there is no possible universe of which the two premisses are true jointly with the contradictory of the original conclusion.)

What extra rules are needed to simplify the atomic quantificational statements so that we can evaluate arguments in the section of Predicate Logic that is confined to monadic predicate formulae? The clue to simplification lies in the fact that a universally quantified one-place predicate expression is a true statement only if *every* instantiation of that one-place predicate expression is true, and an existentially quantified one-place predicate expression is true only if *at least one* instantiation is true. Thus with regard to any monadic predicate formula: either it already links a predicate with a *definite individual* in the universe, or it can be instantiated to *any* individual (if its quantifier is universal) or to *an indefinite individual* (if quantification is existential). This makes it possible for the decision procedure to assume the added form of a search for a universe which could verify all predications contained in the premisses and contradictory of the conclusion, i.e. a universe in which the same individual would not have both a predicate, *F*, and its negation, ~ *F*. The usual numerals (1, 2, 3...) for the positive integers may be used as constants referring to individuals in this universe.

Ackermann gives the following extra rules for simplifying predicative statements down to predicates linked with positive integers:

Rules 18: This enables us to go through all the predicative expressions replacing the individual constants (*a, b, c*...) by positive integers, the same positive integer being used for each recurrence of the same constant. This gives us expressions like *F*1, *G*2, *G*1 for *Fa, Gb, Ga*.

Rule 19: 'If any line of a proof is a universally quantified form, a line may be added which is the instantiation of the formal one-place predicate expression following the quantifier in terms of any numeral already appearing in the proof, or of the first numeral not already appearing in the proof. The new line is justified on the far right by citing "*U*—elimination".'

Obviously the useful instantiations for a decision procedure are those in terms of numerals linked with the same predicate as is in the universal statement.

Rule 20: 'If any line of proof is an existentially quantified form, a line may be added to the proof which is the instantiation of the formal one-place predicate expression following the quantifier in terms of the next numeral appearing in the proof. The new line is justified by citing "*E*—elimination" on the far right.'

We use a new numeral because the reference in an existential statement is indefinite. Further if there are other existential statements equivalent to the one we have instantiated [e.g. (*Ex*) (*Fx*), (*Ey*) (*Fy*), (*Ez*) (*Fz*) are equivalent] we cross them out, citing '*RED*' on the far right as our reason (this is shorthand for 'redundant')—these are simply three different ways of making the same indefinite reference to 'at least one individual' and to instantiate them with separate numerals would be to claim that there was more than one individual with the predicate.

The above 20 rules constitute a complete set for a decision procedure that does not go beyond truth-functional structure and monadic predications. The following test illustrates their use:

(1) $(x)\ (-\ Wx \vee Rx)$	First premiss of argument
(2) $(y)\ (-\ (-Cy) \vee Wy)$	Second premiss of argument
(3) $(Ez)\ (-Cz\ .\ -Rz)$	Contradictory of original conclusion
(4) $-C1\ .\ -R1$	(3) *E*—elimination
(5) $-(-C1) \vee W1$	(2) *U*—elimination
(6) $-\ W1 \vee R1$	(1) *U*—elimination
(7) $-\ R1$	(4) CS_2
(8) $-\ W1$	(6), (7), DS_2
(9) $-(-C1)$	(5), (8), DS_2
(10) $-\ C1$	(4), CS_1

With Lines (9) and (10) in formal contradiction the proof is blocked, and so the original argument is shown to be valid.

Chapter-10

The Traditional Theory of the Syllogism presented as a Fragment of Modern Predicate Logic

Chapter 10

INTRODUCTION

In the preparatory section of this book we presented Aristotle's theory of the syllogism substantially as it has been handed down for over 2000 years. It has been of great importance in the history of logic and it is of interest to see how it has been integrated into both axiomatic and natural deduction systems of predicate logic.

AXIOMATIZING THE SYLLOGISTIC

The formal system presented here is that of Lukasiewicz who was the first to axiomatize Aristotle's theory. It does not go beyond the non-modal or assertoric syllogisms, the theory of which is the most important part of the Aristotelian Logic. That is a study of four types of predicative propositions which are distinguished by quantity and quality—*A, E, I* and *O.* Alternatively we might describe it as the simplest known system of name w\variables, the constants, *A, E, I and O,* being sentence-forming functors of two-name arguments. Lukasiewicz pointed out (*Aristotle's Syllogistic,* Preface) that until the 1930s there was not a trustworthy exposition of the Aristotelian syllogistic: 'all expositions have been written not by logicians but by philosophers or philologists who either, like Prantl, could not know or, like Maier, did not know modern formal logic. All these expositions are in my opinion wrong. I could not find, for instance, a single author who realized that there is a fundamental difference between the Aristotelian and the traditional syllogism.' (The traditional syllogism *All B is A; All C is B; therefore All C is A* is not Aristotelian; an Aristotelian syllogism is represented in the form of an implication such as *If A is predicated of all B, and B is predicated of all C, then A must be predicated of all C.*) The traditional type of syllogism is encountered for the first time in the works of Alexander, and Lukasiewicz believes that 'this transference of the Aristotelian syllogisms from the implicational form into the inferential is probably due to the influence of the Stoics.' (Ibid., p. 21) Boethius was certainly one of the main figures in the transmission of the tradition.

Towards the end of his life, Lukasiewicz (d. 1956) studied Aristotle's theory of the modal syllogism and he constructed a system of modal logic. The following is his axiomatization of the non-modal syllogisms (the *C–N* system of the theory of deduction being assumed) as presented by him in *Aristotle's Syllogistic:*

1. *Primitive terms:* the constants *A* and *I*.

2. *Definitions:* The constants *E* and *O* are defined by *A* and *I*:

Df. 1. *Eab* = *NIab*
Df. 2. *Oab* = *NAab*

3. *Rules of Inference:*

In order to abbreviate the proofs I shall employ instead of the above definitions the two following rules of inference:

Rule *RE*: *NI* may be everywhere replaced by *E* and conversely.
Rule *RO*: *NA* may be everywhere replaced by *O* and conversely.

Besides the rules *RE* and *ROI* accept the two following rules of inference for the asserted expressions:

(a) Rule of substitution: If α is an asserted expression of the system, then any expression produced from a by α valid substitution is also an asserted expression The only valid substitution is to put for term-variables, *a, b, c* other term-variables, e.g. *b* for *a*.

(b) Rule of detachment: If *C* α *β* and α are asserted expressions of the system, then *β* is an asserted expression.

4. Axioms:

The four theses of the system axiomatically asserted are the two laws of identity and the moods Barbara and Datisi:

1. *Aaa*;
2. *Iaa*;
3. *CKAbcAabAac* (Barbara);
4. *CKAbcIbaIac* (Datisi).

As an auxiliary theory I assume the *C-N*-system of the theory of deduction with *K* as a defined functor. For propositional variables propositional expressions of the syllogistic may be substituted, like *Aab*, *Iac*, *KEbcAab*, etc. In all subsequent proofs I shall employ only the following fourteen theses denoted by roman numerals:

I.	*CpCqp*	(law of simplification)
II.	*CCqrCCpqCpr*	(law of hypothetical syllogism, 2nd form)
III.	*CCpCqrCqCpr*	(law of commutation)
IV.	*CpCNpq*	(law of Duns Scotus)
V.	*CCNppp*	(law of Clavius)
VI.	*CCpqCNqNp*	(law of transposition)
VII.	*CCKpqrCpCqr*	(law of exportation)
VIII.	*CpCCKpqrCqr*	
IX.	*CCspCCKpqrCKsqr*	
X.	*CCKpqrCCsqCKpsr*	
XI.	*CCrsCCKpqrCKqps*	
XII.	*CCKpqrCKpNrNq*	
XIII.	*CCKpqrCKNrqNp*	
XIV.	*CCKpNqNrCKprq*	

5. *Deduction of syllogistic theses:*

(In all syllogistic moods the major term is denoted by *c*, the middle term by *b*, and the minor term by *a*. The major premiss is stated first.)

A. THE LAWS OF CONVERSION

VII. *p/Abc, q/Iba, r/Iac* × *C*4–5

5. *CAbcCIbaIac*

5. *b/a, c/a, a/b* × *C*1–6

6. *CIabIba* (law of conversion of the *I*-premiss)

III. *p/Abc, q/Iba, r/Iac* × *C*5–7

7. *CIbaCAbcIac*

7. *b/a, c/b* × *C*2–8

8. *CAabIab* (law of subordination for affirmative premisses)

II. *q/Iab, r/Iba* × *C*6–9

9. *CCpIabCpIba*

9. *p/Aab* × *C*8–10

10. *CAabIba* (law of conversion of the *A*-premiss)

6. *a/b, b/a* × 11

11. *CIbaIab*

VI. *p/Iba, q/Iab* × *C*11–12

12. *CNIabNiba*

12. *Re* × 13

13. *CEabEba* (law of conversion of the *E*-premiss)

VI. *p/Aab, q/Iab* × *C*8–14

14. *CNIabNAab*

14. *RE, RO* × 15

15. *CEabOab* (law of subordination for negative premisses)

B. THE AFFIRMATIVE MOODS

X. *p/Abc, q/Iba, r/Iac* × *C*4–16

16. *CCsIbaCKAbcsIac*

16. *s/Iab* × *C*6–17

17. *CKAbcIabIac* (Darii)

16. *s/Aab* × *C*10–18

18. *CKAbcAabIac* (Barbara)

8. *a/b, b/a* × 19

19. *CAbaIba*

16. *s/Aba* × *C*19–20

20. *CKAbcAbaIac* (Darapti)

XI. *r/Iba, s/Iab* × *C*11–21

21. *CCKpqIbaCKqpIab*

4. *c/a, a/c* × 22

22. *CKAbaIbcIca*

21. *p/Aba, q/Ibc, b/c* × *C*22–23

23. *CKIbcAbaIac* (Disamis)

17. *c/a, a/c* × 24

24. *CKAbaIcbIca*

21. *p/Aba,q/Icb, b/c* × *C*24–25

25. *CKIcbAbaIac* (Dimaris)

18. *c/a, a/c* × 26

26. *CKAbaAcbIca*

21. *p/Aba, q/Acb, b/c* × *C*26–27

27. *CKAcbAbaIac* (Bramantip)

C. THE NEGATIVE MOODS

XIII.*p/Ibc, q/Aba, r/Iac* × *C*23–28

28. *CKNIacAbaNIbc*

28. *RE* × 29

29. *CKEacAbaEbc*

29. *a/b, b/a* × 30

30. *CKEbcAabEac* (Celarent)

IX. *s/Eab, p/Eba* × *C*13–31

31. *CCKEbaqrCKEabqr*

31. *a/c, q/Aab, r/Eac,* × *C*30–32

32. *CKEcbAabEac*

XI. *r/Eab, s/Eba* × *C*13–33

33. *CCKpqEabCKqpEba*

32. *c/a, a/c* × 34

34. *CKEabAcbEca*

33. *p/Eab, q/Acb, a/c, b/a* × *C*34–35

35. *CKAcbEabEac* (Camestres)

30. *c/a, a/c* × 36

36. *CKEbaAcbEca*

33. *p/Eba, q/Acb, a/c, b/a* × *C*36–37

37. *CKAcbEbaEac* (Camenes)

II. *q/Eab, r/Oab* × *C*1538

38. *CCpEabCpOab*

38. *p/KEbcAab, b/c* × *C*30–39

39. *CKEbcAabOac* (Celaront)

38. *p/KEcbAab, b/c* × *C*32–40

40. *CKEcbAabOac* (Cesaro)

38. *p/KAcbEab, b/c* × *C*35–41

41. *CKAcbEabOac* (Camestrop)

38. *p/KAcbEba, b/c* × *C*37–42

42. *CKAcbEbaOac* (Camenop)

XIII. *p/Abc, q/Iba, r/Iac* × *C*4–43

43. *CKNIacIbaNAbc*

43. *RE, RO* × 44

44. *CKEacIbaObc*

44. *a/b, b/a* × 45

45. *CKEbcIabOac* (Ferio)

31. *a/c, q/Iab, r/Oac* × *C*45–46

46. *CKEcbIabOac* (Festino)

X. *p/Ebc, q/Iab, r/Oac* × *C*45–47

47. *CCsIabCKEbcsOac*

47. *s/Iba* × *C*11–48

48. *CKEbcIbaOac* (Ferison)

31. *a/c, q/Iba, r/Oac* × *C*48–49

49. *CKEcbIbaOac* (Fresison)

10. *a/b, b/a* × 50

50. *CAbaIab*

 47. *s/Aba* × *C*50–51

51. *CKEbcAbaOac* (Felapton)

 31. *a/c, q/Aba, r/Oac* × *C*51–52

52. *CKEcbAbaOac* (Fesapo)

As a result of all these deductions one remarkable fact deserves our attention: it was possible to deduce twenty syllogistic moods without employing axiom 3, the mood Barbara. Even Barbari could be proved without Barbara. Axiom 3 is the most important thesis of the syllogistic, for it is the only syllogism that yields a universal affirmative conclusion, but in the system of simple syllogisms it has an inferior rank, being necessary to prove only two syllogistic moods, Baroco and Bocardo. Here are these two proofs:

 XII. *p/Abc, q/Aab, r/Aac* × *C*3–53

53. *CKAbcNAacNAab*

 53. *RO* × 54

54. *CKAbcOacOab*

 54. *b/c, c/b* × 55

55. *CKAcbOabOac* (Baroco)

 XIII. *p/Abc, q/Aab, r/Aab, r/Aac* × *C*3–56

56. *CKNAacAabNAbc*

 56. *RO* × 57

57. *CKOacAabObc*

 57. *a/b, b/a* × 58

58. *CKObcAbaOac* (Bocardo)

Aristotle calls first figure syllogisms perfect, self-evident arguments and he devises methods for reducing the syllogisms of other figures to these. It is not unreasonable to interpret this reductionism as a form of axiomatization. Lukasiewicz is quite definite: 'Aristotle reduces the so-called imperfect syllogisms to the perfect, i.e. to the axioms. Reduction here means proof or deduction of a theorem from the axioms.'

(*Aristotle's Syllogistic,* p.74) However, this is an area in which Aristotle's thinking seemed to suffer from an overestimate of the range of application of the syllogism, in which he is not entirely free from obscurity and inconsistency, and in which, at times, principles used intuitively by him are never formulated explicitly. These facts make it quite difficult to evaluate reductionism in Aristotle.

He was indeed the first person to formalize the structure and properties of an axiomatic system. This was the achievement of his chapters on demonstrative science in the *Posterior Analytics.* In his view the syllogism is the only medium of proof, and he defines the deductive sciences as those in which the formal medium of every proof is the syllogism. This is the explicit teaching of the *Prior Analytics* and *Posterior Analytics.* Thus, within this view, proving syllogisms and axiomatizing the syllogistic not only means deriving the imperfect from the perfect first figure syllogisms but using the latter as the medium of derivation. 'The syllogisms should therefore be proved not only *from* but also *by means of* syllogisms.' (Patzig in *Aristotle's Theory of the Syllogism,* p. 133) However, proving a syllogism (which states a relationship between propositions) is quite different from proving the conclusion of a syllogism (where it is terms that are related), and as forms of proof the reductive procedures of Aristotle must draw on principles of propositional logic for their force and credentials. Aristotle used these principles intuitively without ever formally discerning, apparently, the existence of a logical theory more basic than his syllogistic. The net result is that his theory of proof and his practice of it do not coincide here.

This inconsistency which could not be resolved without the formal discovery of propositional logic—a latter,Stoic, achievement—explains much of the obscurity in Aristotle's texts where the broad concern seems to be proof but the procedures are frequently presented in the lesser role of 'perfecting', 'transforming' syllogisms that are already intrinsically valid.

Patzig sums up the matter: 'The historical fact that Aristotle, understandably overstimating, not the value, but the range of application of his discovery, believed the syllogism to be the only possible form of proof, explains the difficulty he encountered when he tried to prove the syllogisms themselves. His terminology straddles two different ways of evading this difficulty: on the one hand he assumes the first figure syllogisms as undemonstrable and evident axioms and "reduces" the other moods to them, thus avoiding the word "proof"; on the other, he acknowledges that not all syllogisms can be perfected in this way (notably baroco and bocardo) and that their that their validity must therefore be *proved*...The contradictory tendencies of Aristotle's language show that he felt the inconsistency between his theory of proof and his practice [in *PriorAnalytics*] but that he could not steel himself to revise the theory.' (Ibid., p. 136)The central facts are that Aristotle regarded his syllogistic as a deductive system, but that a broader conception of proof than his and a propositional calculus (which he lacked) were necessary to complete the formal task of axiomatization. This, in essence, is Lukasiewicz's view.

PROVING THE SYLLOGISTIC THESES IN A NATURAL DEDUCTION SYSTEM

The traditional syllogistic which is traceable mainly to Boethius, although it antedates him, is closer to a natural deduction system than is Aristotle's theory which consists of implicational propositions and lends itself to axiomatization. The contrast is very striking to Lukasiewicz:

> The difference between the Aristotelian and the traditional syllogism is fundamental. The Aristotelian syllogism as an implication is a proposition, and as a proposition must be either true or false. The traditional syllogism is not a proposition, but a set of propositions which are not unified so as to form one single proposition. The two premisses written usually in two different lines are stated without a conjunction, and the connection of these loose

premisses with the conclusion by means of 'therefore' does not give a new compound proposition. The famous Cartesian principle, 'Cogito, ergo sum', is not a true principle, because it is not a proposition. It is an inference, or, according to a scholastic terminology, a consequence. Inferences and falsity belong only to propositions. They may be valid or not. The same has to be said of the traditional syllogism. Not being a proposition the traditional syllogism is neither true nor false; it can be valid or invalid. The traditional syllogism is either an inference, when stated in concrete terms, or a rule of inference, when stated in variables. The sense of such a rule may be explained by the example given above: When you put such values for *A, B* and *C* that the premisses '*A* belongs to all *B*' and '*B* belongs to all *C*' are true, then you must accept as true the conclusion 'A belongs to all *C*'.

If you find a book or an article where no difference is made between the Aristotleian and the traditional syllogism, you may be sure that the author is either ignorant of logic or has never seen the Greek text of the *Organon.* Scholars like Waitz, the modern editor and commentator of the *Organon,* Trendelenburg, the compiler of the *Elementa logices Aristoteleae,* Prantl, the historian of logic, all knew the Greek text of the *Organon* well, but nevertheless they did not see the difference between the Aristotelian and the traditional syllogism. Only Maier seems to have felt for a moment that something is wrong here, when he asks for permission to replace the Aristotelian syllogism by the more familiar and more convenient form of the later logic: immediately afterwards he quotes the mood Barbara in its usual traditional form, neglecting differences he has seen between this form and that of Aristotle, and does not even say what differences he has seen. When we realize that the difference between a thesis and a rule of inference is from the standpoint of logic a fundamental one, we must agree that an exposition of Aristotelian logic which disregards it cannot be sound. We have to this day no genuine exposition of Aristotelian logic. (*Aristotle's Syllogistic,* pp. 21-2).

In a natural deduction system, proof of Aristotle's syllogistic consists not in deriving each thesis from axioms but in showing that within each the movement from premisses, as assumptions, to conclusion, as derivative, is reducible to movements of natural deduction. The process of doing this reveals a presupposition in the Aristotelian theory that is not shared by modern predicate logic, namely that no term is empty, that corresponding to names, individual variables and predicate letters there are always real objects, properties or relations.

Dealing firstly with Aristotle's language, it is quite clear that he chose it very deliberately in order to display as clearly as possible the logical structure of premisses, conclusion and relationship of implication. Instead of the conventional scheme, *S* is *P*, he generally uses the expressions '...belongs/does not belong to all/some...' or '...is said/is not said of all/some...'; in all his expressions the predicate is in the nominative case, the subject in the dative or genitive. Thus his language suggests a process relating subject and predicate rather than an identity, and he looks on this relationship from the direction of the predicate. Linguistically, his approach is remarkably similar to that of modern logic; indeed in the *Prior Analytics* (Book I, 49b 14-31) he formalizes the universal affirmative as 'the *A* belongs to all to which *B* b belongs' which is very close to $(x)\ (Bx \to Ax)$. Modern formulae for the other simple categorical proposions are $(x)\ (Bx \to -Ax)$ for *E*, $(Ex)\ (Bx\ .\ Ax)$ for *I*, and $(Ex)\ (Bx.\ -\ Ax)$ for *O*.

These formulae map on to the traditional Square of Opposition as follows:

$(x)\ (Bx \to Ax)$ $\qquad$ $(x)\ (Bx \to -\ Ax)$

$(Ex)\ (Bx\ .\ Ax)$ $\qquad$ $(Ex)\ (Bx\ .\ -Ax)$

The traditional relationships of contradiction admit of formal proof, e.g. if *A* is false, *O* is true; if *O* is true, *A* is false; if *E* is false, *I* is true; if *I* is true, *E* is false.

Example: Proof that if A is true, O is false

1	(1) $(x)\ (Fx \rightarrow Gx)$	*A*
1	(2) $Fa \rightarrow Ga$	1, *Uo*
	(3) $p \rightarrow q \ \equiv -(p \ . -q)$	*TI* (from propositional logic)
	(4) $(Fa \rightarrow Ga) -|| - -(Fa. -Ga)$	Specialization of 3
1	(5) $-(Fa \ . - \ Ga)$	4, 2, *Co*
1	(6) $(x) - (Fx \ . - \ Gx)$	5, *Ui*
1	(7) $-(Ex)\ (Fx \ . - \ Gx)$	6, *SI* (i.e.one of the laws, presented earlier, which express relations betwe-en universal and existe-ntial quantifiers)

However, traditional implications of relationships other than contradiction do not admit of formal proof without an existential assumption. Thus the propositions that contraries (*A* and *E*) are not both true, that one of a pair of subcontraries (*I* and *O*) is true, that *A* implies *I* and *E* implies *O*—these appear in modern logic as conclusions under an existential assumption:

$$(\text{Ex})\ Fx \ |- -((x)\ (Fx \rightarrow Gx)\ .\ (x)\ (Fx \rightarrow -Gx))$$
$$(\text{Ex})\ Fx \ |- (Ex)\ (Fx\ .\ Gx) \vee (Ex)\ (Fx\ .\ -Gx))$$
$$(\text{Ex})\ Fx \ |- (x)\ (Fx \rightarrow Gx) \rightarrow (Ex)\ (Fx\ .\ Gx)$$
$$(\text{Ex})\ Fx \ |- (x)\ (Fx \rightarrow -Gx) \rightarrow (Ex)\ (Fx\ .\ -Gx)$$

Similarly, while there is formal proof that the converses of *I* and *E* propositions are of logical consequence, the conversion of an *A* proposition, (x) (*Fx→Gx*), into an *I* proposition (Ex) (Gx . Fx) is not, demonstrably, of logical consequence without the presupposition that (Ex) Fx.

Most of the moods of the syllogism admit of formal proof. The following, e.g. are demonstrably valid sequents:

$(x)\ (Fx \rightarrow Gx)\ .\ (Hx \rightarrow Fx) |- (x)\ (Hx \rightarrow Gx)$ [Barbara]

$(x)\ (Fx \rightarrow -Gx)\ .\ (x)\ (Hx \rightarrow Fx) \mid -\ (x)\ (Hx \rightarrow Gx)$ [Celarent]
$(x)\ (Fx \rightarrow Gx)\ .\ (Ex)\ (Hx\ .\ Fx) \mid -\ (Hx\ .\ Gx)$ [Darii]
$(x)\ (Fx \rightarrow -Gx).(Ex)(Hx.-F(x)) \mid -(Ex)\ (Hx.-Gx)$ [Ferio]

However, any standard or weakened mood in which the premisses are universal and the conclusion particular requires an existential presupposition and this is included in the modern representation of the mood. Nine of the twenty-four traditional moods require such a (single) presupposition:

$(Ex)\ Hx.(x)\ (Fx \rightarrow Gx).(x)\ (Hx \rightarrow Fx) \mid -\ (Ex)(Hx.Gx)$ [bardari]
$(Ex)\ Hx.\ (x)(Fx \rightarrow -Gx).(x)(Hx \rightarrow Fx) \mid -(Ex)(Hx\ .\ -Gx)$ [Celaront]
$(Ex)\ Hx\ .(x)(Gx \rightarrow -Fx).(x)\ (Hx \rightarrow Fx) \mid -(Ex)(Hx.-Gx)$ [Cesaro]
$(Ex)\ (Hx).(x)\ (Gx \rightarrow Fx)\ .\ (x)\ (Hx \rightarrow -Fx) \mid -(Ex)(Hx\ .\ -Gx)$ [Camestros]
$(Ex)\ Fx.(x)\ (Fx \rightarrow -Gx).(x)\ (Fx \rightarrow Hx) \mid -\ (Ex)\ (Hx\ .\ Gx)$ [Darapti]
$(Ex)\ Fx.(x)\ (Fx \rightarrow -Gx).(x)\ (Fx \rightarrow Hx) \mid -\ (Ex)\ (Hx\ .\ -Gx)$ [Felapton]
$(Ex)\ Gx.(x)\ (Gx \rightarrow Fx).(x)\ (Fx \rightarrow Hx) \mid -\ (Ex)\ (Hx\ .\ Gx)$ [Bramantip]
$(Ex)\ Fx.(x)\ (Gx \rightarrow -Fx).(x)\ (Fx \rightarrow Hx) \mid -\ (Ex)\ (Hx\ .\ -Gx)$ [Fesapo]
$(Ex)\ Hx.(x)\ (Gx \rightarrow Fx).(x)\ (Fx \rightarrow -Hx) \mid -\ (Ex)\ (Hx\ .\ -Gx)$ [Camesnos]

CONCLUSION: ARISTOTLE'S SYLLOGISTIC AS A FRAGMENT OF PREDICATE LOGIC

Modern logic does not invalidate Arostptle's is tatle's theory: it simply displays its cnaracter and its presuppositions very clearly. Aristotle selected four forms of propositions for special study and he presupposed that the terms appearing in these forms are non-empty. These are only some of the forms expressed and studied in modern predicate logic whose scope is not restricted by the assumption that corresponding to its names, individual variables and predicate letters, there are always real objects, properties or relations. Because of this assumption some of the traditional implications in the broader framework of modern logic, and some of the traditional valid syllogistic moods are seen to require, in formal proof, a special single existential presupposition. Thus modern logic has integrated Aristotle's theory, as a fragment, into its predicate logic.

This predicate logic is not entirely free of presuppositions. It has not devised any way for expressing or dealing with the peculiar formal properties of empty universes, and built into its language and rules is the presupposition that there is at least one thing in any universe it deals with. This becomes evident when the following expressions work out as theorems:

$$\vdash (x)\ Fx \rightarrow (Ex)\ Fx$$
$$\vdash (x) - Fx \rightarrow (Ex) - Fx$$
$$\vdash (Ex)\ Fx \vee (Ex) - Fx$$

If there was nothing at all these expressions would be false; they depend, for truth, on interpretation in some non-empty universe of discourse.

Although modern logic presupposes that at least one individual exists in any universe it deals with, it does not presuppose that any particular property is realized there. Thus while $(x)\ Fx \rightarrow Gx$ does imply $(Ex)\ Fx \rightarrow Gx$, it does not imply $(Ex)\ (Fx\ .\ Gx)$ and it is this latter which is the *I* proposition of Aristotle's theory. In the modern notation, the universal and existential propositions differ not only in quantification but also in the propositional function quantified ($Fx \rightarrow Gx$ on the one hand, $Fx\ .\ Gx$ on the other). Thus a universal may be true and the corresponding existential false. This was not possible in the Aristotelian and traditional syllogistic where not only is the universe of discourse non-empty but every term has a real correspondent in it, this being reflected in formalizing *A* and *I* propositions as differing only in quantity. The Aristotelian presupposition, natural to a logic that was *abstractive* from living object language, is transcended by modern logic whose point of departure is an artificial logical language and whose method is *constructive*.

Günther Patzig (in *Aristotle's Theory of the Syllogism*) concludes a very thorough exegesis with the observation (p. 193) that 'it is not unaristotelian to consider the logical constants, *a, e, i* and *o* as relations between terms' and that from this viewpoint 'Aristotle's syllogistic is the theory of the relative product of these binary relations between terms.' In explanation it should be noted that if *R* denotes the relation of x to y, and S the relation of y to z then the relative product of these two relations, xRy and ySz, is the relation of x to z and it is symbolized R/S. Thus if R denotes 'husband of' (in xRy) and S denotes 'daughter of' (in ySz), R/S denotes 'son-in-law of', i.e. the relation which exists between the husband (x) and parent (z) of a person (y). For Patzig Aristotle's theory displays the cases in which the relative products of the binary relations, *a, e, i* and *o* have the character of being one of these relations; there are procedures for establishing whether a relative product has a definite *a, e, i* or *o* value and when it lacks any such definite value. For example with *SaM, MaP* the relative product $S\ a/a\ P$ has the value *a* (Barbara); with *SaM, MeP* the relative product $S\ a/e\ P$ has the value *e* (Celarent). In the latter case the relative product lacks a definite *a, e, i* or *o* value and tells us nothing logically about its terms; in the former case it does, and the set of three binary relations is called a syllogism. He concludes that Aristotle's theory can be presented as 'a special part of the logic of binary relations'. (Ibid., p. 194)

Chapter-11

Class Calculus

Chapter 11

INTRODUCTION

Logically (as distinct from psychologically) the concept of class is not generated by a process of collecting and arranging individuals but by the fact that a propositional form has a field of applicability. Thus it is possible to focus an expression such as *Fx* extensionally, in terms of the field of its applicability. Monadic predicates constitute, indeed, the simplest basis for classification: e.g. specifying *F* as 'must die', the propositional form, *Fx* ('*x* must die'), may be said to define the class of mortal beings since it furnishes the criterion for membership—a member is any true value that can be substituted for the variable *x*. A system or calculus in which monadic predicates are focused extensionally as classes is called a calculus of classes or a class calculus. It may be described as being parallel to the logic of monadic predicates or as being an extension of it.

This chapter presents the symbols, classes, statements and inferences that characterize the calculus; it shows how truth-tables are replaced by a box diagram of classes and sub-classes as a mechanical decision procedure for validity, and it includes a formalization of the Boole-Schröder Algebra (devised by Boole and given its definitive form by Schröder)—interpreted of course as a class calculus, for this algebra is a highly generalized system patient of other interpretations, both logical and extralogical, besides the classal one.

THE SYMBOLISM OF CLASS CALCULUS

The variables are *a, b, c,* etc. and they designate classes. The universe of discourse (the total space containing objects, classes being the collections of objects) is represented by the number 1, and 0 represents the limiting null class (containing no objects). Where extension only is taken into consideration there is no distinction between classes that have identically the same membership. Thus while the term 'unicorn' and the term 'centaur' have very different meanings or intensions, the classes of things denoted by them are identical: they are both the class of nothing existent. Similarly, there is only one class 'nothing' (the null class or empty class, symbolized 0) and only one class 'everything' (the universe class, symbolized 1). The term 'universe of discourse' denotes a device adopted to make the determinateness of the class, $\acute{a}$ (the negate of a), completely unambiguous: the members of $\acute{a}$ are outside the class a but within the same universe of discourse. Thus if one class a (red things) is given, its negate $\acute{a}$, is automatically determined as the things which are not red in the universe of discourse (coloured things).

There are no proper names apart from *1* and *0*, except those used for individuals in the context of their being members of a class. In the course of Boolean operations on simple classes (to be discussed in the next section) the basic variables, *a, b, c,* etc. are used in the construction of complex variables, e.g. ab represents the class of things which belong to both a and b; $\acute{a}$ represents the class of things which are not members of a; $a + b$ represents the class of things which belong to a or b or both.

The constants or functors which express relationships between classes are as follows:

= symbolizes identity of membership or material quivalence; $a = b$ is a statement saying that the class a and the class b have identically the same membership; $a \neq b$ denies such an identity or equation of membership: it expresses an inequation.

→ symbolizes the relation of inclusion; $a \rightarrow b$ is a statement saying that the class a is included in the class b.

← symbolizes sub-inclusion; $a \leftarrow b$ states that b is included in *a*.

⇆ symbolizes joint inclusion and sub-inclusion; $a \leftrightarrows b$ states that *a* is included in *b*, and *b* in *a*.

∧ symbolizes the relation of exclusion; $a \wedge b$ states that *a* is excluded from *b*.

∨ symbolizes the relation of sub-contrariety; $a \vee b$ states that the class *a* is sub-contrary to the class *b*: this implies that everything is either in *a* or in *b* or in both.

◊ symbolizes the relation of contradiction; *a* /*b* states that *a* is contradictory to *b*: this implies that everything is either in *a* or in *b* and cannot be in both.

↑ symbolizes partial inclusion; $a \uparrow b$ states that *a* is partially included in *b*.

↛ symbolizes partial exclusion; $a \nrightarrow b$ states that *a* is partially excluded from *b*.

c (the Greek letter epsilon) symbolizes the relationship of membership of a class, *P c a* states that the individual, *P*, is a member of the class *a*.

Functors expressing relationships between statements about classes are as follows:

→ will be used to symbolize the relationship of implication; $(a \rightarrow c) \rightarrow (ab \rightarrow c)$ says that the statement, 'the class *a* is included in *c*' implies the statement, 'the class *ab* is included in *c*'.

≡ symbolizes equivalence; $(a \quad b) \equiv (ab \neq 0)$ says that the statement, 'the class *a* is partially included in *b*', is equivalent to the statement, 'the class *ab* is not identical in membership with the null class'. The equivalence here of course is of truth conditions (it is the connective from propositional logic): each statement is true when the other is true, false when the other is false. It is interesting to note that, with regard to statements about classes, truth-conditions are not displayed in truth-tables but in equations or inequations: thus the essential condition for the statement, $a \rightarrow b$, being true is that $ab' = 0$, the condition under which it is false being $ab' \neq 0$; thus we can say simply that $a \rightarrow b$ is true if and only if $ab' = 0$.

Quantified predicative statements can be translated into the language of class calculus. A singular statement affirmative or negative formalizes as a statement about class membership (Chicago is a member of the class of ports; it is also a member of the class of non-Asiatic cities). Particular statements ('at least one...') are formalized as partial class inclusion or partial class exclusion; and universal statements as total class inclusion or total class exclusion. Thus taking a as the class of things which are A, and b as the class of things which are B.

{	All A is B is formalized as $a \rightarrow b$	(equivalent to the equation $ab' = 0$)
	No A is B is formalized as $a \wedge b$	(equivalent to the equation $ab = 0$)
{	Some A is B is formalized as $a \not\wedge b$	(equivalent to the inequation $ab \neq 0$)
	Some A is not B is formalized as $a \not\rightarrow b$	(equivalent to the inequation $ab' \neq 0$)

BOOLEAN OPERATIONS GENERATING COMPLEX CLASSES FROM SIMPLE ONES

Boolean operations are performed on the membership of classes, since the calculus of classes does not deal with what a class means, with the properties or form which define it. Classes are designated by variables which have no specific meaning. The operations performed on these variables designate, unambiguously, all the classes and sub-classes in the universe of discourse. Basic operations are as follows:

(1) *Unary operations,* i.e. operations upon one variable; there is one, negation. Given a class a, by performing this operation on it we get its negate, $\acute{a}$ (the class of things that

are not a).

(2) *Binary operations,* i.e. operations upon two variables. The operation of conjunction on the classes a and b results in a class (called the conjunct) which comprises things that are members of both a and b. The conjunct is symbolized $a \cap b$ or $a \times b$ (abbreviated often to ab). The operation of disjunction on these classes results in a class (called the disjunct) which comprises things that are members of either a or b. The disjunct is symbolized $a \cup b$ or $a + b$ (which symbolism is used in this chapter). Boole defined his operation of disjunction exclusively (either...or...but not both) But jevons in England, Peirce in the United States and Schröder in Germany all showed that the inclusive disjunct (either. . . or . . . or both if there are any of both) is more useful and now disjunction is always conceived inclusively. (One of the reasons for this is the usefulness of De Morgan's theorems (*infra*) which will not work if the disjunct is defined exclusively.)

The class ab is a sub-class of a: all its members belong to a; it is also a sub-class of b. The classes a, b and ab are all sub-classes of $a + b$. The negate or complement of ab is $(ab)'$ or $á + b'$; the complement of $a + b$ is $(a + b)'$.

Several other binary operations are possible but they can all be symbolized in terms of conjunction, disjunction and negation. Thus the operation rejection performed on the classes a and b, resulting in the class of things which are neither members of a nor of b can be symbolized $(a + b)'$, i.e. the negate of the disjunct, or $á \times b'$, i.e. the conjunct of the negate of a and the negate of b.

Further, any conjunct can be symbolized as a disjunct and vice versa, if the classes are negated in the correct manner. Each term is negated and then the whole is negated: thus the transformation formula for disjunction is $a + b = (á \times b')'$; for conjunction it is $a \times b = (á + b')'$. (If a thing belongs to the class of object that are both P abd Q it cannot possibly beling to the class of things that are either P' or Q'. These transformation formulas or equivalences are called *De Morgan's theorems* after their discoverer Augustus De Morgan. Fully listed for classes *a, b, á* and *b'*, they are:

$$\begin{array}{ll} a \times b = (\acute{a} + b')'; & a + b = (\acute{a} \times b')'; \\ \acute{a} \times b = (a + b')'; & \acute{a} + b = (a \times b')' \\ a \times b' = (\acute{a} + b)'; & a + b = (\acute{a} \times b)' \\ \acute{a} \times b' = (a + b)'; & \acute{a} + b' = (a \times b)' \end{array}$$

Reversing the sides of the above equivalences one may state De Morgan's Theorem as follows: The negative of a product, e.g. $(a \times b)'$ is the sum of the negatives of its terms, $\acute{a} + b'$; and the negative of a sum, e.g. $(a + b)'$ is the product of the negatives of its terms, $\acute{a} + b'$; The correspondence in Boolean Algebra between principles in terms of × and principles in terms of +, is called the Law of Duality.

Many of these operations follow the same laws or protocol as analogous operations of arthmetic:

(1) Just as (2 + 3) + 4 = 2 + (3 + 4) = 2 + 3 + 4 (i.e. the grouping does not affect the final result and need not be indicated so the class $(a + b) + c$ = (in membership) the class a + (b + c) = a + b + c; and as (2 × 3) × 4 = 2 × (3 × 4) = 2 × 3 × 4 so (a × b) × c = a × (b × c) = a × b × c. These are laws of association and both disjunction and conjunction in Boolean algebra are associative.

(2) Just as 2 + 3 = 3 + 2 and 2 × 3 3 × 2 (i.e. it does not matter in what order the numbers are added or multiplied) so we can commute $a + b$ to $b + a$, and $a \times b$ to $b \times a$ (without affecting the referential value of these class names). These are laws of commutation and both disjunction and conjunction are commutative.

Following the practice of Boole himself, disjunction is often called logical addition and symbolized +, the disjunct being called the logical sum. Similarly, conjunction is often called logical multiplication and symbolized ×, the conjunct being called the logical product. It is interesting to note that 'in two papers dated 1867 Peirce clearly differentiated between the arithmetical and the logical operation upon classes. This led to a dropping of Boole's division and a reinterpretation of his subtraction.' (Lee's *Symbolic Logic*, p. 8)

A SAMPLING OF STATEMENTS EXPRESSING RELATIONS BETWEEN CLASSES

In the calculus of classes which considers extension only, the most basic thing we can say about a class is that it has or has not members. Given this information about the classes of a universe we can define the relationships between them.

For example, if the conjunct $a \times b$ designates an empty or null class then the classes a and b are mutually exclusive. If the class of objects which belong to a but not to b is empty, then a is included in b; if $a \times b'$ has members, then there is a relation of non-inclusion. When $\acute{a} \times b' = 0$ (i.e. when there is nothing which is neither a member of a nor a member of b) then the classes, a and b, jointly exhaust their universe. If the classes $a \times b$ and $\acute{a} \times b'$ are both empty then the simple classes, a and b are mutually exclusive and collectively exhaustive. There is a relationship of mutual inclusion between a and b when the classes $a \times b'$ and $b \times \acute{a}$ are both empty. Finally, a class a is said to be a proper part of the class b when there are no members of a which are not members of b but there are members of b which are not members of a (i.e. when $a \times b'$ is empty while $b \times \acute{a}$ has members).

The following is a summary list of formulae expressing the basic Boolean relations with those equivalent expressions which express the essential truth conditions for each formula (Note that '.' symbolizes the propositional connective 'and', and '∨' symbolizes the propositional connective 'either or'):

Formulae	Relations expressed	Equivalences (expressing truth conditions)
$a \wedge b$	exclusion	$a \times b = 0$
$a \uparrow b$	non-exclusion (or intersection)	$a \times b \neq 0$
$a \rightarrow b$	inclusion	$a \times b' = 0$
$a \nrightarrow b$	non-inclusion (or protrusion)	$a \times b' = 0$
$\acute{a} \wedge b'$	exhaustion	$\acute{a} \times b' = 0$
$\acute{a} \uparrow b'$	non-exhauston	$\acute{a} \times b' \neq 0$
$a \overset{\wedge}{\vee} b$	mutual-exclusion and joint exhaustion	$(a \times b = 0)$ $(\acute{a} \times b' = 0)$
$(a \uparrow b) \vee (\acute{a} \uparrow b')$	non-mutual-exclusion-and-joint exhaustion	$(a \times b \neq 0) \vee (\acute{a} \times b' \neq 0)$
$a \quad b$	co-extension(mutual inclusion)	$(a \times b' = 0) . (b \times \acute{a} = 0)$
$(a \rightarrow b) \vee (b \rightarrow a)$	non-co-extension	$(a \times b' \neq 0) \vee (b \times \acute{a} = 0)$
$(a \rightarrow b) . (b \rightarrow a)$	proper part	$(a \times b' = 0) . (b \times \acute{a} \neq 0)$
$(a \rightarrow b) \vee (b \rightarrow a)$	non-proper part	$(a \times b' \neq 0) \vee (b \times \acute{a} = 0)$

In class calculus a statement is a tautology if its truth condition is self-evidently fulfilled. Thus the statement, $ab \rightarrow a$, has as its essential truth condition that $ab\acute{a} = 0$; this is self-evidently fulfilled as the logical product of the class a and its complement $\acute{a}$ is necessarily empty; similarly, the statements $\acute{a} \rightarrow \acute{a}$ and $c' \wedge c$ are also tautologies. The denial of $ab \rightarrow a$ is a logical inconsistency as it is equivalent to an assertion that the product of a and $\acute{a}$ is non-empty; it is necessarily false not just accidentally so. On the other hand, $ab \rightarrow c$ is a contingent statement; a formal analysis of its truth condition, $abc' = 0$, does not reveal whether it is, or is not, actually fulfilled.

In the Aristotelian class calculus, $a \neq 0$ is a variable mode of expressing the postulate that no simple class is empty; its truth condition is this postulate and so it is a tautology,formally necessitated by the logical system itself. In modern logic, $a \neq 0$ is a contingent statement, as is the statement $a = 0$; consequently $a \wedge a$ is also a contingent statement as its truth condition is that $aa = 0$ (i.e. that the class aa, which is the class a, is empty—a contingent fact in modern logic).

DIAGRAMING STATEMENTS ABOUT CLASSES AND USING SUCH DIAGROM AS A METHOD OF DISPLAYING THE VALIDITY OR INVALIDITY OF ARGUMENTS

Diagramming statements. If  is the universe of discourse, the complementary classes a and $\acute{a}$ exhaust it thus:. a $\acute{a}$  The two classes are exclusive and exhaustive: every object in the universe belongs to one class and no object belongs to both.

Two sets of complementary classes exhaust their universe thus:

	b	b'
a	ab	ab'
á	áb	áb'

	b	b'
a		0
á		

$a \rightarrow b$

	b	b'
a	*	
á		

$a \uparrow b$

	b	b'
a	?	?
á		

$a \neq 0$

Given that $a \rightarrow b$, then the class ab' is empty ($ab' = 0$ is the essential truth condition of $a \rightarrow b$); we signify this by putting a zero in the upper right-hand box. The essential truth condition of $a \uparrow b$ being $ab \neq 0$ (i.e. ab has one member at least) it can be diagrammed by putting an * in the upper left-hand box. Given simply that a has members we put a? in each of the boxes for the complementary sub-classes ab and ab' until further information reveals membership or emptiness.

Thus what is diagrammed is the essential truth conditions for class statements:

For $a \wedge b$, a zero is put in box ab.
" a ← b, a zero is put in box ab.
" $a \leftarrow b$, zeros are put in ab' and $\acute{a}b$.
" a ∧ b, a zero is put in áb'.

" $a \vee b$, zeros are put in *ab* and *áb'*.
" $a \overset{\wedge}{\vee} b$, the box *ab* has an asterisk, signifying that the class has at least one member.

For $a \nrightarrow b$, *ab'* has an asterisk.

For $P \varepsilon a$, *P*? is put in each of the boxes ab and ab' to signify diagrammatic ambiguity as it is not clear to which sub-class *P* belongs.

Three and four sets of complementary classes exhaust their universes as follows:

a	*C*	*abc*	*ab'c*
	C'	*abc'*	*ab'c'*
á	*C*	*ábc*	*áb'c*
	C'	*ábc'*	*áb'c'*

a	*C*	*abcd*	*ab'cd*	*ab'cd*	*ab'cd'*
	C'	*abc'd*	*ab'c'd*	*ab'c'd*	*ab'c'd'*
á	*C*	*ábcd*	*ábcd'*	*áb'cd'*	*áb'cd'*
	C'	*ábcd'*	*ábc'd*	*ábc'd'*	*áb'c'd'*

The sub-classes are exclusive and exhaustive: every member of the universe belongs to one and only one of these sub-classes. Thus if *a* is the class of black objects, *b* of round objects, *c* of tall objects and *d* of thick objects, and if there is nothing which is white, round, tall and thin, ker, a zero is put in the square *ábc'd'*. If only tall objects are black, thin and round, a zero is put in the square *abc'd'*.

We have already seen that any statement asserting a relation between classes may be translated into an equivalent claim that certain classes are, or are not, empty (note that universal statements are equivalent to equations and particular statements to inequations):

	Vernacular Equivalent
$a \wedge b \equiv ab = 0$	No *a* is *b*
$a \uparrow b \equiv ab \neq 0$	Some *a* is *b*
$a \rightarrow b \equiv ab' = 0$	All *a* is *b*
$a \rightarrow b \equiv ab' \neq 0$	Some *a* is not *b*
$a \leftarrow b \equiv \acute{a}b = 0$	Only *a* is *b*
$a = b \equiv (ab' = 0) . (\acute{a}b = 0)$	All *a* and only *a* is *b*
$a \vee b \equiv \acute{a}b' = 0$	Everything is *a* or *b* or both.
$a \overset{\wedge}{\underset{\vee}{}} b \equiv (\acute{a}b' = 0) . (ab = 0)$	Everything is *a* or *b* but not both.

The above equivalences can present very clearly and powerfully the truth conditions of vernacular statements. For example 'No one but a very simple person would believe that' translates (with *a* as the class of simple people and *b* as the class of people that would believe that) into $\acute{a}b = 0$. Again 'The only criticism made referred to style' translates (with *a* as the class of criticisms made, and *b* the class of things that referred to style) into $ab' = 0$.

Statements in the above list can be opposed by asserting that a class declared to be empty is non-empty, or one declared non-empty is empty. Thus the range of possible conflict and compatibility can be clearly displayed in a diagram: a statement that is diagrammed as putting a zero in a box is in conflict with a statement diagrammed as putting an * in the same box. Both statements are compatible with any third statement which is diagrammed either as not saying anything about the box in question or as putting a ? in it (i.e. denying neither that it is empty nor that it has members).

It follows that where arguments are analysable into statements of the above kind (as, e.g. in the Aristotelian syllogistic), the evidential force of the premisses can be diagrammed and the diagram inspected to see if the conclusion is really necessitated. In other words, the diagram displays the essential truth condition for each and all the premisses to be true, and we can inspect it to see if, as a consequence, the essential truth condition for the conclusion is fulfilled. This is a powerful method of displaying validity or invalidity, a decision procedure as simple and effective as truth tables in propositional logic.

Table of the valid immediate inferences in class calculus

Conversion (an operation in which subject and predicate classes interchange positions with a new and valid relationship):

Converse	Essential truth conditions for both expressions
$(a \wedge b) \equiv (b \wedge a)$	$ab = 0$
$(a \vee b) \equiv (b \vee a)$	$\acute{a}b' = 0$
$(a \,\hat{\vee}\, b) \equiv (b \,\hat{}\, a)$	$(ab = 0) \,.\, (\acute{a}b' = 0)$
$(a \uparrow b) \equiv (b \uparrow a)$	$ab \neq 0$
$(a = b) \equiv (b = a)$	$(ab' = 0) \,.\, (\acute{a}b = 0)$

Obversion (an operation which replaces the predicate class with its complement, expressing the valid class relationship present):

Obverse	Essential truth conditions for both expressions
$(a \wedge b) \equiv (b \rightarrow a')$	$ab = 0$
$(a \uparrow b) \equiv (a \rightarrow b)$	$ab \neq 0$
$(a \Diamond b) \equiv (b \leftarrow a)$	$\acute{a}b' = 0$
$(a \vee b) \equiv (a = b)$	$(ab = 0) \,.\, (\acute{a}b' = 0)$

Contraposition (an operation which validly replaces the subject class with the complement of the original predicate class, and the predicate class with the complement of the original subject class):

Contrapositive	Essential truth conditions for both expressions
$(a \rightarrow b) \equiv (b' \rightarrow \acute{a})$	$ab' = 0$
$(a \leftarrow b) \equiv (b' \rightarrow \acute{a})$	$b\acute{a} = 0$
$(a \Diamond b) \equiv (b' \Diamond \acute{a})$	$(ab = 0) \,.\, (\acute{a}b' = 0)$
$(a = b) \equiv (b' = \acute{a})$	$(ab' = 0) \,.\, (\acute{a}b = 0)$
$(a \rightarrow b) \equiv (b' \rightarrow \acute{a})$	$ab' \neq 0$

Inversion (an operation which validly replaces both subject class and predicate class with their complements):

Inverse	Essential truth conditions for both expressions
$(a \wedge b) \equiv \acute{a} \vee b'$	$ab = 0$
$a \vee b \equiv b \wedge a$	$\acute{a}b' = 0$

Diagramming Aristotelian operations of immediate inference displays the fact that some conclusions are valid only on the special Aristotelian postulate that no simple class term is empty (i.e. that none refers to an empty class). Without this postulate, *Some b is a* is not a valid converse of *All a is b*, for the essential truth condition of the latter is $ab' = 0$, and of the former $ba \neq 0$; the diagram displays these truth conditions as being simply compatible (a zero in box ab', an *in box ab). A similar lack of logical necessitation is shown between *No a is b* and its Aristotelian contrapositive *Some non-b is a* (the truth conditions being, respectively, $ab = 0$ and $b'a \neq 0$); also between *All a is b* and its inverse, *Some non-a is not b* (the truth conditions being $ab' = 0$ and $\acute{a}b' \neq 0$).

The validity of inferences based on the traditional Square of Opposition.

A — All a is b $(a \rightarrow b)$

E — No a is b $(a \wedge b)$

I — Some a is b $(a \uparrow b)$

O — Some a is not b $(a \nrightarrow b)$

The A and O propositions are contradictory: from the truth of either we can infer the falsity of the other and vice versa.

Their truth conditions are, respectively, $ab' = 0$ and $ab' \neq 0$

E and I are also contradictory.

Their truth conditions are $ab = 0$ and $ab \neq 0$.

A and E may not only both be false, they may also both be true if one does not postulate, with Aristotle, that the basic class *a* is non-empty.	Their truth conditions are different but compatible, being respectively $ab' = 0$ and $ab = 0$.
The A proposition does not imply the I proposition, sub-alternating it, unless one postulates, with Aristotle, that the simple class *a* cannot be empty.	Their truth conditions are $ab' = 0$ and $ab \neq 0$. Notice that *a* is conjoined here with the complementary classes *b* and *b'*. If *a* has members, and one of these sub-classes is empty, the other must have members.
Similarly, without the Aristotelian postulate that *a* is not empty, *E does not imply O* sub alternating it.	The truth conditions of *E* and *O* are respectively $ab = 0$ and $ab' \neq 0$.
Logically, *I* and *O* may not only both be true, they may also both be false, except in a system which operates the Aristotelian postulate that no simple class is empty.	Their truth conditions are $ab \neq 0$ and $ab' \neq 0$.

Sample arguments containing statements which have complex subjects or predicates. We have seen that a class calculus which is Aristotelian postulates that every simple class has at least one member, and that some Aristotelian theorems would not hold for a world which did not provide a real correlate for every simple class. However, even Aristotetian calculus does not postulate that a complex class (generated by a Boolean operation on simple classes) has members; e.g. *ab* may be empty, although it is not possible for both *ab* and *ab'* to be empty, since *a* must have members and these classes are the product in turn of *a* and the complementary classes b and b'. The existential postulate of modern calculus is simply that the universe of discourse is not a totally empty one, and so it accepts that any class, simple or complex, may be empty.

Argument 1: $(a \wedge b) \rightarrow (ab \wedge c)$

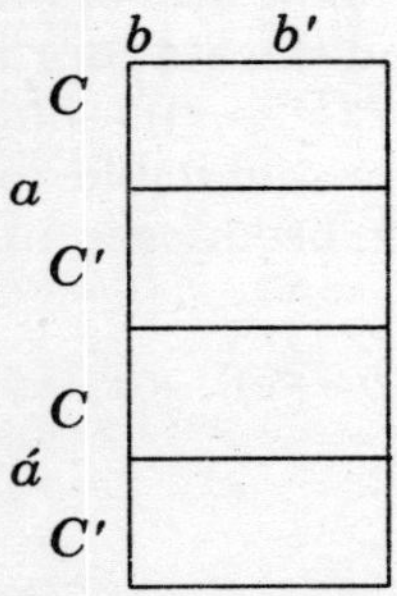

The essential truth condition for $a \wedge b$ is $ab = 0$. This means that $abc = 0$ and $abc' = 0$. The former is the essential truth condition for the consequent, $ab \wedge c$. Thus the argument is valid. However, the converse does not hold, i.e. it is not the case that $(ab \wedge c) \rightarrow (a \wedge b)$. The truth conditions demanded by the consequent are more extensive than those fulfilled by the antecedent: although the box abc is empty (we are given $ab \wedge c$), abc' might not be empty.

Argument 2: $(ab \uparrow c) \rightarrow (a \uparrow b)$

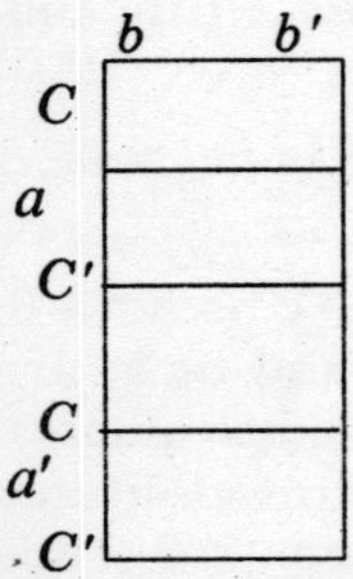

The essential truth condition for $ab \uparrow c$ is $abc \neq 0$. Since the members of the sub-class abc are also members of the wider class ab this means that the class ab is non-empty. This is the essential truth condition for the conclusion $(ab \neq 0)$. Again the converse, $a \uparrow b \rightarrow (ab \uparrow c)$, does not hold: given that $ab \neq 0$, it is possible that the members of ab are concentrated in the sub-class abc'; we are not entitled to conclude that abc has members, which is the essential truth condition for the conclusion. Thus granted that some employees pay taxes it does not follow that there are some employees over 60 years of age paying taxes.

Standard forms of syllogistic argument. In seeking valid forms of syllogistic reasoning, the information provided by each premiss can be represented in a box diagram, and the diagram can then be inspected to see if the premisses have furnished the essential truth condition for the conclusion. One has to be clear whether or not we are postulating (with Aristotle) that no basic class is empty; if so then when, e.g. the class *ab* is empty, the class *ab′* cannot be empty also.

In modern calculus (where the Aristotelian postulate is not made), the standard form of argument for a universal conclusion is $((a \rightarrow b) \,.\, (b \rightarrow c)) \rightarrow (a \rightarrow c)$, and the standard form for a particular conclusion is $((a \uparrow b) \,.\, (b \rightarrow c)) \rightarrow (a \uparrow c)$. Any argument in one of these forms or reducible to one of them (by, e.g. obverting, converting premisses or conclusion) is valid.

Proof of standard argument form 1: $((a \rightarrow b).(b \rightarrow c)) \rightarrow (a \rightarrow c)$

		b	*b′*
a	*C*		0
	C′	0	0
á	*C*		
	C′	0	

The truth condition of the premiss $a \rightarrow b$ is $ab' = 0$; $\therefore$ $ab'c = 0$ and $ab'c' = 0$ (if a class is empty then all its sub-classes are empty).

The truth condition of the premiss $b \rightarrow c$ is $bc' = 0$; $\therefore$ $abc' = 0$ and $\acute{a}bc' = 0$.

The truth condition of the conclusion, a → c, is ac′ = 0; this is fulfilled if both the sub-classes *ac′b* and *ac′b′* are empty (for a class is empty if all its sub-classes are empty). Actually, as we have seen, the first premiss necessitates $ab'c' = 0$, and the second premiss necessitates $abc' = 0$. Thus the truth of the premisses involves fulfilment of the truth condition for the conclusion.

Proof of standard argument form 2: $((a \uparrow b) \,.\, (b \rightarrow c)) \rightarrow$ (a ↑ c).

The truth condition of the premiss $a \uparrow b$ is $ab \neq 0$; $\therefore$ one of the sub-classes *abc* or *abc′* has members. (In the diagram a ? is put in each of these boxes.)

The truth condition of the premiss $b \rightarrow c$ is $bc' = 0$; $abc' = 0$ and $\acute{a}bc' = 0$ since sub-classes of an empty class must also be empty. (In the diagram the ? in box abc' is now replaced by a zero, and the ? in box abc is replaced by an *, since we now know that abc must have members.)

		b	b'
a	C	?*	
	C'	?0	
$\acute{a}$	C		
	C'	0	

The truth condition required for the conclusion, $a \uparrow c$, is $ac \neq 0$; this is fulfilled if one of its sub-classes acb or acb' is shown to have members. Actually, we have just seen that in the light of the first premiss, the second one necessitates that abc is not empty.

Aristotelian moods, standard or weakened, in which the premisses are universal and the conclusion is particular, cannot be reduced to either of the standard forms in modern class calculus. This draws our attention once more to the existence of a special postulate in Aristotle's calculus permitting the inference of a particular conclusion from universal premisses—the postulate, namely, that simple classes are never empty and that consequently, particular propositions are simply less extensive statements about their membership than universal propositions.

Simple arguments in the vernacular

First argument:

No successful lawyers are dull	$(a \wedge b)$
P is a successful lawyer	$(P \in a)$
∴ *P is not dull*	$(P \in b)$

a = the class of successful lawyers; b = the class of dull people. The premisses of the above argument may be represented in a box diagram as follows:

Since the truth condition of the major premiss is that ab is empty, P (a member of a) must be placed in ab'. The truth condition of the conclusion is indeed that P is a member of b'. Thus the argument is valid—the premisses being true necessitate the truth of the conclusion.

Second argument:

	b	b'
a	O	P
$á$		

'None of the expenses which John cited in his tax claim were for personal expenses or for depreciation in value of property. Now all other relevant claims are acceptable. Therefore, John's claims are acceptable.'

Let a = the class of claims John made
b = the class of claims that are for personal expenses
c = the class of claims that are for depreciation in value of property
d = the class of all other claims relevant to John
e = the class of claims that are acceptable

The argument, fully expressed, may be formalized as follows:

$$(a \wedge (b + c) \,.\, (d \rightarrow b'c') \,.\, (a \rightarrow d) \,.\, (d \rightarrow e)) \rightarrow (a \rightarrow e).$$

The truth condition of $a \wedge (b + c)$ is $a(b + c) = 0$
The truth condition of $d \rightarrow b'c'$ is $dbc = 0$
The truth condition of $a \rightarrow d$ is $ad' = 0$
The truth condition of $d \rightarrow e$ is $dé = 0$

The force of this evidence may be represented in a box diagram thus:

The truth condition for the conclusion, $a \rightarrow e$, is $aé = 0$. The class space occupied by aé is represented in the upper half of the diagram by the two rows of boxes designated $é$. The premisses have been diagrammed as filling these boxes with zeros. Thus they are displayed as logically necessitating the truth condition of the conclusion ($aé = 0$), and the argument has been validated.

			b d	b d'	b' d	b' d'
a	C	e	0	0	0	0
		e'	0	0	0	0
	C'	e	0	0		0
		e'	0	0	0	0
a'	C	e	0			
		e'	0		0	
	C'	e				
		e'	0		0	

AXIOMATIZING THE CLASS CALCULUS—A FORMALIZ ATION OF THE BOOLE-SCHRÖDER ALGEBRA OF CLASSES

Different codifications have been worked out by Whitehead, Huntington (who in 1904 and 1933 published five), Sheffer (whose codification in 1913 remains the most concise and simple perhaps), Lewis and Langford, and Eaton. These codifications have exactly the same content and are consequently equivalent—the same elements, operations and relations are organized under varying sets of primitive terms, definitions and postulates. The formal system presented in this chapter is that of Lewis and Langford; in their *Symbolic Logic* (chapter 2) it is completely and meticulously worked out for about one hundred representative theorems. Only the basic structure and some of the theorems (with commentary) are presented here:

Primitive term. Any term of the system, '*a, b, c,* etc.', will represent some class of things, named by some logical term.

'$a \times b$' for the class composed of these things which are members of a and members of b, both.

'—a' for the negative of a, for the class of all things which are not members of the class a.

'0' for the unique class 'nothing', the 'null class'.

'$a = b$' for the proposition: the terms a and b have the same extension; the class a and the class b have identically the same members.

Definitions

1.01 $1 = -0$

That is, 1 represents the class of all things which are not members of the null class; thus 1 represents 'everything' or 'everything being considered' or 'the universe of discourse'

1.02 $a + b = -(-a \times -b)$ Def.

That is, $a + b$ represents the class of things which are either members of a or members of b (or members of both). Since $-a \times -b$ is the class of what is both not-a and not-b (neither a nor b), the negative of this, $-(-a \times -b)$, will be what is either a or b or both.

1.03 $a \subset b$ is equivalent to $a \times b = a$ Def.

This is the relation of class-inclusion: $a \subset b$ represents 'a is contained in b' or 'Every a is also a b'. The class 'both men and mortals' is identical with the class 'men' if and only if all men are mortals.

Postulates

1.1 $a \times a = a$.

What is both a and a, is identical with a. Since this law holds, there are no exponents in this algebra.

1.2 $a \times b = b \times a$.

What is both a and b is the same as what is both b and$a$.

1.3 $a \times (b \times c) = (a \times b) \times c$.

Since this law holds, parentheses in 'products' can be omitted.

1.4 $a \times 0 = 0$

What is both a and nothing, is nothing.

1.5 If $a \times -b = 0$, then $a \subset b$.

If nothing is both a and not $-b$, then all a is b.

1.6 If $a \subset b$ and $a \subset -b$, then $a = 0$.

If all a is b and all a is not $-b$, then a is a class which has no members.All the laws of the algebra can be rigorously deduced from these three definitions and six postulates, given above.

Theorems ($\subset$ signifies class inclusion; the symbol $\times$ is generally omitted, e.g. $a \times b$ is abbreviated to ab; in some cases it is replaced by., e.g. instead of $o \times a$ the symbolism is $0 \,.\, a$)

2.1 If $a = b$, then $ac = bc$ and $ca = cb$.

2.12 If $a = b$, then $a + c = b + c$ and $c + a = c + b$.

These two laws follow immediately from the meaning of the relation = .

2.2 $a = b$ is equivalent to the pair, $a \subset b$ and $b \subset a$.

If a = b, then by def. 1.1, ab = aa = a; and ba = bb= b. But by def. 1.03, ab = a is a $\subset$ b; and ba = b is b $\subset$ a. Conversely, if $ab = a$ and $ba = b$, then [1.2]

$$a = ab = ba = b.$$

If two classes are identical, then each is contained in the other; and classes such that each is contained in the other are identical.

2.3 $a \subset a$.

This follows from 2.2, since $a = a$. Every class is contained in itself: 'All a is a' holds for every a.

2.4 $ab \subset a$ and $ab \subset b$.

By 1.1, 1.2 and 1.3, $(ab)a = a(ab) = (aa)b = ab$.
And by 1.03, $(ab)a = ab$ is $ab \subset a$.

What is both a and b, is contained in a, and is contained in b.

2.5 $a - a = 0 = -aa$.

By 2.4, $a - a \subset a$, and $a - a \subset - a$.

Hence by 1.6, $a - a = 0$.

This theorem states the Law of Contradiction: Nothing is both a and not-a.

2.6 $0 \subset a$.

By 1.2 and 1.4, $0 \cdot a = a. 0 = 0$.

But [1.03] $0 \cdot a = o$ is $0 \subset a$.

Theorem 2.6 states the principle that the null class is contained in every class. This follows from the law, $a \times 0 = 0$, together with the definition of the relation $a \subset b$. It expresses an extensional relationship between the memberships of classes and would not hold if the intension or meaning of classes weere taken into consideration.

Some other interesting theorems are:

3.5 $a + -a = 1$.

This is the Law of the Excluded Middle Term: Everything is either a or not-a.

3.6 $-a + b = 1$ is equivalent to $a \subset b$.

'Everything is either not-a or b' is equivalent to 'All a is b'

The next two principles, concerning the relation $\subset$, are of fundamental importance:

3.7 If $a \subset b$ and $b \subset c$, then $a \subset c$.

[1.03] If $a \subset b$ and $b \subset c$, then $ab = a$ and $bc = b$.

Hence $ac = (ab)c = a(bc) = ab = a$.

But [1.03] $ac = a$ is $a \subset c$.

If all a is b and alal b is c, then all a is c: the relation $\subset$ is transitive.

3.8 $a \subset b$ is equivalent to $-b \subset -a$.

[2.8] $a \subset b$ is equivalent to $a - b = 0$.

[2.9] $a -b = -(-a) = 0$ is equivalent to $-b \subset -a$

And [2.8] $-b = -(-a) =0$ is equivalent to $-b \subset -a$.

'All a is b' is equivalent to 'All not-b is not-a'. The terms of any relation $\subset$ may be transposed by negating both. This is called the Law of Transposition. These last two laws are the fundamental principles underlying the validity of the syllogism. (From *Symbolic Logic* by C. I. Lewis and C.H. Langford, Dover Publications, Inc., New York, 1959. Reprinted through the permission of the publisher.)

CLASS CALCULUS SPECIFIED TO A CALCULUS OF RELATIONS

Whatever the adicity of a relation it may always be expressed as a predication: a dyadic relation is a predication made of an ordered couple, a triadic of an ordered triad, etc. The internal order of the dyad, triad, etc. defines each as a group, i.e. the defining function of each such group or class is a relation. Thus the dyad or triad itself is the relation in extension. The extension of a dyadic relation R is focused when we exhibit it as the class of couples (x, y) such that xRy. Common notation is $R = \hat{x}\hat{y}(xRy)$, $S = wz$ (wSz)—the circumflex has the force of higher abstraction or generalization, i.e. R = the class of x's y's such that xRy. This notation is simpler and more suggestive than equivalent notation using dyadic functors, e.g. $R = \hat{x}\hat{y}$ $(x, y)]$. A triadic relation T is symbolized $T = xyz \mid T(x, y, z) \mid$, i.e. T is the class of triads (x, y, z) for which the propositional form $T(x, y, z)$ is true.

The symbolism represents, quite definitely, the members of, e.g. a dyad (x, y) or triad (x, y, z), the relations which constitute them as dyads or triads (R, S, T), and the classes of dyads or triads so constituted (the letters R, S, T are agaian used here, commonly). Boolean operations can be performed on simple classes of dyads, triads, etc. to generate complex classes and the general laws of class calculus can be seen to hold specifically (or analogically) for these classes. Thus a good deal of any present-day calculus of relations is constructed by simply translating laws of general class calculus into the specific concepts and symbols required by an explicit calculus of relations. Many concepts in the latter are simply adaptations of ones in the general calculus; some are proper.

Sample concepts, postulates and theorems of the class calculus specified to a calculus of relations. *Examples of concepts adapted from the general calculus are:*

'Universal' and 'null': the universal relation (symbolized $\vee$) holds between every two individuals in the universe of discourse; the null relation ($\wedge$) does not hold between any two.

'Inclusion': the relation R is said to be included in the relation S if, for any x and y, xRy implies xSy. Thus 'less than' is included in 'unequal to'—whenever x is less than y, x is unequal to y.

'Identity': R and S are identical relations when they are mutually inclusive: xRy implies xSy; and xSy implies xRy.

'Sum' or 'disjunct': the sum or union of two dyadic relations can be symbolized $x(R + S)y$. Two things x and y form an ordered couple of this class if either xRy or xSy.

'Product' or 'conjunct': the product or intersection of two dyadic relations can be symbolized $x(R \times S)y$. Two things x and y form a dyad of this class if both xRy and xSy. Thus if R denotes fatherhood and S denotes motherhood the relation $x(R \times S)y$ is the null relation, for in no couple can one individual be both father and mother of the other.

'Negate' or 'complement': the negate of a relation R is symbolized R' and holds between two things if, and only if, R does not hold between them: $xR'y \equiv \sim (xRy)$.

The following is a sampling of analogous laws, i.e. expressions in the calculus of relations which are analogues of theorems demonstrated in the calculus of classes. (The symbols 0, 1, +, × have different—but analogous—meanings for relations from their meaning for classes.):

(x, y) $[(x, y) \in 1]$: every couple is a member of the universe of couples or has the universal (dyadic) relation.

$(x, y) \sim [(x, y) \in 0]$: no couple has the null relation.

$R \subset 1$ and $0 \subset R$: every class of couples is included in the universe class of couples and the null class of couples is contained in every class of couples. The latter express an extensional relationship and would not hold if intension or meaning were taken into consideration.

$R \subset S = (x, y) [(xRy) (x Ry)]$: the class of couples related by R is contained in the class of couples related by S, means that every (x, y) couple related by R is also related by S.

$(R = S) = (x, y) [xRy) = (xSy)]$: the expression, the class of couples related by R is coextensive with the class related by S, is equivalent to the expression that every couple related by R is also related by S.

$[(R \subset S) \times (-S \subset -R)$: if R is contained in S then the negate of S is contained in the negate of R.

$[(R \subset S) \times (S \subset T)] \subset (R \subset T)$: the class of couples such that R is contained in S and S in T is itself included in the class of couples in which R is contained in T. This displays the transitivity of inclusion.

$[(R = S) \times (S = T)] \subset (R = T)$: the class of couples related by R ad the negate fo S is the null class of couples, then the class of couples, the the class of couples ordered by R and S is equivalent to T. This displays th transitivity of equivalence.

If $(R \times -S) = 0$ then $(R \times S) = R$: if the class of couples related by R and the negate of S is the null class of couples, then the class of couples ordered by R and S is equivalent to the class of couples ordered by R.

$(R \subset S) = [(R \times S) = R]$: the class of couples in which R is contained in S is equivalent to a class which fulfills the condition that $(R \times S) = R$, i.e. that the class of couples ordered by both R and S is coextensive with the class ordered by R.

The following are analogues of the postulates used by Lewis and Langford in formalizing the calculus of classes:

$$(R \times R) = R$$
$$(R \times S) = (S \times R)$$
$$(R \times S) \times T = R \times (S \times T)$$
$$(R \times 0) = 0$$
$$\text{If } (R \times -S) = 0 \text{ then } R \subset S$$
$$\text{If } R \subset S \text{ and } R \subset -S \text{ then } R = 0$$

The analogues of De Morgan's theorems are as follows ($-R$ signifying the class of couples not ordered by the relation R):

$$(R \times S) = -(-R + -S)$$
$$(-R \times S) = -(-R + -S)$$
$$(R \times -S) = -(-R + S)$$
$$(-R \times -S) = -(R + S)$$
$$(R + S) = -(-R \times -S)$$
$$(-R + S) = -(R \times -S)$$
$$(R + -S) = -(-R \times S)$$
$$(-R + -S) = -(R \times S)$$

Concepts that are not adapted, by analogy, from the calculus of classes. The following are examples of concepts that are proper to the calculus of relations: (a) 'Identity' and 'diversity' between individuals: these relations have special symbols xIy and xDy respectively. (The symbols = and ≠ are pre-empted for identity and diversity between relations or classes.)

(b) A special operation performed on the two relations, R and S, yields a third relation which is called the Relative Product or Composition of R and S, and is symbolized R/S. It is the relation which exists between x and z if and only if there is a y such that xRy and ySz. Thus if R denotes 'husband of' and S denotes 'daughter of', R/S denotes 'son-in-law of', i.e.the relation which exists between the husband (x) and parent (z) of a person (y). This concept is very important in the study of series.

(c) A special operation performed on R yields the converse of R (symbolized $\cup R$). The relation $\cup$ R holds between x and y if, and only if, the relation R holds between

y and x.

In the early years of modern mathematical logic, Augustus De Morgan believed that any ultimate formal explanation of the syllogism must be in terms of transitive and convertible relations, and he believed that, for logic generally, a theory of relations was of ultimate and fundamental importance. In the event, modern logic has not grown in accordance with such a vision: it has been more concerned with 'relatives' than with 'relations'; its theories have been constructed as extensions and applications of predicate logic and class calculus; and its concepts, distinctions and laws have their individual values (especially in applied logic) without constituting a section of primary explanatory importance.

Chapter-12

Modal Logic and Many-Valued Logic

Chapter 12

INTRODUCTION

Standard Logic is, historically, the most developed branch of logic; it operates on the principle that a proposition is either true or false (the Law of Bivalence). However, truth and falsity are actually subject to modes;some propositions must be true, others cannot be true, others again may be actually but not necessarily true or false. In ancient logic these modalities were named *alethic modalities.* Again our knowledge of facts is subject to modalities: we grade our assertions in modes of determinancy from certainly true to certainly false and we quantify these modes in a probability calculus. This evident presence of *alethic* and *epistemic* modalities in human speech and thought has been a motivating force in the development of modal and many-valued logics, i.e. logics which, not being restricted to simple true-false evaluations, are called non-standard.

Modal Logic is concerned with modal statements, e.g. *S* is necessarily *p*; it is impossible that *S* is *P*; *S* mayor may not be *P*. It studies the modalities or modal functors—necessity,impossibility, possibility and contingency. Not only does it deal with the meaning of these functors, it endeavours also to formalize their logical features into a system of propositions, a calculus. In many-valued logic propositions are abstracted from their traditional epistemological framework, whcih simply evaluated truth and falsity; they are conceived as entities which can have three, four... *n* values, and the objective of many-valued logic is (a) to work out tables or calculi for logics of three, four ... infinite propositional values; and (b) to seek for possible interpretations of these values and useful applications of their calculi.

MODAL LOGIC

The basic history of its development. Aristotle's pioneer work on modal logic was done, as we shall see, in the context of his syllogistic. Modern work is technically quite different and comparatively recent: it began in 1918 with C. I. Lewis's concern that mathematical logic should extend its primitive language (substantially presented in the *Principia Mathematica*) so as to include a symbol for a stronger form of implication than material implication—such a form indeed as would be free from paradox and could be identified as the implication which governs human argumentation when it is perfect. The definition of material implication (called Philonian because it can be traced back to Philo in the third century B.C when according to Callimachus even the Greek crows cawed about the nature of conditionals) is such that it makes any conditional automatically true if the antecedent is false or the consequent true:

$$p \supset (q \supset p)$$
$$-p \supset (p \supset q)$$

Lewis suggested the introduction into mathematical logic of the type of implication that holds not merely materially but in strict consequence. He used the symbol ϒ and suggested as definitions: 'It is necessary that $(q \supset p)$', or 'it is necessary that $(-p \vee q)$', or 'it is not possible that (p and $-q$)'. The alternative definitions are based on the fact that $p \supset q$ is equivalent to $-p \vee q$ and to $-(p \, . -q)$.

The relationship defined by Lewis and generally called *strict implication* or *entailment* has paradoxes of its own:

(1) If p cannot be true, it is automatically not possible that $(p.-q)$; thus an impossibility strictly implies any proposition, just as in the case of material implication a simply false proposition (p) materially implies any proposition (q).

(2) If q is necessarily true, then it is strictly implied by any proposition, because it is not possible that $(p \, . -q)$. This paradox is similar to the one of material implication where a simply

true proposition (*q*) is implied by any proposition (p).

Since Lewis's time various systems of modal logic have been constructed.

Basic concepts and definitions in modal logic. The basic concepts of Modal Logic are necessity, possibility, impossibility and contingency. They are expressed, grammatically, by adverbs, auxiliary verbs and verb phrases, e.g. *S* is necessarily *P*; it is necessary that *S* is *P;* it is necessarily true that *S* is *P*; *S* must be *P*; it is bound to be the case that *S* is *P* *S* is possibly *P* it could be that *S* is *P*; it is possible that *S* is *P*.It is not surprising that there are important metalogical problems in interpreting modal statements: are they to be treated as sentences stating necessary, possible, impossible or contingent facts (the modality being predicated *de re*) or as sentences whose truth or falsity is necessary, possible, impossible, contingent (the modality being predicated *de dicto*)? While recognizing that a modality *de re* and a modality *de dicto* differ in meaning, for the moment the simplest procedure is to interpret modalities as being primarily *de re,* and to regard the necessity,etc. of sentences being true or false as derivative and secondary.

Necessity can be taken as an undefined functor and the remaining modalities be defined in terms of it. In the notation of the Polish School:

'*LP*' means '*p* is necessary' or '*p* is necessarily true'.
'*MP*' reads '*p* is possible' and is equivalent to *NLNp*.
'*Up*' reads '*p* is impossible' and is equivalent to *LNp*.
'*Zp*' reads '*p* is contingent' (this latter term coming from Marius Victorinus who used it to translate one of Aristotle's meanings of 'possible'—that which is not necessary and the supposed existence of which implies nothing impossible, i.e. that which is neither necessary nor impossible); it is equivalent to *KNLpNUp*.

Possibility could also be taken as the undefined functor with *Lp* defined as *NMNp*, *Up* as *NMp*, and *Zp* in terms of *Lp and Up*.

The basic modal equivalences are:

$$Lp = UNp = NMNp$$
$$LNp = Up = NMp$$
$$NLp = NUNp = MNp$$
$$NLNp = NUp = Mp$$

In the above notation *L, M, U, Z* are modal functors with *p* as their argument, i.e. they signify modalities *de dicto.*

Modal laws in the context of Aristotle's syllogistic and the logic of modal syllogisms. Relations displayed within the traditional Square of Opposition and the operations of conversion, etc. give rise to basic modal laws when *A*, *E*, *I* and *O* propositions are arguments of modal functors. For example, the following are laws of Aristotelian logic:

(a) *Modal laws of sub-alternation:*

CLAabLIab	(Law of Sub-alternation of *LI*—premiss)
CMEabMOab	(" " " " " *MO*—premiss)
CLEabLoab	(" " " "*LO*—premiss)
CMAabMIab	(" " " " *MI*—premiss)

(b) *Modal Laws of Conversion:*

CLIabLIba	(Law of conversion of *LI*—premiss)
CMEabMEba	(" " " " *ME*—premiss)
CLEabLEba	(" " " " *LE*—premiss)
CMIabMIba	(" " " " *MI*—premiss)
CLAabLIba	(" " " " *LA*—premiss)
CMAabMIba	(" " " " *MA*—premiss)

(c) *Laws of Modal Subordination:*

CLAabAab
CLIabIab
CLOabOab
CLEabEab
COabMOab
CEabMEab
CAabMAab
CIabMIab

It would be easy to derive further relations from these,e.g.

CNAabNLAab
CNIabNLIab
CNOabNLOab
CIabMIba
CNMIabNIab

With regard to Aristotle's theory of the syllogism it is not easy to formalize the extension of it to modal propositions and the consistency of Aristotle's own ideas is controverted. In a modal proposition, one at least of the constituent propositions is modal (symbolized *L*, *M*, *U*, *Z* according to the mode it expresses). Since the propositions may also differ in quantity and quality (i.e. be *A*, *E*, *I* or *O*) the number of possible combinations is very great indeed. Thus using *X* to symbolize a categorical proposition and restricting ourselves to *L* and *M* modals, it is clear that there are 27 different general forms of the *L—X—M syllogism:*

LLL, LLX, LXL, XLL, LXX, XLX, XXL, XXX,
LLM, LML, MLL, LMM, MLM, MML, MMM,
XXM, XMX, MXX, XMM, MXM, MMX,
LXM, XLM, LMX, MLX, XML, MXL.

Within each of these modal arrangements propositions can be further varied in quantity and quality. Sifting out the valid moods is made difficult not only by the number of combinations to be considered but also by the problems asscociated with particular combinations. In his *Aristotle's Modal Syllogisms,* Storrs McCall arrives at the figure 333 for the total number of valid *L—X—M* moods; extending the range of modal propositions to include the contingent type, he arrived at 464 further valid moods—a grand total of 797. In the Middle Ages, Ockham Visualized syllogisms in which the mode of one premiss was *de re* and of the other *de dicto*—the number of valid moods in his whole modal syllogistic was about a thousand. (cf. Bochenski's *A History of Formal Logic*, pp. 229–30)

Jan Lukasiewicz was the first to organize modal syllogisms

into a complete deductive system. His system was published in 1953; while 'built up upon Aristotle's ideas' it did not attempt to reproduce his modal syllogistic as Lukasiewicz felt that 'in contrast to the assertoric syllogistic which is perfectly clear and nearly free of errors, Aristotle's modal syllogistic is almost incomprehensible because of its many faults and inconsistencies'. (*Aristotle's syllogistic,* p. 133) As a contrast Storrs McCall presents a formalized system which he believes agrees with Aristotle's at all important points, the agreement being complete with regard to the apodeictic or necessary moods. Nicolas Rescher, however, believes that Aristotle's doctrine does not admit of complete fomalization.

Aristotle's own treatment demosntrates the difficulty one may encounter in finding an adequate formal proof of modal moods. In the *prior Analytics* (his treatment covers chapters 3 and 8–22) he maintains that when there are two necessary premisses, a necessary conclusion follows in exactly those cases in which an assertoric conclusion follows from two assertoric premisses. An example is the first-figure mood with universal affirmative premisses: If all *B* is necessarily *A* and if all *C* is necessarily *B*, then all *C* is necessarily *A*. (This is known as Barbara *LLL*.) Aristotle says: 'There is hardly any difference between syllogisms from necessary premisses and syllogisms from premisses which merely assert. When the terms are put in the same way, whether something belongs or necessarily belongs (or does not belong) to something else, a syllogism will or will not result alike in both cases, the only difference being the addition of the expression "necessarily" to the terms.' (ch. 8. 29b36–30a 1 in the Oxford translation) Turning to moods with one necessary and one categorical premiss (chapters 9-11) he holds that a necessary conclusion is valid in the case of Barbara *LXL*: If all *B* is necessarily *A*, and if all *C* is *B*, then all *C* is necessarily *A*. However, a necessary conclusion is not valid in the case of Barbara *XLL*: If all *B* is *A* and if all *C* is necessarily *B*, then all *C* is necesarily *A*.

Since the time of Theophrastus who held that a valid

conclusion must always follow the weaker premiss (the order of strength being: necessary, assertoric, possible), Barbara *LXL* and *XLL* have occasioned controversy both as to their validity and as to the cogency of Aristotle's arguments for his rule that in the first figure an apodeictic major and an assertoric minor may yield an apodeictic conclusion, while an assertoric major and an apodeictic minor cannot. Lukasiewicz says: 'The controversy shown by the example of the mood Barbara can be extended to all other moods of this kind.' (*Aristotle's Syllogistic,* p. 188) He believes that Aristotle is wrong in rejecting Barbara *XLL* as invalid and, of course, that Theophrastus is doubly wrong in rejecting both Barbara's.

Modern systems of modal logic. Well-known systems are:

System T: constructed essentially by Kurt Gödel, subsequently named T by Robert Feys. It uses *L* as the undefined modal operator (for necessity) along with the language of propositional logic. The definitions for strict entailment and equivalence are:

$$p \; \Upsilon \; q \;\equiv\; \mathrm{Df}\; L(p \to q)$$
$$p \equiv q \equiv \mathrm{Df}\; (p \Upsilon q).\; (q \;\Upsilon\; p)$$

Its axioms are:

1. $(p \vee p) \to p$
2. $q \to (p \vee q)$
3. $(p \vee q) \to (q \vee p)$
4. $(q \to r) \to ((p \vee q) \to (p \vee r))$
5. $Lp = p$ (axiom of necessity)
6. $L\,(p \to q) \to (Lp \to Lq)$

There is a special transformation rule, called the rule of necessitation. If *p* is a thesis, then *Lp* is a thesis, i.e. $(\vdash p) \to (\vdash Lp)$. The basis of this rule is that a thesis being either an axiom or a theorem has a complete guarantee within the system, i.e. the system as such necessitates it.

Systems S1, S2, S3, S4, S5, S6, S7, S8: These were alternative systems constructed by C. I. Lewis. *S1* and *S2* are weaker than *T*: *S4* and *S5* are stronger; the rest have laws that *T* does not establish and *T* has laws which they do not have.

Using possibility as the undefined modal functor, defining strict implication (*p* *q*) as –*M*(*p*. –*q*). and using a set of six axioms each of which expresses a relationship of strict implication, *S1* derives among its theorems a set of laws from which the whole of propositional Calculus can be deduced and it derives also the rule of detachment for materrial implication. Thus *S1* contains Propositional Calculus.

S4 and *S5* formalize iterated modalities. *S4* adds to the six axioms of System *T* the axiom, $Lp \rightarrow LLp$ (necessarily *p* is the case materially implies that it is necessary that necessarily *p* is the case). *S5* adds a different axiom. namely $Mp \rightarrow LMp$ (possibly *p* is the case materially implies that it is necessary that possibly *p* is the case). Since $Lp \rightarrow LLp$ can be proved as a theorem in *S5*, it follows that *S5* includes *S4*. Some example of theorems in these systems are:

$$Mp \leftrightarrow MMp$$
$$Lp \equiv LLp$$
$$MLMp \rightarrow Mp$$
$$LMp \leftrightarrow LMLMp$$
$$MLp \equiv MLMLp$$

The operatiors, $\leftrightarrow$ (biconditional) and $\equiv$ (equivalence), have the same truth conditions.

System M: Constructed by G. H. von Wright and, like Lewis's systems, *using M* as the undefined modal operator, this system is equivalent to *T*.

Systems which include quantifiers and/or postulates about identity: Since the 1940s these more extended systems have been evolving seeking to combine modal logic with quantification theory and the theory of identity. W. V. Quine does not believe that these efforts can have any valid outcome—the formal conditions and meaninigs of necessity and concrete individual existence have too little in common. The main work has been done by Ruth Barcan Marcus, A. N. Prior, R. A. Bull, S. A. Kripke and Jaakko Hintikka.

Modern modal logic has revived the medieval and Peircean conception of material implication as a limiting case of strict implication: actual states of affairs (the domain of material implication) are a boundary for possible states of affairs (over the entire range of which strsct implication operates). Further since modal language is strongly linked with our language of past, present and future time (the impossible, e.g. is that which can never be, the possible that which may have been in the past or may be in the future), modern modal logic has developed an interest in formalizing the conditions and laws which govern tense. For Prior, tense-logic is a genuine modal system: 'if we define *M* (or "possibly") as "It either is or will be the case that", and *L* (or "Necessarily") as "It is and always will be the case that", these operators will meet Lukasiewicz's conditions for being modal operatons and, furthermore, will have all the formal properties of the *M* and *L* of the Lewis system *S4*. "Possibly" and "Necessarily" were used in this sense by the Megarian logician Diodorous, and I have pointed out the resemblance between Diodoran modal logic and *S4*...' (*Time and Modality*, p.12).

MANY-VALUED LOGIC

The basic history of its development. In Greek and medieval times there was speculation as to whether there might be more than two truth values. This was bound up with philosophical problems posed by propositions which refer to future contingent events. Aristotle speculated on the possibility of some propositions having a neuter value, e.g. on the proposition 'there will be a seabattle tomorrow' being neither true nor false now (chapter 9 of *On Interpretation*). Many commentators interpret Aristotle as holding that the Principle of Bivalence (*tertium non datur*) does not govern such propositions. It is clear, on the other hand, that Stoic Logicians such as Chrysippus, being determinists, insisted on the absolute validity of this principle; for this reason Lukasiewicz referred to systems which do not use a Law of Excluded Middle as non-Chrysippian systems where earlier writers referred to them as non Aristotelian ones. In medieval times the possibility of a third truth-value had a significant place in debates on the extent of God's foreknowledge. Various logicians, especially Duns Scotus and William of Occam, relied on Aristotle's treatise in arguing for the need of a third, neuter, truth-value to express a truth indeterminancy of future contingent events.

In modern times, the Scot logician Hugh MacColl (1837-1909) constructed a 'logic of three dimensions' in deference to the reality of probabilistic modalities. Every proposition was the bearer of one of three possible values: certainty (necessity), impossibility and variability (contingency). In effect he anticipated the interest of the 1930 in using many-valued logic to formalize probability theory.

By 1909, Charles Sanders Peirce (1839-1914) had achieved a definite conception of a three-valued logic to which the truth-table method would be extended and he had considered some of the special three-valued operators which were later developed by Lukasiewicz, Post, Slupecki, Bochvar and Kleene. In a letter to William James he worte (1909).

> I have long felt that it is a serious defect in existing logic that it takes no heed of the limit between two realms. I do noty say that the Principle of Excluded Middle is downright *false;* but I do say that in every field of thought whatsoever there is an intermediate ground between *positive assertion* and *positive negation* which is just as Real as they.Mathematicians aways recognize this, and seek for that limit as the presumable lair of powerful concepts; while metaphysicians and old-fashioned logicians—the sheep and goat separators—never recognize this. The recognition does not involve any denial of existing logic, but it involves a great addition to it.

The Russian logician, Nikolai A. Vasil'ev (1880-1940) was writing on 'imaginary non-Aristotelian logics' in the 1910s. In his view all Aristotelian systems of logic include principles which are grounded in the laws of the world in which we live. When any of these principles is eliminated we have an 'imaginary logic'; such a logic could visualize any object as having the predicate *A*, or the negation of this predicate, non-*A*, or both *A* and non-*A*, where the law of excluded middle would allow only two possibilities. The logic of the imaginary world would be three-valued. Vasil'ev, however, did not develop any logical system.

Neither did the American, Edwin Guthrie, who wrote in 1916:

> Not only can logic include more than the logic of Aristotle, as the modern logistic does, there might have been non-Aristotelian logics with principles different from the familiar laws of contradition and excluded middle. What final authority would judge between the ultimate 'correctness' of Aristotle's logic which offers two contradictories, obeying the laws: $x.x' = 0$, $x + x' = 1$, $(x')' = x$, and a logic which would provide three contradictories, obeying the laws: $x.x' . x'' = 0$, $x + x' + x'' = 1$, $(x')' = x''$, $(x'')' = x$? It is true that we can only discuss other logics in terms of one logic, but this is no more a proof that they are therefore unreal than is the fact that an Englishman in discussing German must use English, a proof that English is the *a prior* condition of communication, valid for all times and all places.

It was the ancient philosophical discussion about propositions concerning the future which stimulated Jan Lukasiewicz. At a meeting of the Polish philosophical Society held at Lwow in June 1920 he delivered a paper entitled 'On three-valued logic'. He indicated how principles concerning two-values could be supplemented by principles concerning a third value, and he concluded, firstly, that three-valued logic has great theoretical significance in being the first attempt to create a non-Aristotelian logic, and tht its practical significance, if any, would depend on the acceptability of an indeterministic view of the world, this being the metaphysical basis of the new logic. In later papers he formalized his three-valued system in detail, generalizing it to the many-valued case and even to the infinite-valued case. In 1931 Mordchaj Wajsberg succeeded in giving L_3 (Lukasiewicz's three-valued system) an elegant axiomatic format—through a set of four axioms together with the rules of inference: modus ponens and substitution.

Independently of Lukasiewicz, the American Emil Leon Post presented a generalization of *m*-valued truth-tables as part of a doctoral dissertation, for Columbia University, on a general theory of elementary propositions (completed in 1920, the dissertation was published in 1921). In contrast with Lukasiewicz, Post's interest was almost exclusively mathematical and in the introduction to his paper he notes that this non-Aristotelian logic 'seems to have the same relation to ordinary logic that geometry in a space of an arbitary number of dimensions has to the geometry of Euclid.' Post's treatment was more generalized than Lukasiewicz's in 1920 (he dealt with *n*-values and allowed for an arbitrary number of designated—truth-like—truth values) but he did not produce any further development of his work.

In the past fifty years many-valued logic has become an important branch of logic. The literature on it is very extensive indeed, covering not only developments of the Lukasiewiczian systems by logicians of the Polish school (such as Mordchaj Wajsberg, Jerzy Slupecki, Alfred Tarski, Boleslaw Sobocinsk) but also fundamentally new systems such as those of D. A. Bochvar, Stephen C. Kleene, Kurt Gödel and Hans Reichenbach. A good deal of attention has been given to the special operators in many-valued logic above all to its negator (which is not governed by a *tertium non datur* principle); also to adapting quantification theory to it and to systematizing is both on an axiomatic and on a natural-deduction basis. It has been used to formalize modal logic, to provide a logical groundwork for mathematical intuitionism (which does not accept the *tertium non datur* principle), to analyse paradoxes and to formalize probabiltiy theory.

Of course it has remained associated with philosophical questions about future contingent events, and recent literature has provided 'tense logics' (from e.g. A.N. Prior) i.e. logical systems in which tense plays an important part in determining the truth-value of propositions. In Physics, Quantum theory has presented its need for a logic of indeterminancy and three-valued logic has been applied to this context of indeterminancy situations. Very concretely, many valued logics are used for the formal analysis of electronic circuitry and for the formalization of swithcing theory.

Nicholas Rescher points out: 'Many-valued logic is a very new subject whose original development in effect goes back only a single generation...It is built up by a great mass of often rather isolated findings resulting from the work of a diverse group of contributors approaching the subject from many different directions. All this makes the task of integration...a particularly urgent one.' (*Many-Valued Logic,* p. 15)

Basic observations about values, operators, proofs and theorems in many valued systems. *Values.* In standard logic the calculation of the truth-value of propositions is a central operation; in the calculi it uses, the range of values assignable to propositional variables is restricted to two, truth and falsity. Many-valued calculi can have a range of values from three to infinity. It is a matter for metalogic (*infra*) to deal with the logical significance of such calculi, i.e. whether or not they can be an integral part of *logical* evaluation. Certainly many of them have been constructed with a built-in semantical interpretation that links them in some way to a general enquiry into truth. Technically, too, many-valued truth-tables, very useful for showing that some formula is not derivable from certain axioms, are used in independence proofs (one axiom being 'independent' of the rest when it cannot be derived from them) and in consistency proofs (its is not the case that every formula is a theorem, *p* and not *p*).

A many-valued system is said to be *normal* when the 'matrices of two-valued logic extend into it, i.e. for all 0, 1 combinations of values (or the symbolic equivalent) the matrices are the same. The simple three-valued system constructed by Lukasiewicz in 1917 is an extension of the *C–N* tables in two valued logic. Its primitive symbols are *C*, *N*; all other expressions can be reduced to *C–N* type ones and can be evaluated by the matrix tables for *C* and *N*. The tables are as follows (1, ½, 0, symbolizing the three values possible):

p	*q*	*Cpq*
1	1	1
1	½	½
1	0	o
½	1	1
½	½	1
½	0	½
0	1	1
0	½	1
0	0	1

p	*Np*
1	0
½	½
0	1

Lukasiewicz justifies the extra evaluations made as being 'very intuitive'. Since the extremes *C 0* 1 and *C* 0 0 have the value 1, it is evident that the intermediate *C 0* ½ should be given the same value; as long as *q* is not less in value than *p* (as happens in *C* 1 0) the table gives *Cpq* the value 1—thus *C* ½ 1 and *C* ½ ½ = 1; finally *C* 1 ½ and *C* ½ 0 are given the intermediate value ½ between the extremes *C* 1 0 and *C* 0 0. In the *N* table, *N* ½ has also an intermediate value.

The tables for *C* and *N* constitute a matrix. All expressions in Lukasiewicz's system can be reduced to a *C–N* form and can be evaluated by applying these tables. Thus *Apq* is defined as *CCpqq* and *Kpq* is reduced to *NANpNa.* In 1931, Lukasiewicz's student, Mordchaj Wajsberg, axiomatized the system on the basis of the following axioms:

CpCqp
CCpqCCqrCpr
CCNpNqCqp
CCCpNppp

While every sentence of this three-valued logic is also a sentence of two-valued logic, the converse does not hold. Indeed neither *ApNp* (the law of excluded middle) nor *NKpNp* (the law of contradiction) have the value 1: both are evaluated ½, and thus three-valued logic lacks a law of excluded middle and a law of contradiction. However, no laws of two-valued logic have ever the value 0 in the Lukasiewicz system and many have the value 1. In summary, this three-valued logic is a proper part of two-valued logic: internally consistent and distinct its theses are contained within the other simpler and more extensive logic.

In two-valued logic we are primarily interested in wff's which always have the value 1 no matter what values are assigned to the variables. The set of such wff's is called the *designoted* set (1 being the designated value). In many-valued logics, where 0 and 1 are the value limits, 1 is frequently taken as the designated value (and the term, *designated value,* takes on the force of truth-like value). Accordingly, the designated set of wff's contains those wff's which have the value 1 for any and every value assigned to the variables. Since the range of values is greater than two, it follows that while all theorems of many-valued logic are theorems of two-valued logic (they preserve the value 1 over a greater range of values for the variables) the converse does not hold (what holds wihin a framework of two values for the variables may not hold in a framework of many values). Thus many-valued systems assess fewer arguments as correct than do two-valued ones. This makes it worth while to entertain the possibility that these systems may provide a better grammar of correctness of argument than a two-valued one with its paradoxes of material implication.

It is interesting to note that Stanislaw Jaskowski devised

a technique for extending any n-valued logic into an (n + 1)-valued one. He also devised a way of forming a new many-valued system from any two other systems that have more than one value—the Cartesian product of the two.

The family of Lukasiewicz—Tarski calculi have a good variety of formal systems with {1} as designated set.

Operators: in standard calculi one has basic operators and later one introduces other operators defining the latter in terms of the former. Thus in the *C–N* calculus one introduces *A* and *K* through the definitions

$$Apq = \text{Df. } CNpq$$
$$Kpq = \text{Df. } NCpNq$$

These definitions would not be suitable for introducing *A* and *K* into a *C–N* calculus that was many-valued as the properties of *A* and *K* which are provable in the two-valued calculus cannot be totally preserved in the many-valued one. Thus we must choose and stipulate, from the sum of requirements which 'disjunction' and 'conjunction' meet in standard logic; otherwise our many-valued operators will have no relevance at all to disjunction and conjunction. In Lukasiewiczian systems it is customary to retain the intuitive properties that the value of a disjunction be the maximum value of its disjuncts ($A\ 10 = 1$) and the value of a conjunction should be the minimum value of its conjuncts ($K\ 10 = 0$). Suitable definitions for this purpose are:

$$Apq = \text{Df. } CCpqq$$
$$Kpq = \text{Df. } NANpNq$$

Thus we see there is room for variety of definition in introducing many valued operators that are analogues of two-valued ones.

The negation operator is particularly interesting. In two-valued logic where a designated wff has the value 1 and an undesignated wff has the value 0, the negation of a designated wff is an undesignated wff and vice versa. Taking L_3 (Lukasiewicz's simple three-valued system) we notice that while the negation of a designated (1) wff is undesignated (0), the converse does not hold: ½ is also an undesignated value and the value of *Np* where $p = ½$ is itself ½. Thus this three-valued analogue does not meet the stringent requirements of two-valued *N*. In order to have a negative function, *p*, which would reverse the designated or undesignated value of *p*, Rosser and Turquette introduced *J*-functions. Taking two-valued negation as primitive, one can introduce the *J*-functions defining them in terms of it and *C* and then introduce the new negative function defining it in terms of *J*-functions.

Thus in many-valued logic, various types of negation are possible according to the kind and number of properties we choose to stipulate. In his systems, Post stipulates for the negator that it make a cyclic shift in the values as the following table shows:

p	not-*p*
1	2
2	3
3	4
.	.
.	.
$m-2$	$m-1$
$m-1$	m
m	1

This of course is a radical departure from standard negation.

It is evident that the number of functors possioble is considerably greater than in two-valued logic. The number of *n*-adic truth functors in a logic of *m* values is ${}^{n}m^{m}$. Thus while only 4 monadic functors are possible in a two-value logic, 27 are possible in a three-valued one and 256 in a four-valued one; the respective figures for dyadic functors are very disparate: 16; 19,683; and 4,294,967,296. In spite of this kind of complexity Lukasiewicz and others have studied infinitely-valued logic which admits an infinity of values instead of just three or four.

Quantification may also feature of course in many-valued systems.

Proof: In two-value logic, the rule of inference, ***modus ponens,*** is central in proof and meets the two following conditions:

(1) Whenever p has the value *1 and* Cpq has the value 1 then q has the value 1;

(2) Whenever p and *Cpq* are tautologies, q is a tautology. In many-valued logic the second condition may be met in circumstances in which the first condition is not met. (In Lukasiewicz's three-valued system, if 1 and ½ are both designated values then *C*½0 has the designated value ½ even though q has the value 0.) Thus *modus ponens* is defined precisely there as a rule of inference governing a movement from tautologies to tautology. Of course the fact that it guarantees the tautologous nature of a conclusion that is derived, by it, from tautologies justifies it as a genuine rule of inference.

Again, turning from the axiomatic approach to that of natural deduction, one finds that not all of the primitive logical argument forms hold in a many-valued framework. For instance, due to the fact that *CCpCpqCpq* is not a theorem in Lukasiewicz's three-value system, we cannot use the argument form: If $p \mid - q$ then $\mid - Cpq$.

Theorems: It is clear that the Principle of Bivalence (the *tertium non datur* principle) cannot be a theorem in many-valued logic. Other versions of the Law of Excluded Middle may be preserved at will, however, as may various possible versions of the Law of Contradiction. The literature includes much precise discussion on possible formulations of these laws.

Examples of theorems in two-valued logic which do not hold in Lukasiewicz's simple three-valued system are:

CCNppp
CCpNpNp
CCpqCCpNqNp
CCpKqNqNp
CCpEqNqNp

Theorems may be characterized as such on the basis of truth-table procedure (this is called the matrix-characterization of theorems), or on the basis of being derived either axiomatically or by natural deduction. While the theorems of modal calculi are usually derived by the axiomatic method, those of many-valued calculi are more usually developed by the use of matrix truth-tables. Wajsberg has shown that the systems of Lukasiewicz are finitely axiomatizable, and very elegant axiomatic systems have been constructed. Completeness proofs have been provided by Wajsberg and by Rosser-Turquette.

The main systems of many-valued logic. Nicholas Rescher's book *Many-Valued Logic* provides an excellent survey of these systems and of the literature that has grown up about them. They are:

(a) *The Lukasiewiczian family*

This includes both finite and infinite systems. There are also systems which are radically different from this family and yet are generalizations of Lukasiewicz's three-valued system.

(b) *The three-valued system of Bochnar*

This was published by the Russian logician, D.A. Bochnar in 1939, and interprets the third value as 'undecidable' (because of being paradoxical or meaningless). Some infinitely-valued systems are based on the guiding principles of this system.

(c) *The three-valued systems of Kleene*

S.C. Kleene's work was published in 1938. His approach is similar to Bochvar's as he interprets the third value in a knowledge-related way as denoting the unknown.

(d) *Other three-valued systems*

These include Reichenbach's Quantum Logic (1946); Slupecki's system (1946) completely axiomatized and with a proof of its truth-functional completeness; Sobocinski's system (1952) also axiomatized.

(e) *The Gödelian family of many-valued systems*

These were the work of Kurt Gödel (published in 1932).

(f) *'Standard system' of many-valued logic*

These seek to generalize into a many-valued framework a sequence of rules derived from orthodox two-valued logic. They may be symbolized S_3, S_4...S_n (n indicating the number of values involved).

(g) *The Postian family of many-valued systems*

These were the work of Emil L. Post (1921).

(h) *Stanislaw Jaskowski's systems*

These include systems based on his technique for extending any given *n*-valued logic into an (n + 1)- valued logic, and those based on his method of forming the product of two pluri-valued systems (1936).

(i) *Boolean systems*

These product systems are due mainly to Church (1953) and are based on an *alternative possible worlds* approach with propositions having truth-values with respect to each world

(j) *Quasi-truth-functional systems*

These systems need not have a single value entry in each place: they permit in any place an alternative indicating entry, e.g. '*T*, *F*' meaning: 'the truth-value at issue here may be *T* or it may be *F*'.

(k) *Probability logic*

This is a non-truth functional approach assigning likelihood values or probabilities to statements. The development of such systems was begu in the 1930s by Hans Reichenbach and

Zygmunt Zawirski. Values are symbolized by the real numbers from 0 to 1 inclusive; it is stipulated that 1 is a designated value thus ensuring the incorporation into the system of the tautologies of two-valued propositional logic. Further designation is left open.

Chapter-13

Arguments

Chapter 13

We have seen roughly what makes arguments good or bad. We must improve on that.We must also consider how we can tell whether any particular argument is god or bad. This is no easy matter. Most people are competent to tell whether fairly simple arguments are acceptable, but, perhaps surprisingly, there does not seem to be anything that deserves to be called a *method* behind that skill. That is, if you ask people whether simple arguments such as those used in the previous chapter are good, they can usually give the correct answer without much difficulty. I depended on that when I asked you to decide whether those arguments were good. However, if you ask people how they arrived at their answer, the chances are that they would be at a loss to say. The main business of this chapter will be look more deeply into the nature of arguments. The ultimate goal (realized in the next chapter) will be to draw up a strategy for *testing* whether any argument is good or bad. But first things first.What precisely is a good argument and how is it different from a bad one?

VALIDITY

Two things were said about what makes an argument good:

(a) if its premises are true; then its conclusion is bound to be true:

(b) it is suitable as a means of persuading someone of the truth of its conclusion.

Let us concentrate first on (a).An argument which is good in this sense will be called *valid.*In order to see precisely what makes an argument valid we have to look more deeply into the form of words used in (a).

What does it mean to say that the conclusion of an argument is *bound to be true.* When its premises are true?

Below is a particularly clear way of putting the thought.

An argument is valid when

(P) it is *not possible* that the premises of the argument are true and the conclusion is false.

In spite of its apparent simplicity. (p) can give rise to misunderstandings. To prevent this, it is best if we see how (p) is applied to specific examples.

Examples 1

(1) All oak trees have roots.
(2) All the trees that grow in England have roots.

Some oak trees grow in England.

Is this a valid argument? One's immediate reaction is to deny that it is–to say that it is *invalid.* But we have to try to understand why. We begin by seeing whether the premises and conclusion of the argument are in fact, true.

It doesn't require a great deal of knowledge of botany and geography to see that they are indeed all true. However, (P) requires that, for an argument to be valid, it is not *possible* for the premises to be true and the conclusion false. Merely knowing that the premises and conclusion are *actually* true does not tell us that. What is required is some thought about the possibilities in this case.

The world is such that all oak trees have roots, all trees that grow in England have roots, and some oak trees grow in England. That much we know. But the world could have been different. It could have been the case that the world was created in such a way that all oak trees have roots and all the trees that grow in England have roots, but that there were no oak trees in England. Things are not that way but *it is possible for them to have been that way.* That is, it is possible for the world to be such that the premises are true and the conclusion of the argument is false. It is this possibility which makes Example 1 invalid, even though its premises and conclusion are actually true.

Many people have very little patience with mere possibilities. Why, they would ask, do we bother with the possibility that the world might have been created with an England devoid of oak trees? England does have oak trees, so that's that.

The reply to this goes right back to our original discussion of arguments in chapter 1. An argument is a particular way in which our thoughts move. If it is a good argument, then it can be justified. What better way could there be of justifying it than by showing that it could not happen that its premises are true and its conclusion false? And here talk of what 'could be' the case is talk of possibilities. If an argument has the sort of goodness we have called *validity,* it offers a guarantee that the conclusion is true if the premises are. This is a very good reason for being interested in the sort of possibility we need for validity.

Example 2

(1) Oak trees grow only in places where it rains with some degree of regularity.

(2) It does not rain in the Sahara with any degree of regularity.

Oak trees do not grow in the Sahara.

By now you should anticipate the inevitable questions: are the premises and conclusion true? Is the argument valid? Interestingly,in this case, the answer to both quetions is 'Yes'. Here we have a case where an argument is valid and has true premises and conclusion. It is not possible for (1) and (2) to be true and the conclusion false, *and*, as a matter of fact, all three thoughts are true.

Is it the truth values of the premises and conclusion which leads you the say that this is a valid argument? Of course not ! Remember, Example 1 had true premises and conclusion. In that respect, it is just like Example 2. Nonetheless, Example 1 is invalid and Example 2 is valid.This difference between them does not turn on the actual truth or falsity of their premises and conclusions, but on certain possibilities. What is important is not that the premises and conclusion of Example 2 are actually true, but that it is not possible for its premises to be true and its conclusion false. It is this fact about possibility which leads us to say that Example 2 is valid.

How does one decide these possibilities? This question will occupy us more fully in the next chapter. There we will begin to work out a strategy for enabling us to tell whether any given argument is valid. Our present concern is more with what it means to say that an argument is valid than with working out means of telling whether this is so. For that reason, I have chosen examples which you can easily classify as valid or invalid.

Example 3

(1) All fish swim.

(2) All whales swim.

All whales are fish.

The premises of this argument are true and its conclusion is false, so we do not have to look deeply into possibilities to tell that it is invalid. Validity requires that it not be possible for the premises to be true and the conclusion false. Since the premises are actually true and the conclusion false, we know straightaway that the argument is invalid. After all, what is actually the case surely counts as a possibility.

However, you should be careful here. In most cases, we have to think about non-actual possibilities in order to tell whether an argument is valid. Here, it suffices to know the actual truth values of the premises and conclusion. In this respect, Example 3 seems to contrast with Example 1 and 2, but do not let this mislead you. The invalidity of Example 3 is as much connected with possibility as, for instance, Example 1. It is just that, as I noted above, the way things actually are counts as a way things could be, as a possibility.

Example 4

(1) The Earth is either round or not round.

(2) If the Earth is round, then many things would just fall off it.

(3) Things do not just fall off the Earth.

The Earth is not round.

This is a valid argument, but its conclusion is certainly false. How can this happen? Validity requires that it not be possible for the premises to be true and the conclusion false. It does not require that the premises and conclusion actually be true. In this case, since the conclusion is false and the argument is valid, at least one of the premises must be false. The culprit is quite clearly premise (2).

If you followed the Examples you should understand the relationship between validity, possibility and truth. We now turn to consider an interesting feature of validity.

VALIDITY AND TRUE THOUGHTS

In order to tell whether an argument is valid, you do not have to know whether the premises and conclusion of the argument are true. It isn't even required that they be true, whether or not you know it. Of course, if you happen to know that the premises are true and the conclusion is false, then you know the argument is invalid. But, this is a special case—one in which the counter-example is actual. Validity turns on what is possibly the case rather than what is actually the case, but in saying this we are not ruling out the actual. What is actually the case counts as one of the possibilities. All of this is familiar from our previous discussion. What I want to point out here is something about the relationship between truth and validity which is both puzzling and important.

Our thoughts are true, when they are, in virtue of their subject matter. If I think that trees have roots, then my thought is true because of 'how it is' with trees. It would be useful if my thoughts could be made true merely in virtue of my thinking them, but this just isn't so. In order to tell whether a thought is true, I have to go and see whether the world is as it is held to be by my thought. Or so it would seem. Let's look more closely at validity.

Here is an example of an argument that was used in the earlier discussion of validity.

(1) Oak trees only grow in places where it rains with some degree of regularity.

(2) It does not rain in the Sahara with any degree of regularity.

Oak trees do not grow in the Sahara.

In that earlier discussion, I asked you to examine the argument and say whether it was valid. I had very little doubt that you could see that it was, even though you as yet have not been taught any procedures for testing validity. Try to remember what your examination of this argument involved. Did you have to ask yourself whether each of the premises and conclusion were true? Did you have to consult encyclopedias or try to imagine what the Sahara is like? Certainly not. Very likely it was a matter of just reading through the argument and seeing how it struck you. Notice that in doing this, you were in effect examining the thoughts in the argument; you were not consulting the world to see whether the thoughts were true of it.

However, in so far as the argument did strike you as valid, your inspection showed you that

Oak trees do not grow in the Sahara

could be checked for being true by checking the truth of

Oak trees only grow where it rains with some degree of regularity

AND

It doesn't rain in the Sahara with any degree of regularity.

This is because, since the argument is valid, the truth of the conclusion is a necessary consequence of the truth of the two premises. But this is really quite amazing. The standard way of checking whether oak trees grow somewhere is by looking in that place for oak trees. The existence of the above valid argument gives us a different way of checking: just do whatever looking is needed to tell whether the premises are true. It is surprising that, by examining the argumentative relationship between certain thoughts, we can come up with ways of checking the truth of some thought in other than the standard way. That is, we can check the truth of the conclusion of a valid argument by checking the truth of its premises.

How can this happen? That very deep question is certainly beyond the scope of this chapter, and is one for which there is nothing like an agreed answer. This is a question for discussion in the branch of philosophy called the 'philosophy of logic'.I have raised it to give you both some idea of the importance of the notion of validity and an inkling of the deeper issues that lie behind this notion.

VALIDITY AND OTHER-THAN-TRUE THOUGHTS

I said earlier that the definition of validity raised two issues. It is time to consider the second of them. Here is an argument:

(1) If you go out, you'll get wet.

(2) You do not want to get wet.

Do not go out !

Is it valid? Be careful here. There is certainly something natural about this progression of thoughts. (1) and (2) seem to offer a very good *reason* for the conclusion. Nonetheless, given our definition of validity, we cannot really say that this argument is either valid or invalid. To see why, remind yourself what validity is, and take a closer look at the conclusion.

To say that an argument is valid is to say that it is not

possible for the premises to be true and the conclusion false. The trouble is that the conclusion of this argument isn't the sort of thought that is either true or false. I would expect you to be puzzled if someone were to ask you if the advice

do not go out

were true. As advice, it could be described as 'useful' but not as 'true', or 'unhelpful' but not as 'false'. Because of this, the notion of validity simply doesn't apply to the above argument. Here we have hit on a feature of our understanding of validity which makes it somewhat restrictive. *An argument is a candidate for validity only if its premises and conclusion are the sort of thing which it makes sense to describe using the words 'true' and 'false'.* The following are a few examples of thoughts that might figure in arguments but which would not be described using these words:

Where shall I go on holiday?
Pass the sugar!
Would that I were happy.

Many people dislike restrictions. Why not define validity so that it does not impose this restriction on possible premises and conclusions of valid arguments? The short answer is that it is very difficult to see how to go about it. The long answer – and it is the one I prefer – comes roughly to this. By defining validity the way we have, we end up with a clear notion which can be studied further. When we are able to understand arguments valid in this sense. We will be better placed to understand more general forms of argument. In other words, our definition of validity is best viewed not so much as restrictive, but as a way of not biting off more than we can chew.

ARGUMENTS AND PERSUASION

Being valid is one way in which an argument could be said to be good. We are now ready to consider the other way. Here is the formulation given earlier:

An argument is good when it is suitable as a means of persuading someone of the truth of its conclusion.

It doesn't take much of an argument to convince some people of things they are predisposed to believe, and we can hardly allow gullibility to feature in our understanding of what makes an argument good. It might help a bit if we changed 'someone' to 'anyone', but the benefit would be very limited. On the one hand, it might be the case that some form of argument *seemed* convincing to all of us, even though it was defective. On the other hand, we would hardly want to reject an argument as good simply because some exceedingly stubborn individual refused to be convinced by it.

The first of these possibilities can be illustrated by an analogy. Suppose we defined two lines to be of equal length just in case everyone would perceive that they were. Are the *horizontal* lines in the drawing below of equal length?

I have no doubt that you perceive them as unequal. So do I, even though I know, and perhaps you do too, that they are equal. It seems to be a fact about our perceptual system that it unavoidably misleads us about these lines. But, is it really a mistake? It wouldn't be if we stuck to the definition of equal

length proposed above, and this shows that there is something wrong with the definition. The same could be the case about the convincingness of arguments. There might be an argument which convinced everyone who came across it, even though it might be one which we came to think of as a bad argument. However, if we *defined* a good argument as one which convinced everyone, then we would have defined out of existence the very real possibility that we could be systematically mistaken. This won't do.

One thing we might do is revise our definition of a good argument so it read:

> An argument is good just in case it could be used to persuade any rational thinker of the truth of its conclusion.

This certainly avoids all the problems raised above. We can stipulate that a rational thinker is one who is not gullible, not prone to systematic errors, and not given to insupportable stubbornness.The trouble with this new definition is that, while it is correct, it isn't very helpful. We are trying to understand what connection there is between goodness and persuasiveness in arguments. Introducing the rational thinker helps only if we can say what such a thinker would be like. Saying that a rational thinker is one who is persuaded only by good arguments is true, but is doesn't tell us what makes an argument good.

Why not use 'good argument' in the sense described earlier? We would expect a rational thinker to be one who wouldn't allow himself to be persuaded by any but valid arguments. So, why not equate persuasiveness with validity? If this were accepted, we would have shown that the two senses of 'good argument' come to pretty much the same.

We certainly do not want to allow that the rational thinker can be persuaded by an invalid argument: a thinker would not be rational if he could be convinced of the truth of a conclusion by an invalid argument. However, we cannot directly define a convincing argument as one which is valid because there are many cases in which it would not be at all rational to accept as true the conclusion of an valid argument. Here is one:

(1) Unicorns have been depicted in tapestries.

(2) If something has been depicted, then that thing exists.

Unicorns exist.

Remember that a valid argument might very well have false premises and a false conclusion. The conclusion of this argument is almost certainly false and, since it is valid, it must have at least one false premise–in this case, premise (2). It would hardly do for a rational thinker to be convinced that there are Unicorns by this valid argument. Here is another example:

(1) There has never been an authenticated sighting of a Unicorn.

(2) Unless something has been authentically sighted, it doesn't exist.

Unicorns do not exist.

If you accepted that the conclusion of the previous argument was false, then you certainly accept that the conclusion of this argument is true. However, even though it is true and the argument is valid, it would not be rational to accept it on the basis of this argument. Premise (2) here is certainly false; there are any number of things of which no one yet had an authenticated sighting, but which nonetheless exist.

These examples simply reiterate the point made earlier: validity is a way of guaranteeing that the conclusion is true *if the premises are.* It is in no way a guarantee that either the conclusion or the premises are actually true. If an argument is to convince the rational thinker then we want that argument to have features in addition to validity.

PERSUASION AND TRUTH

Why not take the hint of these examples and define an argument as good just in case it is valid *and* has premises that are actually true? Surely, this would do the trick since these two properties together guarantee that the conclusion is actually true. Even this, though, will not do.

An argument that is valid and has true premises is called *sound.* This is a very important combination of features for an argument, and it is to be aimed at in our thinking. A sound argument, as opposed to a merely valid one, is certainly closer to what is intended when we think of an argument as persuasive. However, ask yourself is the following valid? Sound?

Persuasive?

(1) Money cannot guarantee happiness.

Money cannot guarantee happiness.

This argument is certainly valid. How could it fail to be, since the premise and conclusion are one and the same? Also, in so far as you accept the received wisdom of the premise, you will regard it as sound. (If you dissent from this, then it is easy to see how to construct your own example.) Finally, is it persuasive? Would it be a good way to convince a rational thinker that money cannot guarantee happiness? Obviously, not. Of course, if the person to whom you addressed the argument agreed that it was sound, he would thereby be accepting the truth of the conclusion. But, since the conclusion and the premise are the same, the acceptance could hardly be seen as the result of the *argument.* A rational thinker will require that a conclusion be supported by a valid argument with true premises, but he will also require that the premises be sufficiently different from the conclusion. That is, the premises must be distinct enough from the conclusion for us to see the movement from premises to conclusion as a genuine movement of thought.

This is admittedly very vague, but it is not easy to improve on it. It might be tempting to require that an argument is persuasive only if the conclusion is not already contained in the premises. This is a little less vague but it gets us into a different sort of trouble. There is a sense in which the conclusion of any valid argument is 'contained' in the premises. At this stage of discussion, I do not expect you to fully understand this; we are at this point getting into very deep philosophical waters. However, compare the above unconvincing argument with this one:

(1) Happiness requires self-fulfilment.

(2) Money cannot guarantee self-fulfilment.

Money cannot guarantee happiness.

This argument is valid and is, I think, sound. It is also plausible to see it as persuasive. Yet, there is a clear sense in which (1) and (2) already contain the conclusion; embracing these premises is embracing the conclusion, or it certainly would be for an ideally rational thinker. Saying this seems no more than syaing that the argument is valid.

There is a tension between requiring that a convincing argument is valid, and requiring that its conclusion is other than a repetition of the premises. Validity seems to demand that the conclusion not stray too far from the premises. While persuasiveness demands that it be some distance away.

THE SUBJECT MATTER OF LOGIC RECONSIDERED

Our discussion of good and bad arguments has uncovered three possible distinctions. Arguments can be:

(i) Valid or invalid,
(ii) sound or unsound,
(iii) persuasive or unpersuasive.

The study of logic in this book is the study of (i). The reason for the restriction follows.

In order for an argument to be either persuasive (to a rational thinker) or sound, it must at least be valid. This certainly gives us the best possible reason for studying validity. Additionally, there are grounds for thinking that our study cannot sensibly go beyond the study of validity.

We never did discover any criterion for distinguishing persuasive from unpersuasive arguments, but that by itselt is no reason for abandoning the search. What is more to the point are the difficulties with the notion of soundness. Persuasive arguments have to be sound whatever else they are. Remember, we discussed persuasiveness in connection with the ideal of the rational thinker, and such a thinker could only be persuaded by arguments which were at least sound. A sound argument is defined as a valid argument which has true premises. The study of soundness is therefore clearer than the study of persuasiveness, but it has one very great disadvantage. To decide whether an argument is sound, we have to decide whether the premises are true. Since premises can be about anything that we happen to be thinking of, the study of soundness would be the study of every subject matter—and even that would not be enough. After all, there are no doubt many truths which are at present unknown to us. There may even be truths we will never know. All of this means that the study of soundness within the bounds of one book is simply not a real option.

Validity can be investigated without our having to bother unduly as to whether any given specific thought is true. This is just as well since logicians can lay no claim to being omniscient.

The Main Points of Chapter 13

(1) Arguments can be *valid, sound* or *persuasive.* These are three related sorts of goodness in arguments.

(2) An argument is valid just in case it meets the following condition:

> it is necessarily the case that if the premises are all true, then so is the conclusion.

This condition is equivalent to one that can be stated using the notion of possibility:

> it is not possible for all the premises of the argument to be true and the conclusion false.

(3) The following two important observations about validity were made:

(i) A valid argument for a conclusion provides a way of telling whether the conclusion is true which can differ from the usual direct way, Normally, we tell whether a thought is true by comparing it with how things are in the world. However, if the thought is the conclusion of a valid argument. We can determine its truth by finding out whether the premises of the argument are true.

(ii) Validity as defined only applies to arguments whose premises and conclusions are thoughts that can be true or false.

(4) An argument is sound just in case it is *both* valid *and* its premises are all true. Given this, it is clear that sound arguments are more likely to be persuasive than merely valid ones.

(5) It is very difficult to spell out just what is required of an argument if it is to be persuasive. Part of the trouble is that it is unclear *who* is the intended object of the persuasion. Also, there seemed to be no way to spell out what features, in addition to soundness, are needed for persuasiveness.

(6) The subject matter of the remainder of the book is the validity of deductive arguments.

Chapter-14
Strategy

Chapter 14

Our thoughts sometimes move in ways that are describable as deductive arguments. Among other things, such arguments can be either valid or invalid. The discussion in the last chapter provided an account of these notions. Given these elements, we now have to plan a strategy for working out whether any given argument is valid.

This is not to say that you now lack all ability to tell whether an argument is valid. I depended on your views about typical cases of valid and invalid arguments in my discussion of these notions, and this discussion would not have served its purpose unless you already had some skill in telling whether arguments are valid. Our first task will be to take a closer look at this skill.

VALIDITY IN EVERYDAY LIFE

Below is a sample argument. I want you to say whether it is valid *and* ask yourself how you arrived at your answer.

SAMPLE (1) Cats have backbones.
(2) Most pets have backbones.
―――――――――――
Most pets are cats.

The argument is transparently invalid. What is more interesting is the question of how we come to know this. There seem to be two ways in which we manage the task. One can be called *Visualizing,* and the other *Analogizing*.

NOTE There is considerable interest among psychologists in the question of how we actually decide that cert ain arguments are valid. For more on this see the Rea ding List. My remarks are, in effect, an attempt to spell out ways which seem plausible candidates for explaining how we perform this task. I think that you will recognize some of your own thinking in these ways, but I do not claim that we always use them—that they fully characterize the actual working of the human mind. Nor would you expect me to be able to do this without detailed experimental investigation.

Visualizing

The Visualizing method works like this: you imagine what it would be like for the premises of an argument to be true and, at the same time, you try to imagine that the conclusion is false. Applied to the above argument, the method might come out as follows.

I picture cats as having backbones. This is easy since they do have backbones.I next picture various pets—goldfish. dogs, cats, etc.as having backbones and I try not to picture too many pets as lacking backbones. This is also fairly easy since it is likely that most pets do have backbones. The truth is often, but not always, easier to picture. Finally, I picture cats as very rare pets. They are, of course, not rare at all, but I find that I can picture them this way without upsetting my previous efforts to picture the premises of the argument. It is this that convinces me that the argument is invalid—that the premises can be true and the conclusion false.

The method is called 'Visualizing' and I used the word 'picturing' in applying it, but it is not strictly and literally visual. It is more a method based on our sensitivity to possibilities. My justification for the use of the visual metaphor is that such words as 'see' and 'picture' are not solely visual: I can *see* a reason no less than a landscape.

Analogizing

When required to say why they think the SAMPLE argument is invalid, many people are apt to say something like this: if the SAMPLE argument were valid, then I could just as well argue in the following way.

(1) People have fathers.

(2) Most frogs have fathers.

Most frogs are people.

But, it is as plain as can be that the premises of this argument are true and its conclusion is false, it is blatantly invalid. Since the argument about frogs is just like the argument about cats, the invalidity of the frog argument shows the invalidity of the original one.

NOTE By the way, not all frogs have fathers. Consult a zoology text for confirmation of this—look under 'parthe- nogenesis'. I mention this because some people may think that if all frogs have fathers, the (2) is false. I think that they would be wrong, but there is no need to argue about it here, given the biological facts.

Crucial to this procedure is the idea of certain arguments being *just like* or *analogous* to one another. For anyone who is excessively literal-minded, the argument about cats is not just like the one about frogs. After all, one is about cats and the other is about frogs. However, I suspect that most of us would understand what is meant by the claim that the two arguments are alike, and would agree. What the arguments share is not a content, but a *form* or *structure.* Implicit in Analogizing is the idea that what makes the above arguments invalid is that are of the same structure, and that this structure is in some way defective.

We can spell out what goes on in Analogizing as follows. First, a structure for the argument is isolated. In the SAMPLE argument case, this structure can be displayed as follows:

(1) As have Bs.
(2) Most Cs have Bs.

Most Cs are As.

Next, there is a search for an argument which has just this structure, but which has true premises and a clearly false conclusion. This is where the argument about frogs came in. It is analogous in structure to the SAMPLE argument, but it doesn't require any effort to see that its premises are true and its conclusion is false.

Comparison

Visualizing and Analogizing are alike in two important respects.First, imagination plays a key role in their operation; and second, validity is demonstrated in both of them by a certain sort of failure. Let me expand on these points.

In Visualizing, you keep fixed the thoughts expressed by the premises and conclusion, while you use your imagination to vary the way the world is, to think of it as how it might have been. If this exercise of the imagination convinces you that the world could have been such as to make the premises true and the conclusion false, you will judge the argument invalid. The world in which the premises are true and the conclusion false constitutes a *counter-example* to the argument.

In Analogizing, you do not keep the thoughts expressed by the premises and conclusion fixed, but you do keep fixed a structure which you discern in those thoughts. You then exercise your imagination in a search for an argument which shares that structure, but whose premises are true and conclusion false. If this search is successful, then you have found in the new argument a counter-example to the original one.

In both cases, the judgement that an argument is *valid* depends upon a *failure* to find a counter-example. This is a weakness of everyday methods which I will discuss shortly.Before that, I want to highlight a difference between the two methods.

The method of Visualizing comes directly from the definition of validity. An argument is valid when it is not possible for its premises to be true and its conclusion false. Visualizing is the exercise of imagination to see whether this is so of particular arguments. In contrast, the method of Analogy introduces a new and important idea--structure.

It seems obvious that the arguments we have discussed so far in the book have structure—logical structure—and that their validity (or invalidity) is closely tied to this. What could be more natural than the way in which the SAMPLE argument was shown to have a logical structure that rendered it invalid? Yet, there is no mention of logical structure in the definition of validity itself. The definition speaks only of possibility and truth.

We have here the beginnings of what will grow into the governing idea of this book. It can be expressed as follows: one way to tell whether an argument is valid is to discern in it a logical structure which can then be assessed. The method of Analogy works by employing imagination in this assessment, and this has many disadvantages. It shares these disadvantages with the method of Visualizing. Nonetheless, once we have discussed the failings of both everyday methods, the way will be clear to explore the connection between logical structure and validity. The aim will be to develop a method for isolating and assessing logical structure which does not suffer from the disadvantages imposed by our reliance on imagination.

NOT GOOD ENOUGH?

Some of you might be thinking:if what he calls Visualizing and Analogizing have served us in our assessment of arguments up to this point in our lives, why do we need to acquire further ways of assessing arguments? This seems to me a question worth answering. In fact, it seems worth two different answers.

The first answer comes roughly to this: everyday methods have practical and theoretical limitations which the methods of logic overcome. The second answer will have to wait until the next section. You will be better placed to understand it when you have considered the first answer in more detail.

Practical Limitations

Everyday methods are limited by these three facts.

(i) Our memories are very limited.
(ii) We sometimes lack imagination.
(iii) Structure is sometimes hard to discern.

All three merit discussion.

(i) Visualizing requires memory: you have to see each premise as true, and keep that in mind, while imagining the conclusion is false. An argument with a number of premises, and/or complex premises, is going to exhaust most people's memory capacity. Here is a fairly simple argument—as arguments go. Can you decide its validity by Visualizing? By any method you now know?

(1) If unemployment keeps on increasing and investment declines, then interest rates will go up.
(2) Either productivity will go down or unemployment will keep on increasing.
(3) If interest rates go up, then investment will decline.
(4) Productivity will go down unless investment increases.

If investment declines, then unemployment will keep on increasing.

I suspect that by the time you got to premise (3) you had already lost your grip on (1) and (2): it is very difficult to picture simultaneously such thoughts as true.The problem is one of memory.

Does Analogizing fare any better? I won't try to guess what sort of device you might use to describe a structure for this argument. I will simply assume that you have worked out that structure for yourself. However, even if you have managed to do this satisfactorily, you still face the formidable task of searching for an argument with the same structure, but with true premises and a false conclusion. The burden which this places on your memory is no less prodigious than it was for Visualizing.

(ii) Not everyone is blessed with a powerful imagination. Even if you had unlimited memory, if you lacked the requisitie imagination, you would be unable to assess many arguments for validity using the everyday methods. This is obviously true for Visualizing, but it applies to Analogizing as well. Even after you isolate a logical structure in an argument, you still must use your imagination to search for a counter-example.

(iii) We are all sensitive to the structure of thoughts: the thoughts of others, and arguably our own, are expressed in the medium of language and we are quite good at producing and understanding sentences of our native language. However, it is one thing to understand a sentence as expressing a thought, and another to specify the features of that sentence which are relevant to the validity of an argument. To see this, reconsider the argument about employment given earlier.

Each premise and the conclusion are expressed in sentences of English. Anyone who understands English should have no difficulty in understanding each of these sentences. Yet, it is not always clear which features of these sentences contribute to the structure of the *argument.* In the simpler example,

(1) Cats have backbones.

(2) Most pets have backbones.

Most pets are cats.

it was fairly obvious how to isolate the structure of the argument; that is what makes it a simple example. In more complex cases, it is not obvious. We have all learned ways in which to see structure in sentences.Sentences have words and these can be described by grammatical terms such as 'noun', 'verb', 'adjective', etc. Most of us learned about this when we learned English. However, the sort of structure we need in making decisions about validity is the *logical* structure of whole arguments, and this is not something that is explicit in our linguistic training.

So even if our imagination was up to the task, it is not

always easy to say what the task is. For, our imagination can only provide counter-examples to arguments whose structure we have laid out.

A Theoretical Limitation

Things are even worse. Let us suppose that our memory and imagination are no hindrance, and our ability to discern logical structure is keen. What if the argument we are trying to evaluate is valid? Notice that I never did say whether the longer of the two sample arguments is valid. If it is valid, then no counter-example can be constructed, all your attempts would fail. Yet, can we really think we are justified in moving from

(1) I have not been able to construct a counter-example to

(2) no counter-example can be constructed?

There is a world of difference between failing to construct a counter-example, and knowing that one cannot be constructed.

Of course, we do quite confidently claim that certain arguments are valid. No doubt we are able to do this for these arguments because, having discerned a logical form in them, we are able to assess it directly as one which would never allow the construction of a counter-example. But, this reliance on our intuitions is not much of a method, and is liable to lead us astray in more difficult cases.

DEEPER REASONS

At this point, I have probably said enough to convince you of the severe limitations of everyday methods. By itself, that might be enough to get you interested in the less limited methods offered by logic. Logic would be like a new car which a salesman has talked you into buying by pointing out all the defects of your present car. There are, however, more profound reasons for interest in the methods of logic.

In order to replace the everyday methods we use for testing arguments we will have to develop systematic ways of displaying the logical structures of arguments. When I asked you about this argument:

(i) Cats have backbones.
Most pets have backbones.
———
Most pets are cats.

I depended on your sensitivity to linguistic and logical structure to convince you that such structure could be (partly) revealed in this way:

(ii) As have Bs.
Most Cs have Bs.
———
Most Cs are As.

However, (ii) is only really of use if it engages with a *method* of showing something about the validity of (i). Unless it does so, there can be no reason to think that (ii) does genuinely exhibit the appropriate logical structure of the original argument. The imagination gets to work on the basis of structures such as (ii), but it does not offer any guarantee that (ii) really does give the correct logical structure of (i). Also, any way of revealing logical structure must be general: it must show us logical structure in a whole range of arguments. It was noted earlier that the structural proposals in (ii) do not carry over to more complex arguments such as the one about unemployment. So, what we need is a way of displaying logical structure which is both general and goes hand in hand with a method for deciding whether a given structure is valid.

The interest of such a general way of displaying logical structure goes much deeper than its connection with testing for validity. Understanding the structure of arguments is an ability very closely connected with the ability to understand and use language. The development of methods of logic will give us insights into the nature of language, and through this, into the nature of thought. This is a second, and more important, reason for pursuing logic.

LANGUAGE AND STRUCTURE

Language has figured prominently in our discussion of arguments and validity in two ways:

(1) The thoughts which make up an argument have to be expressed in sentences of a language if the argument is used in a public way, for example to influence someone else. It may also be true that our thoughts are dependent on language, even in cases where we are not making our arguments public. Perhaps there cannot even be thought without language.

(2) Our sensitivity to the structure of arguments which is used to assess validity is something like, and may be part of, our sensitivity to linguistic structure.

Let us consider each of these in a bit more detail.

Sentences and Thoughts

To be confronted by an argument is to be confronted by sentences. (We can rule out telepathy here since even its most enthusiastic supporters do not claim that it can be used to 'transmit' complex arguments.) This means that we need to understand sentences in order to so much as understand what argument is being offered.

The arguments used so far in this book were expressed using sentences chosen for ease of comprehension. Because of this, you may now think that there is no real problem in moving from sentences to the thoughts expressed by them. This would be a mistake. There are many intricacies in our use of language, and these intricacies often make it difficult to tell what is being expressed in a sentence, and how it is related to what is expressed in other sentences. For example, suppose you are told:

(1) if John saw an old friend on his bicycle, he was late for his appointment.

Suppose (1) to be a first premise in a *valid* argument the

conclusion of which is:

(3) John was late for his appointment.

Which of the following thoughts could serve as the second premise in this argument? That is, which of them can be combined with (1) so as to validly lead to (3)?

(2a) John saw his friend Ralph who at 80 was still riding around on his bicycle.
(2b) John saw Michael, his childhood friend, sitting on John's bicycle.
(2c) John saw michael, his childhood friend, ridingJohn's bicycle.
(2d) John saw his 80-year old friend, Alice, riding his bicycle.
(2e) John saw his 80-year old friend, Ralph, sitting on John's bicycle.

All of these *might* justify the drawing of the inference, and this list is only partial. Whether they would actually lead to the conclusion depends on how we are to understand the 'if' part of (1), viz. 'John saw an old friend on his bicycle'. Let me expand on this by considering (2a).

Does the following exhibit a valid argument structure?

(A) (1) If John saw an old friend on his bicycle, he was late for his appointment.

(2a) John saw his friend Ralph who at 80 was still riding around on his bicycle.

---

(3) John was late for his appointment.

Quite clearly, we would count arguments with this structure:

(B) If M then
M

N

as valid. The question is whether we are correct in thinking that (B) gives the structure of (A), and this, in turn, depends on how we are to understand

John saw an old friend on his bicycle

in (1). What (2a)–(2e) show is just how ambiguous this sentence is.

This is an extreme case. Most of the sentences we use are not open to quite so many intepretations. However, (1) illustrates very clearly just how careful one has to be about moving from sentences to thoughts. Moreover, it illustrates how ambiguity can infect the study of arguments and validity. Unless you know what thought is expressed by a sentence, you will be at a loss to say whether an argument using the sentence is valid.

Linguistic and Logical Structure

How did you know that 'John saw an old friend on his bicycle' could be used to express the very different thoughts which (23a)–(2e) suggested? In outline, I suspect the answer is this: in learning English, you acquired a sensitivity to the linguistic forms used in (1), and this sensitivity makes it possible for you to understand the different interpretations that are indicated by (2a)–(2e). For example, the word 'old' in the phrase 'old friend' can be understood either as an adjective describing the person in question, or as an adjective describing the nature of the friendship. Either someone is said to be old and a friend, or someone is said to have been a friend for some time.

Sensitivity to linguisitic structure does not require that you have mastered all sorts of grammatical terms: you could perfectly well see what is going on in (1) without even knowing what an adjective is. However, grammar does provide us with a way of describing and explaining such cases. Knowing a grammar for a language enables you to explain why certain sentences express certain thoughts, and to chart the relationships between different sentences.

The logical structure of arguments depends upon and is closely related to linguistic structure. As you have seen, you need to have some idea of linguistic structure in order to be able to identify arguments. However, it should be clear that linguistic and logical structure are not the same.

The linguistic structure of a given sentence is describable by a grammar for a specific language. Sentences are in English, French, Italian, etc., and the grammars of all these languages are different. The logical structure of an argument, however, is largely independent of the grammatical quirks of particular natural languages. If you translate a valid argument from English to French, you would expect the translation also to be valid. If it was, so to speak, valid in English then it should remain so when translated into any language. If this were not so in a given case, you should suspect the translation.

This means that any attempt to display the logical structure of an argument must be independent of many of the grammatical features of the language in which the argument is couched. This is not to deny that we have to have a command of the grammars of specific languages in order to discern logical structure. It is just that logical structure should not depend on the individual differences between languages.

THE STRATEGY

Ideally, what we want is a very general language—a language of logical structure. This *language of logic* would have its own grammar and would be independent of any particular natural language. The idea would be this: we could use our knowledge of natural language to translate arguments from, say English, into the language of logic. Once this is done, we could apply the yet-to-be-described methods of logic to the result to test for validity. In fact, this is such a good idea, it is worth spelling it out very carefully. Here are the elements of the what I will distinguish (in upper case) as the Strategy:

(1) *Construct a structural language—a language of logic.*

This language will have its own grammar and you should be able to master it regardless of which natural language you use.

(2) *Work out a method or methods of testing the validity of arguments which are expressed in the language of logic.*

Unlike Analogizing, these methods should not depend on memory and imagination. They should allow us to tell directly whether a given structure makes for validity.

(3) *Describe how to translate arguments from a natural language into the language of logic.*

Translation depends on the understanding of both languages. It is here that logic gives us a great deal of insight into some of the mysteries of language.

Given what the Strategy is a strategy *for,* we must then satisfy ourselves that:

(4) *An argument formulated in the language of logic is valid if and only if its translation into natural language is valid.*

That is, given an argument in natural language, you can test it for validity by *first* translating it into the language of logic, and *second* applying the methods of logic.

The major aim of the rest of this book will be to carry out steps (1)–(3) in an effort to achieve (4). Along the way, more will be said about language, translation and validity.

I hope that you understand how we arrived at the Strategy, but most important is that you understand what it now requires us to do. In the next chapter we will begin to construct a language of logic.

The Main Points of Chapter 14

(1) Everyday methods for testing the validity of arguments include *Visualizing* and *Analogizing.* Both of these methods depend on our imaginative ability with respect to possibility.

(a) In Visualizing, we try to construct a counter-example by imagining that the world is such that the premises of the argument are true and the conclusion is false.

(b) In Analogizing, we try to construct a counter-example by imagining a different argument which has the same structure as the original, but which has true premises and a false conclusion.

(c) An argument is said to be valid if there is no counter-example.

(2) Everyday methods are defective in various ways. They depend too much on our memory and imagination and, most importantly, they let us down when an argument is valid. Such an argument does not allow of the construction of a counter-example, yet we can never be sure, in the specific case, that the failure to find a counter-example is due more to our lack of memory or imagination than to the validity of the argument.

(3) The methods of logic aim to provide more efficient procedures for testing validity. This is valuable in itself. However, a deeper reason for interest in logic comes from the insight that the investigation of logical structure gives us into language and thought.

(4) The Strategy which governs the remainder of the book is, in outline, as follows:

(i) CONSTRUCTION
A language of logic will be constructed. ?Such a language is a language of logical structure.
(Before we are finished, we will construct two languages of logic.)

(ii) DECISION
Methods will be developed to test the arguments formulated in the language of logic.

(iii) TRANSLATION
Ways of translating natural language arguments into the language of logic will be given.

In so far as (i)–(iii) are successful, we should be able to test an argument for validity by simply translating it into the language of logic, and then applying the methods of logic.

Chapter-15

Primitive

Chapter 15

The Strategy outlined in the last chapter requires us to construct a language that has the following two features:

(i) Natural language arguments can be translated into it so as to reveal their logical structure.

(ii) We can test arguments formulated in it by procedures which do not rely on memory or imagination.

This chapter takes a *step* towards constructing such a language. For the present, do not worry about either procedures for testing validity or translation. The language about to be discussed is one of the simplest you are ever likely to come across, but it will serve as the basis for a language that will genuinely help us to realize our goal. Since it is useful to have a name for this language, I will call it 'Primitive'.

THE BASIC SENTENCES OF PRIMITIVE

Primitive has four sentences which form the basis for the whole language. Each of these is completely unstructured. That is, these sentences do not contain what we would recognize as words or other 'sub-sentential' components. They are written like this:

P
Q
R
S

Each of them says something about the weather, and, for our purposes, it will be sufficient if we concentrate on the first two. Speakers of primitive use 'P' to describe the weather when it is like this:

but not when it is like this

they use 'Q' to describe the weather when it is like this:

but not when it is like this:

Given this, it is reasonable to think of 'P' as meaning that it is raining, and 'Q' as meaning that it is windy.

(Indulging in the fantasy which this language conjures up,

we may imagine that speakers of this language have an obsessive interest in the weather—perhaps because it interferes with their most cherished outdoor activities. As to why their language contains, only four basic sentences, we may speculate that they are so reticent they have never had the need for a language which allows more than these comments on the weather.)

ANOTHER SORT OF SENTENCE IN PRIMITIVE

Primitive contains only four *basic* sentences, but these can be used in combination to make more complicated, *non-basic* sentences. These combiantions are best explained one at a time.

Conjoining

Spekers of Primitive sometimes use sentences like

P & Q

which is made by using the '&' symbol and two basic sentences. The symbol is called the *conjunction.* Perhaps the best way to understand what this sentence asserts is to consider those circumstances in which speakers think it applies, and those in which it does not. It applies in this case:

but not in any of these:

This range of application of 'P & Q' makes it seem reasonable to regard the '&' as functioning something like the word 'and', though we will not pause to speculate further about this, since

our concern here is, above all, with the Primitive language, not with its relaetion to natural languages. It is worth considering, though, precisely how it is that the above pictures work to provide an explanation of 'P & Q'.

If you know the circumstances in which 'P' applies, and the circumstances in which 'Q' applies, then you understand these sentences; you can use them in the same way as a native speaker of Primitive. The pictures I gave you earlier were intended to provide you with a (somewhat crude) idea of these circumstances. Exactly the same thing carries over to non-basic sentences such as 'P & Q'. The pictures provide you with an idea of the circumstances in which this sentence could be correctly used, and an idea of those in which it would be incorrect.

Why did I use four different pictures when I introduced the sentence 'P & Q' above?

The answer to this may seem obvious, but the question is not a trivial one, and it is worth pausing over.

POSSIBLE CIRCUMSTANCES

Four pictures were used to represent the possibilities relevant to 'P & Q' because, given what 'P' and 'Q' say, the applicability (or not) of each of these sentences determine four states that the weather might be in. These four ways are depicted below and, underneath each picture, is the information that determines each picture. (I have included approximate translations of the Primitive sentences in brackets.)

(1)

'P' applies (it is raining). 'Q' applies (it is windy).

(2)

'P' applies (it is raining). 'Q' does not apply (it is not windy).

(3)

'P' does not apply (it is not raining). 'Q' applies (it is windy).

(4)

'P' does not apply (it is not raining). 'Q' does not apply (it is not windy).

Given these four possibilities, we can tell what 'P & Q' says by noting whether it applies (or not) in each of the four cases.

In fact, it applies in circumstance (1), but does not apply in (2), (3) or (4). This way of looking at 'P & Q' is merely an application of the common-sense idea that you know what a sentence asserts when you know, in any possible circumstance, whether the sentence applies. The pictures (1)—(4) depict those circumstances.

But do (1)—(4) show *all the possibilities* relevant to 'P & Q' ?

Behind this question are two real worries.

First, couldn't there be cases in which it is indeterminate whether or not 'P' (or 'Q') applies? If there are such cases, these are not shown by the four scenes above, and yet they might be relevant to the applicability of 'P & Q'. For example, what would we say about 'P & Q' in a case where 'P' applies, but it is not clear whether 'Q' applies?

Second, couldn't the function of '&' be more-complicated than we have so far recognized? It allows the construction of a sentence which applies to the circumstances shown, but it might have a meaning which is not fully expressed by this range of application. Suppose, for example, that it meant (roughly) 'and curse the gods'. Since it is still used for conjoining, speakers of Primitive would apply 'P & Q' to (1) and not to (2), (3) or (4), but our knowing this would not, by itself, suffice to tell us what it really meant. The meaning of '&' would contain an extra element of emotive colouring expressing an attitude towards (presumably) the weather gods. (There is a further discussion of this shortly.)

The answers to these questions are as follows.

As to the first question, when speakers use any of their basic sentences, they use them in a way which does not allow that there could be any indeterminacy of application. For them, for example, all circumstances are divided into those to which 'P' applies, and those to which it does not; there is no middle ground. Many speakers of English would be less firm about our sentence: 'it is raining'. That is why I said that the English sentence was only an approximate translation of the sentence 'P'.

As to the second question, the speakers of Primitive use the '&' in such a way that its meaning is fully specified by its effect on the applicability of non-baic sentences in which it occurs. In other words, there is no extra ingredient to the meaning of '&'.

These answers make Primitive a very simple language indeed.

(a) The language contains only four basic sentences.

(b) Each sentence is itself understood as definitely applying or definitely not applying.

(c) A non-basic sentence made with '&' says no more than that it applies in certain cases, and doesn't apply in the others.

TRUE AND FALSE

Everyone knows that a picture is worth a thousand words, but, as with most cliches, there are times when they fail to hold. Indeed, as you'll come to appreciate, this is a time when a word is worth more than a thousand pictures. That word is 'true'.

In explaining what 'P', 'Q' and 'P & Q' assert, I drew a rough sketch of a circumstance, and indicated whether or not the sentence applied.Thus, you learned that 'P & Q' applies to

but does not apply to these:

Instead of drawing such pictures, I could convey the same information by saying:

'P & Q' is true when 'P' is true and 'Q' is true

and

'P & Q' is false when 'P' is false and 'Q' is true
and when 'P' is true and 'Q' is false
and when 'P' is false and 'Q' is false.

Given that you understand what each basic sentence says, you know precisely what circumstances must be like when someone asserts that one or other of them is either true or false. The pictures were helpful for getting started. They can now be replaced by the use of the words 'true' and 'false'. Aside from saving me a lot of space, this change removes some of the artificiality that my pictures imposed. After all, there are very many subtly different pictures that I could draw to represent how things are asserted to be by a basic sentence. Using the words 'true' and 'false' of sentences you understand is a way of telling you what is asserted without having to choose from among these different pictures. For example, if I now tell you that 'P' is true, you know I have said that it is raining. No pictures are required to convey this to you. So, a word (or two if we count 'false') really is worth at least a thousand pictures.

Let us rewrite the explanation of 'P & Q' without pictures.

(1) When 'P' is true, and 'Q' is true, then 'P & Q' is true.
(2) When 'P' is true, and 'Q' is false, then 'P & Q' is false.
(3) When 'P' is false, and 'Q' is true, then 'P & Q' is false.

(4) When 'P' is false, and 'Q' is false, then 'P & Q' is false.
I have used the same numbers here as I did in the explanation given earlier with pictures so that you can compare the two, line by line. (Do that now.)

We can improve this explanation still further by writing it in table form as follows.

	'P'	'Q'	'P & Q'
(1)	true	true	true
(2)	true	false	false
(3)	false	true	false
(4)	false	false	false

Even though the use of 'true' and 'false' makes it much easier to write out explanations of non-basic sentences, you should not forget the relationship between the use of these words and the use of pictures. The pictures portrary the way things are, or might be; their use makes it evident that sentences in Primitive are intended to connect up with reality in appropriate ways. Using 'true' and 'false' of the sentences of Primitive is no less a way of saying something about the relation between these sentences and reality.

TRUTH TABLES AND TRUTH FUNCTIONALITY

You may think that it has taken me a great deal of space to say very little. Many lines of print have been used to introduce a language that has so far been shown to contain only a very few sentences. Nonetheless, as I go on to describe further sentences in Primitive, the ways of talking about the language that have been used above will make explanations clearer and shorter. A further aid to clear and concise discussions in the pages which follow, are certain terms that can be applied to what you now know about Primitive.

The table used on page 285 to explain 'P & Q' (the one without the pictures) is called a *truth table.* It can be abbreviated still further and written in a clearer format as follows.

‘P	‘Q’	‘P & Q’
T	T	T
T	F	F
F	T	F
F	F	F

Read the *rows* of the table. The first row consists of a *truth value* for ‘P’, a truth value for ‘Q’, and a truth value for ‘P & Q’. This last truth value is just what you would expect given the values for ‘P’ and ‘Q’ and the meaning of the ‘&’. Each row gives different possible truth values for the combination of ‘P’ and ‘Q’. The four rows display all the possible ways in which these basic sentences could be true or false. As we have discussed, the truth value of the sentence ‘P & Q’ is fixed by the truth values of its constituent sentences. I have marked the fact that the truth values under ‘P’ and ‘Q’ list the four possibilities by dividing them off from those under ‘P & Q’ with a double vertical line. Each row to the left of the double line describes a way the weather could be at some time.

In section ‘Possible circumstances’ I claimed that, in the Primitive language, the meaning of ‘&’ was fully determined by the effect is has on the applicability (truth values) of the sentences in which it occurs. The truth value of any non-basic sentence made with ‘&’ is completely determined by the truth values of its constituent basic sentences. The term for this is *truth-functional*. In saying that ‘&’ is truth-functional, we are saying that the pattern of truth values illustrated in the table for ‘P & Q’ (above) shows all there is to know about the role of ‘&’ in determining the truth values of non-basic sentences in which it occurs. Moreover, in Primitive, the truth-functional role of ‘&’ is all there is to its meaning. This last comment requires further discussion.

If ‘&’ had meant something like ‘and curse the gods’, then the truth table would not *fully* specify its meaning. The truth table can only tell you what contribution '&' makes to the truth values of sentences containing it. To appreciate this, suppose there was a language which differed from Primitive in one and only one respect: in this language (NotPrimitive), '&' really means 'and curse the gods'. The truth table for '&' in NotPrimitive would be exactly the same as the one for '&' in Primitive. This is because their '&' is used, among other things, for conjoining two basic, sentences in the way given in the truth table. But it also has a further blasphemous use which does not affect truth value, and so does not show up in a truth table. The point about the Primitive use of '&' is that it does not have any such further use. Its meaning is fully specified by the pattern of truth values it determines for non-basic sentences in which it occurs.

First, even though I have never said what 'R' and 'S' mean to speakers of Primitive, you can still write out a truth-table for their conjunction. All you need to know is that these sentences are determinately true or false, and, because they are sentences of Primitive, you can be assured of that. Second, the order in which basic sentences occur does not affect the truth values of a non-basic sentence constructed with '&'. The truth table for 'Q & P' has the same value in each of the relevant rows as the one for 'P & Q'.

REFERRING TO SENTENCES

I have referred to sentences in Primitive by naming them, and I have used a device with which you are familiar to do so. That device is quotation. To form the name of an English sentence, you merely write the sentence inside quotation marks. (They could be single or double quotes. I have used single, but this is merely a matter of which style you prefer.) Failure to be careful about whether you are using a sentence, or referring to it with its quotation name, can lead to confusion. For example, what would you make of the following?

(i) John wrote said Mary.

I wouldn't expect you to make much of it at all. This is because, as written, the above is gibberish. It makes no more sense than:

(ii) John ate wandered sky.

Of course, there is a temptation to think that (i) is more intelligible than (ii), and this is easily explained. (i) can be 'heard' either as:

(i_a) 'John wrote' said Mary,

]or as,

(i_b) John wrote 'said Mary'.

When quotation marks are put around the appropriate parts of (i), we get perfectly intelligible sentences. This is because the quotation marks prevent us reading the words within them as having their ordinary uses; instead, we read them as part of a name of some bit of language. The effect of this, in connection with (i_b) was to convert the last two words into the name of a two word phrase of English. This named thing then served as the grammatical direct object of the verb 'wrote'. With such a direct object, the original sentence could be understood in a way that makes sense.

So, quotation marks are useful – indeed, in many uses of English, they are necessary. The trouble is that, in discussing Primitive, they are a nuisance. Every time I needed to tell you something about the Primitive sentence 'P' I had to enclose it in quotation marks. Yet you wouldn't be confused if I left them out because Primitive is a recognizably foreign language, and there is little chance that you would confuse the sentence and the name. Taking advantage of this fact about Primitive, I am going to drop the use of quotation marks from here on. Primitive sentences can serve as their own names even without quotation marks. Logicians call items with this feature *autonyms*.

DISJOINING

The next sort of non-basic sentence of Primitive looks like this:

P ∨ Q

and has the following truth table.

P	Q		P ∨ Q
T	T		T
T	F		T
F	T		T
F	F		F

The '∨' symbol with which it is constructed is called the *disjunction.* Can you get some idea of what P ∨ Q conveys to a user of Primitive?

Just as for conjunction, the truth table tells you all you need to know to about the meaning of '∨'. To understand disjunction you should read each of the rows of the truth table, seeing what truth value is assigned to the non-basic sentence given the values of the basic sentences. Doing this reveals that P ∨ Q is true in each of the first three rows and is only false when both constituent sentences are false.

Strictly speaking, this should suffice to give you an understanding of P ∨ Q: armed with this information, you would be able to go among speakers of Primitive and use sentences constructed with '∨' correctly. You would know that you could use such a sentence truly in every case except when both of its constituent basic sentences were false. In the specific case of P ∨ Q, you would know that it was false only when it was false that it is raining *and* false that it is windy.

It is often helpful in understanding a foreign language sentence to be able to translate it, perhaps only approximately, into your own. So, granting that. there might be no *exact* equivalent in English, how best could you convey the meaning of '∨' as it occurs in P ∨ Q using the resources of English?

Remembering how we rendered the basic sentences, consider the following as a translation of P ∨ Q:

(i) it is raining *or* it is windy.

How closely does this match the truth table account of P ∨ Q? Put it another way, does the English word 'or' have the same meaning as the Primitive '∨'?

These questions can be answered by examining each row of the truth table above, Rows 2, 3, and 4 seem uncontroversial: the truth values assigned to P ∨ Q in each case are just what you would expect to be assigned to (i). Check this for yourself by asking whether you would be prepared to count (i) as true in each of these cases. I think you will agree that they do match. Thus,

Row 2 Given that it is true that it is raining, and false that it is windy, it is true that: it is raining or it is windy.

Row 3 Given that it is false that it is raining, and true that it is windy, it is true that: it is raining or it is windy.

Row 4 Given that it is false that it is raining, and false that it is windy, it is false that: it is raining or it is windy.

The problems arise in connection with row 1, and might be put as follows. P ∨ Q is true in row 1 (when it is true that it is raining and true that it is windy). This might be taken to show that 'or' is not a good translation of '∨'. Someone might argue: the use of 'or' in a sentence conveys the idea that one or the other constituent sentence is true; when *both* are true, 'or' is not the appropriate word. So, if it is raining and it is windy, it is false that: it is raining or it is windy.

Is this consideration compelling? Think about the following dialogue.

Teacher (disgruntled): Every time we have the school picnic it is raining or windy.

Pupil: No, last year we had the picnic and it was raining *and* windy.

The pupil's remark is (mildly) amusing. Why? Clearly, the teacher did not intend to rule out the possibility of rain *and* wind by his remark. He wanted to make an assertion that included that worst eventuality, but also made provision for the fact that rain alone (or wind alone) had adverse effects on the school picnic. Had the teacher said

(ii) every time we have the school picnic it is raining and windy

he would not have conveyed the thought he considered true. Using 'or' as in (i) seemed the proper way of expressing the thought.

The pupil's remarkj draws attention to a somewhat different use of 'or' as illustrated in this dialogue.

A: What are your holiday plans?
B: I am going for one week to paris or Vienna.

It is implicit in this exchange that B has not spoken accurately if he ends up going to Paris *and* to Vienna. In essence, then, the pupil's remark is a play on the word 'or': the teacher intended it one way, while the pupil interpreted it is another.

Does this mean that 'or' is ambiguous – that it has more than one meaning in English? We cannot fully answer this question now, but we can venture this much: 'or' can be used in different ways, and the use that matches '$\vee$' most closely is that in the teacher's lament about the weather. The teacher used 'or' in an *inclusive* way, whereas it was used in an *exclusive* way in B's remark about his holiday. Speakers of Primitive do not have these different uses – the student's joke could not be made in it. This is because '$\vee$' is given an exhaustive and precise meaning by its truth table. Primitive disjunction is always inclusive.

Would you say that 'or' is a good translation of '$\vee$'? At this point I would hope that you were cautious enough to hesitate before answering. There are uses of 'or' that seem at variance with the use of '∨', but a definite answer to the question requires that we be clearer about the notion of translation. This must wait until the Strategy is more fully developed.

NOTE You may wonder why I did not just come out and say that 'or' is ambiguous, and can mean inclusive or exclus- ive disjunction. My hesitation here is because of the very intricate theoretical issues in linguistics and philosophy which surround the ideas of ambiguity and meaning. We will return to this issue.

NEGATING

Here is another non-basic sentence of Primitive.

$\neg P$

The '¬' in it is called *negation*, and the explanation of its use is simple. (In fact, its very simplicity will call for more explanation than the symbol itself.)

The truth table for the above sentence is.

P		$\neg P$
T		F
F		T

This truth table has only two rows, and thus differs from the truth tables we have used up to this point. Why?

A negated sentence is a non-basic sentence that is constructed from just one basic sentence. As you can see from the truth table, it has the effect of reversing the truth value of the basic sentence it contains. Since this non-basic sentence is formed from just one basic sentence, its truth table is constructed using only the appropriate sentence. Because P only has two possible truth values, the truth table for $\neg P$ need only have two rows.

The most natural translation of $\neg P$ in English is

it is not raining

and I think you can satisfy yourself that there is nothing in the truth table for ¬ P which casts doubt on this translation.

The symbols '&', '∨' and '¬' are called *connectives,* of Primitive. There are two more to come. You may not think that this is the most appropriate word, since '¬' doesn't appear to do much connecting. However, logicians have been used to calling symbols such as '&' *two-place* connectives (for obvious reasons), and they do not therefore find it odd to think of '¬' as a *one place* connective].

CONDITIONALIZING

The next sort of non-basic sentence of Primitive looks like this:

P ⊃ Q

and has this truth table:

P	Q		P ⊃ Q
T	T		T
T	F		F
F	T		T
F	F		T

The '⊃' symbol used in its construction is called the *conditional.* As before, it is quite easy to use the truth table to master the use of '⊃' in primitive. A sentence P ⊃ Q constructed with it can be truly asserted in all cases except where P is true and Q is false. In discussing the conditional, it is helpful to use the following terminology: the first element of the conditional sentence (P in the above) is called the *antecedent*; the second element (Q) is called the *consequent.*

Speakers of Primitive think it correct to use the above example of a conditional sentence in all cases except when, as we would put it, it is raining and it is not windy. Can you think of any close approximation to P ⊃ Q in English? That is, can you think of some form of words in English that translates '$\supset$' in the way that 'or' was used in connection with '$\vee$'? You will come to appreciate that these questions lead to the unfolding of a complex and fascinating story. Here we can only begin the story.

The most plausible translation in English of $P \supset Q$ is:

(i) *if* it is raining *then* it is windy.

Understanding Primitive speakers as using $P \supset Q$ with the sense of (i) goes some way to showing why they assign the truth values they do to the conditional sentences. There are problems, however, so it is best to discuss this in a little detail.

Row 1: It is true that it is raining, and true that it is windy. What verdict would this lead to for (i)?

Many would give the answer 'true', and we would hardly call (i) 'false' in these circumstances. Nonetheless, there may be some hesitancy here. Some people would be reluctant to assert (i) in these circumstances. They think that, in order to feel comfortable about asserting (i), you need to be assured that there is some *connection* between its being rainy and its being windy. Knowing simply that it is both raining and windy does not seem much of a ground for the existence of a connection. But we do not have to examine the merits of this view here. Our question is not 'would you assert (i) in these circumstances?' Rather, it is 'if (i) were asserted would it be true or false?' When we distinguish the question of assertion from the question of a true/false verdict, there seems very little reason to disallow the assignment of 'true' to (i) in row 1.

Row 2: It is raining, and it is *not* windly. What verdict does this demand for (i)?

Here matters are less complicated. The verdict must surely be 'false'.You would neither assert (i) in these circumstances, nor would you think anyone correct who did make such an assertion.

Row 3: It is *not* raining, and it is windy.What verdict does this demand for (i)?

This question seems most peculiar: even more so than in connection with row 1. One is very tempted to protest: what possible sense does it make to use (i) when the antecedent is false? By now you should be able to anticipate the answer. The question before us is whether (i)is true in the circumstances given in row 3. We are *not* interested in whether you would actually use (i) if you knew it was not raining and it was windy.

As in the case of row 1, it is fairly clear that (i) is *not* falsified by having a false antecedent. After all, there could be many other weather conditions that happen to go with its being windy. Sentence (i) does no more than claim that rain is one such condition. It would be unreasonable to think that the truth of

it is snowing and it is windy

makes it false that

if it is raining then it is windy.

Moreover, there is evidence that English speakers would regard (i) as, in fact, true in the circumstances, given in row 3. Consider the following dialogue which makes the point using a different example of an English sentence with 'if...then'.

(On Wednesday)
Smith: If England win the toss then they will win the Test Match.
(A Week Later)
Jones: You were wrong. They lost the toss and won the Test.
Smith: No, I was perfectly right. I never said that winning the toss was the only way they would win the Test. I said that *if* they won the toss, they would win the Match.In saying this, I spoke the truth even as things turned out.

Row 4: It is not raining and it is not windy.
What is the verdict on (i)?

This case shares with row 3 the somewhat puzzling fact that the antecedent is false, but it differs in that the consequent is also false. Does this change things? Not really, though I suspect that the false consequent makes it easier to see (i) as true in this case. Imagine that someone has offered you (i) as a bit of lore about the weather. While out for a walk on a sunny and still day, he says: I told you, if it is raining then it is windy. Isn't what he says true in those circumstances? I expect that many would agree that it is, and certainly would not think it false.

A Concluding Remark About The conditional

Our discussion of the use of 'if...then' as a translation of '⊃' may not have left you completely satisfied. Do not let that cause you to lose sight of this basic point: in Primitive, the meaning of the conditional ('⊃') is clearly set out in the truth table. The issue of translation is, for now, secondary. After all, the aim is to master Primitive.

As a first approximation, we can agree that (i) will do. That is, we can understand '⊃' as something like the English language 'if...then'. I say this even while recognizing that there seem to be differences between these. In struggling with these differences, we were forced to make some very fine distinctions such as that between a sentence being true and our having grounds to assert it. Understanding the use of 'if...then' in English, and its equivalents in other natural languages, requires all the resources of philosophical and linguistic theory. As you will see, the conditional in Primitive plays a crucial role in this issue. So, whilst you should begin to think about 'if...then', the main business of this section has been about '⊃'. Speakers of Primitive are blissfully unaware of the complexities of English language conditionals.

Unlike non-basic sentences constructed with '&' and '∨', the result of this EXERCISE should show you that the order in which basic sentences occur makes a difference to the truth value of a non-basic sentence constructed with '⊃'.

EQUALIZING

The last sort of non-basic sentence of Primitive is constructed with '≡'. An example of such a sentence is

P ≡ Q.

The new symbol is called *equivalence,* and has the following truth table.

P	Q		P ≡ Q
T	T		T
T	F		F
F	T		F
F	F		T

P ≡ Q is true when both basic sentences are true, and when both basic sentences are false. In the other two cases it is false. A first attempt to express P ≡ Q in English might come out as:

(i) it is raining *matches in truth value* it is windy.

The idea would be that (i) will be true in row 1 and row 4, and false in row 2 and row 3. The trouble is that (i) is simply not a sentence of English. This may seem surprising at first, but a moment of thought should convince you. What is the grammatical subject of the verb 'matches in truth value'? You would be correct if you said: the sentence 'it is raining'. The trouble is that these words in (i) do not *name* a sentence; they are used in the ordinary way to say that it is raining. It certainly makes little sense to say: it is raining matches something in truth value. The weather doesn't have a truth value. We could have written:

(ii) the sentence 'it is raining' matches in truth value the sentence 'it is windy'

but, though grammatically acceptable, (ii) doesn't do what is required of a translation of P ≡ Q. P ≡ Q is about the weather;

it is not about sentences and truth values. Because of the explicit mention of sentences and truth values, (ii) does not convey the same, weather-oriented, message as P ≡ Q.

We can get closer to the required translation of P ≡ Q into English using:

(iii) it is raining *if and only if* it is windy.

The phrase 'if and only if' is called the *biconditional.* All the problems that arose in connection with the conditional '⊃', and its translation into English, come up again in regard to (iii). These will be taken up in chapter 10.

The Main Points of Chapter 15

(1) Primitive has four *basic* sentences:

P, Q, R, S.

They are all used to describe the weather, though we have only bothered with translations into English for P and Q. They are:

P it is raining.
Q it is windy.

The basic sentences of Primitive arc, in every situation, determinately true or false.

(2) *Non-basic* sentences of Primitive can be constructed with *connectives.* Below is a list of the connectives, each of which is given with a sample sentence showing how the connective is used in Primitive, and with a suggested English translation for the sample sentence.

(3) Each of the connectives is *truth-functional.* That is, the truth values of non-basic sentences constructed with these connectives are wholly determined by the truth values of the constituent basic sentences. The particular way in which a connective contributes to these truth values is given by constructing the appropriate *truth table* for each connective. Moreover, the meaning of each connective is completely

CONJUNCTION		
&	P & Q	It is raining and it is windy.
NEGATION		
¬	¬ P	It is not raining.
DISJUNCTION		
∨	P ∨ Q	It is raining or it is windy.
CONDITIONAL		
⊃	P ⊃ Q	If it is raining then it is windy.
EQUIVALENCE (or BICONDITIONAL)		
≡	P ≡ Q	It is raining if and only if it is windy.

determined by its characteristic truth table.

(4) The idea of a *truth table* is one of the most important in this chapter. A truth table contains a listing of all possible truth values of the basic sentences relevant to determining whether some non-basic sentence is true. You should be able to write out truth tables for sentences constructed with the connectives of Primitive.